Hiking Maryland and Delaware

Help Us Keep This Guide Up to Date

Every effort has been made by the author and editors to make this guide as accurate and useful as possible. However, many things can change after a guide is published—trails are rerouted, regulations change, techniques evolve, facilities come under new management, etc.

We would love to hear from you concerning your experiences with this guide and how you feel it could be improved and kept up to date. While we may not be able to respond to all comments and suggestions, we'll take them to heart, and we'll also make certain to share them with the author. Please send your comments and suggestions to the following address:

The Globe Pequot Press
Reader Response/Editorial Department
P.O. Box 480
Guilford, CT 06437

Or you may e-mail us at:

editorial@GlobePequot.com

Thanks for your input, and happy trails!

A FALCON GUIDE®

Hiking Maryland and Delaware

A Guide to the Greatest Hiking Adventures
in Maryland and Delaware

Second Edition

David Edwin Lillard

FALCON GUIDE®

GUILFORD, CONNECTICUT
HELENA, MONTANA
AN IMPRINT OF THE GLOBE PEQUOT PRESS

A FALCON GUIDE ®▫

Falcon and FalconGuide are registered trademarks of
Morris Book Publishing, LLC.

Text design by Nancy Freeborn
Maps created by Bruce Grubbs © 2006 Morris Book
Publishing, LLC.
Spine photo © 2004 Michael DeYoung

ISSN: 1558-6308
ISBN-13: 978-0-7627-3635-5
ISBN-10: 0-7627-3635-6

Manufactured in the United States of America
Second Edition/First Printing

To buy books in quantity for corporate use
or incentives, call **(800) 962–0973, ext. 4551,**
or e-mail **premiums@GlobePequot.com.**

For Ann Hall. When her legs failed her, she did her volunteer trail work from her bottom, sitting in the trail to cut brush, clean water bars, and tend the path. How she got herself so far into the woods no one can imagine. That's love.

Contents

Overview

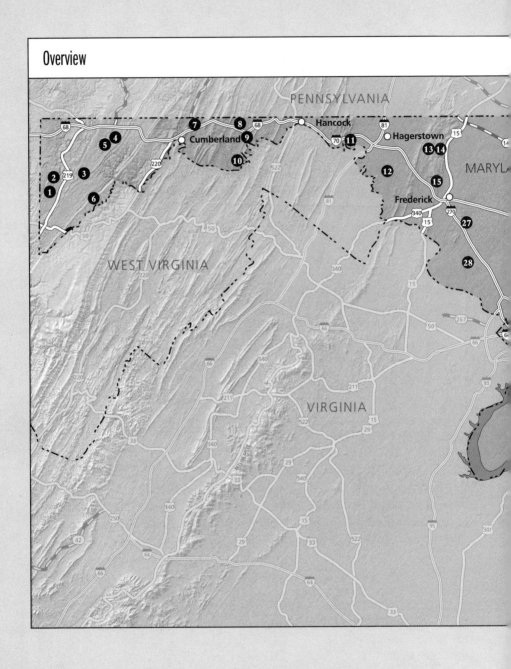

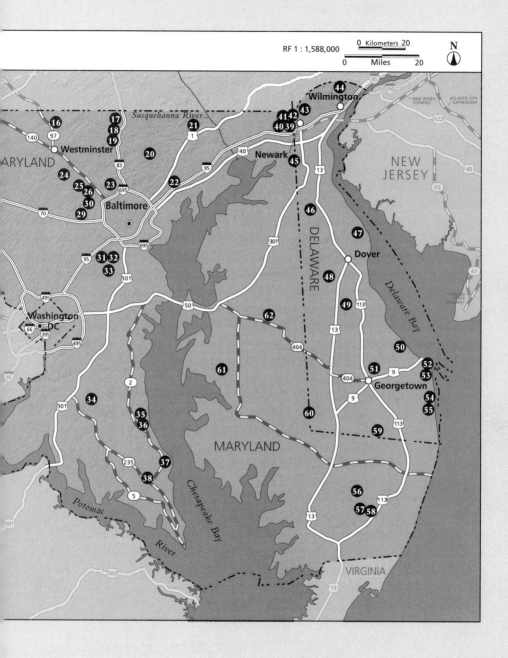

RF 1 : 1,588,000

0 Kilometers 20

0   Miles   20

N

Wilmington

Susquehanna River

NEW JERSEY TURNPIKE

ATLANTIC CITY EXPRESSWAY

95

295

322

16

17

18

19

ARYLAND

97

140

Westminster

20

21

1

40

Newark

45

13

NEW JERSEY

40

55

24

83

25 26

23

695

30

22

DELAWARE

46

47

Dover

43

41 42

40 39

29

70

301

48

Delaware Bay

47

13

31 32

95

33

301

49

113

50

DELAWARE STATE PARKWAY

495

50

301

62

404

51

9

52

53

Washington DC

66

395

495

2

61

60

404

9

Georgetown

54

55

95

34

35

36

235

37

MARYLAND

59

113

301

38

5

Potomac

56

57 58

113

Chesapeake Bay

13

River

301

360

VIRGINIA

13

Acknowledgments

Chris Reiter coauthored the first edition of *Hiking Maryland and Delaware*. His work is represented in this second edition, especially in hikes that appear in the section Land between the Bays.

Thank you to the agency staffs and land managers in Delaware and Maryland who took the time to help ensure the accuracy of information contained in the guide. I am grateful to Susan Moerschel of the Delaware Division of Parks and Recreation and Christina Holden of the Maryland Department of Natural Resources for their assistance in obtaining photographs for this second edition.

Joe Reiter produced the draft maps for the first edition; and Jayson Knott, Ceil Petro, and Lisa Gutierrez of the Maryland Department of Natural Resources offered photographs and photographic research. As always, thanks to Ed Talone for helping find new places to explore on foot, and a big thanks to Lauren Clingan for pretending to be my research assistant.

Introduction

You would not think it could be such a secret to residents, but here it is: Delaware and Maryland are wonderful day-hiking states. It is true that remote backpacking experiences are rare in both states, with the rugged mountains of western Maryland offering the only real places to disappear into the landscape for a few days. But if you are looking to spend a day wandering through hardwood forests, along meandering creeks, or through the mixed scent of salt water and beach pines, both states have plenty to offer.

Although housing development exploded in the Washington, D.C., to Wilmington, Delaware, corridor in the 1980s and 1990s, both states have invested heavily in conserving land for outdoor recreation. Two examples illustrate the types of hiking lands found most often in both states. White Clay Creek State Park, in Delaware's New Castle County, offers hikers several thousand acres of woodland rambles, despite its proximity to tens of thousands of homes. Likewise, the Gunpowder Falls State Park system in Maryland, connected by the riverway, preserves the wild feeling of "fall zone" and piedmont stream valleys. These valleys attracted settlers to the region more than three centuries ago. Now they are within minutes of one of America's largest cities—and yet, you can escape the bustle for a few hours.

Most of the hiking trails in these states are only a few miles in length, with the average being 3 to 5 miles. For many hikers, a hike of that length does not make a destination in and of itself. The truth is, few out-of-staters travel to either of these states just for the hiking, except those hiking the Appalachian Trail, the Chesapeake & Ohio Canal Towpath, or the Allegheny Mountains in Allegany (yes, they are spelled differently) and Garrett Counties of Maryland. Thankfully, there is a lot to see and experience that offers a perfect complement to hiking.

Often it is a small town or crossroads near the trail that rounds out the hiking day. For example, it is hard to think about hiking Snavely Ford Trail in Antietam National Battlefield without considering the ice cream that follows in Sharpsburg.

Most of the trails in both states are managed to accommodate bicycles and horses as well as human feet. Sometimes this can put a damper on the attempt to find solitude, especially when you have hiked several miles into a lonely wood only to have a bicycle whiz past. However, relations among so-called user groups in these states are good for the most part, in no small part due to the education efforts of mountain bicycling groups in the area. Both states do restrict bicycle and horse traffic on a portion of their trails, allowing hikers to find the narrow, quiet footpaths they crave.

The Hiking Regions

This book is divided into three hiking regions: West from Catoctin, West of the Chesapeake Bay and Susquehanna River, and the Land between the Bays.

West from Catoctin. Just west of Frederick, Maryland, the rolling piedmont gives way to a series of northeast-leading ridges. Catoctin Mountain is home to a national park, three state parks, and a municipal forest—all strung together to provide plentiful day-hiking opportunities. The Catoctin Trail, a pathway winding along the length of the mountain, makes possible a short but sweet backpacking trip.

Although the border between Maryland's western, mountainous counties lies atop South Mountain, Catoctin Mountain actually serves as the mental demarcation line between mountain hiking in Maryland and everything to the east. The farther west you go, the taller and more remote the mountains you will find. Green Ridge State Forest, at more than 40,000 acres, and Savage River State Forest, at 53,000 acres, are the two largest land areas devoted to recreation. The backpacking options are limited even in these areas, but there are plenty of trails to take you into the woods where you can find a quiet place to spend a night.

In this West from Catoctin region, you will find the mountainous terrain, waterfalls, and tumbling streams beneath hemlock groves that capture the spirit of any hiker.

West of the Chesapeake Bay and Susquehanna River. The content of this section—covering trails east of Frederick, Maryland, and west of the Susquehanna-Chesapeake waterscapes—is grouped together here as much for its proximity to Baltimore and Washington, D.C., as for any topographic or geologic similarities. From the almost lunar surface of the serpentine grasslands in Soldier's Delight, to the rolling agricultural lands of Baltimore and Carroll Counties, to the brackish still-water creeks of the Chesapeake's western shore, this region has all the physiographic complexity of a small country. There are few trailheads in this region that cannot be reached within two hours on a weekend morning, and the region happens to be home to some of the most overlooked hiking trails in the east. Residents of the Baltimore-Washington metropolis will be amazed at how much hiking there is so close to home.

Most remarkable about hiking in this region are the surprises in store on every hike, such as the open countryside viewed from the Northern Central Railroad Trail and the old carriage road that follows a narrow ridge above Big Pipe Creek in Carroll County. When you watch a blue heron grab a fish dinner out of the ponds at Patuxent River Wildlife Area, you have to remind yourself you are hiking in the epicenter of seven million people.

Land between the Bays. This region encompasses two distinct areas essentially east of the Chesapeake Bay and Susquehanna River. First is Cecil County, Maryland, and northern New Castle County, Delaware—two counties that were transformed from mostly rural to mostly suburban in twenty short years beginning in the 1970s. But for residents, even the workaday routine need not be an impediment to hiking. With Lums Pond, White Clay Creek State Park, and Brandywine Creek State Park nearby, you can stow a pair of boots in the trunk and hit the trail whenever the gift of an extra two hours presents itself.

Below the Chesapeake & Delaware Canal is the Delmarva Peninsula. Here hiking opportunities are found in the salt marsh wildlife preserves, the pine-covered state forests, and the shores of inland bays. Mountain snobs, who believe the quality of the hiking experience is directly proportional to the elevation above sea level, will be amazed to lose themselves amid the tall shore grasses and backwaters. One winter hike in Delmarva is all it will take to turn any hiker into a cool-weather lowlander.

How to Use This Guide

Hikes in this book were selected with a phrase in mind: easy to find, easy to follow. Few things are more frustrating than spending an hour trying to find a trailhead to a two-hour hike or spending half your time trying to match the trail before you to a map in your hand. This guide was assembled with you busy Easterners in mind.

We have selected not only the best day hikes in Delaware and Maryland but also ones that even novice hikers can navigate. Unless otherwise noted, all hikes in this guide have minimal elevation gain. This book is for hikers of all abilities and interests. If you have never hiked before, this book will put you on the trail in safe, beautiful settings. For seasoned hikers, this book will help you discover new destinations.

To put this book to work for you, start with the overview map (pages viii and ix). Each hike is numbered, and its location is represented on the map by its number. Then go to the Trail Finder (pages 13-15) to find a hike that matches your plans for the day—for example, a hike for kids, a walk along the water, a snowshoe hike. Then find your hike listed by number in the table of contents. Go to that hike's pages and read about what you will see.

Be sure to read the entire entry for a hike before you go, in case there is anything special you need to know to enhance your enjoyment of or safety for the trip. For example, in the hike description for Paw Paw Tunnel, you'll find a suggestion to bring along a flashlight. In another example, the trails in Herrington Manor and Swallow Falls State Parks are groomed for cross-country skiing. In other hikes, under the **Special considerations** heading you are told which trails pass through lands managed for hunting in autumn and winter. That is important to know! Read the entire hike description before you leave.

To really make use of this guidebook and discover the best trails in Maryland and Delaware, keep a copy of this book in your car, right next to that extra pair of boots or running shoes in the trunk. Delaware's moniker as the "Small Wonder" holds true for hiking trails in both states. There are many, many fine short hikes that you may never make a destination of but will be glad you visited when you had a chance.

Maps in This Guide

Some of the maps in this book that depict a close-up of an area use elevation tints, called hypsometry, to portray relief. Each gray tone represents a range of equal elevation, as shown in the scale key with the map. These maps will give you a good idea of

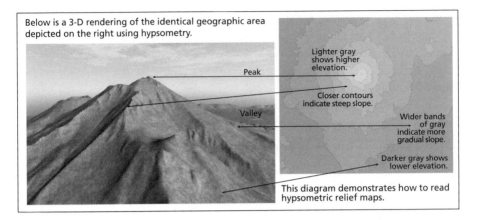

Below is a 3-D rendering of the identical geographic area depicted on the right using hypsometry.

Lighter gray shows higher elevation.

Peak

Closer contours indicate steep slope.

Valley

Wider bands of gray indicate more gradual slope.

Darker gray shows lower elevation.

This diagram demonstrates how to read hypsometric relief maps.

elevation gain and loss. The darker tones are lower elevations, and the lighter grays are higher elevations. Bands of different gray tones spaced closely together indicate steep terrain, whereas wider bands indicate areas of more gradual slope. These maps also show the appropriate GPS coordinates. Relief data was not available for very large-scale maps of shorter nature hikes; some of these are not to scale.

Because all the hikes in this book are accessible by primary and secondary roads and because few of the hikes involve major elevation changes, the maps in this book are all you will need to find your way along the trail. For further research on regional topography, you can consult the U.S. Geological Survey (USGS) maps for each hike. In the beginning section of each hike description, we have noted the USGS topo map for the quadrant or quadrants for each hike's area.

Long-distance Hiking and Backpacking

There are only a handful of truly worthy backpacking trips in Maryland and none in Delaware. By worthy, we mean hikes that will keep you on the trail for more than 25 miles and longer than a couple of days—and that do not include a great deal of road walking. Those few hikes are adequately documented in other sources and are therefore not the subject of this book. Contact information for those sources is available in the appendices of this guide.

Among the most notable backpacking trips in Maryland are the 40-plus miles of the Appalachian Trail in the Free State. The majority of those miles traverse South Mountain from the Potomac to the Pennsylvania line. While there are many opportunities for day hikes along the AT, most involve either a two-car shuttle or hiking in and hiking out. Because of the narrow corridor preserved for the trail by the State of Maryland, the number of loop hikes utilizing the AT and side trails does not compare to, for example, the Virginia sections of the trail.

Like most of the trails in the United States, the AT is maintained by volunteers. The Appalachian Trail Conservancy in Harpers Ferry, West Virginia, is a nonprofit organization charged with overall management responsibility of the "longest

Canoeing is a popular pastime on the quiet waterways of Maryland and Delaware. PHOTO COURTESY OF MARYLAND DNR

national park," under a unique partnership arrangement with the National Park Service. The volunteers of the Potomac Appalachian Trail Club perform the on-the-ground work that keeps the trail open and safe in Maryland.

The longest trail in Maryland is the 184-mile Chesapeake & Ohio Canal National Historical Park. Begun in 1828 as a transportation route between the commercial centers in the East and the frontier resources of the West, the C&O Canal stretches along the Potomac River from Georgetown in Washington, D.C., to Cumberland, Maryland. Remnant canal locks, lock houses, and other historical features interpret the past along the waterway known as the "Nation's River." The trail is the former towpath followed by the mules that pulled the cargo barges downriver. It also provides incredible, up-close contact with the Potomac for many miles while traveling through woodlands and small towns.

It is a wonderful trail, but like the AT in Maryland, there are limited opportunities for loop hikes. Most of the day hikes on it are "in-and-out" walks, and all but one of the backpacking trips along it require a shuttle or two cars. This book does contain a loop hike over part of the C&O Canal, one that travels through Paw Paw Tunnel. The trail is managed by the National Park Service and is supported by the nonprofit C&O Canal Association.

Three other backpacking trips bear noting. A 25-mile loop created from trails in Maryland's Savage River State Forest and New Germany State Park requires a longish stretch of road walking but is otherwise an enjoyable and very popular hike. The Green

Ridge Hiking Trail covers some 19 miles as it climbs from the Potomac River and winds its way north to Pennsylvania, where it connects with Pennsylvania's Mid State Trail to make a hike of more than 200 miles. It is a lovely hike but also one requiring a shuttle arrangement. Finally, one loop utilizes portions of the C&O Canal Towpath and the Green Ridge Hiking Trail to assemble a very nice 50-plus-mile hike. To obtain information on these hikes, contact the Potomac Appalachian Trail Club.

That is the best of it for backpacking. But, again, that does not mean that other "day hikes" in this book do not offer splendid spots for an overnight in the woods, even if you are hiking only several miles.

Being Prepared: Safety and Hazards

Here are a few basic planning strategies and precautions to keep you safe on the trail. For a thorough understanding of backcountry travel and safety, consult these FalconGuides: *Wilderness First Aid* and Will Harmon's excellent *Wild Country Companion*.

Planning and Preparation

The two easiest ways to stay safe when hiking the trails in this book are to plan ahead and to stay on the trail. When you head out for a hike, especially to a backcountry location that is new to you, take a few precautions. Pack a little extra food, warm clothing, rain gear, and anything else you may need if you are forced to rough it for the night. We are not talking about packing a tent and sleeping bag every time you go out for a day hike. But when you're hiking in the West from Catoctin region, it is a good idea to know what you need to survive for a night, even uncomfortably, if you are forced to do so.

A second precaution is to always tell someone where you are going, your basic itinerary, and when you plan to return. If you have told a spouse or roommate that you will be home by noon on Sunday, then you know someone will be looking for you if you do not come home. This is especially important when hiking in western Maryland, where the woods are wonderfully deep. Remember, most tragedies start out simply. All it takes is an unexpected slip on a rock to break an ankle. If you have not left word about where you are, no one will be looking for you.

Although Maryland and Delaware are not known as states with vast wilderness areas, anyone can get lost in the woods by straying from the trail. Experienced hikers can and do get lost. If you do unwittingly leave the trail you are supposed to be on, follow your footsteps back until you find the place where you went astray.

If you are totally lost and you have taken the precautions outlined above, the worst that will happen is that you will spend an uncomfortable night in the woods. Stay put, eat your extra food, find shelter, and wait until morning. If you have left word with someone of your whereabouts, someone will be searching for you soon. Whatever you do, do not go scrambling around in the darkness; that is an easy way to get hurt.

An essential precaution is to carry a first-aid kit. The Hiker's Checklist in Appendix D lists some of the items every hiker should carry. Your personalized first-aid kit should contain a couple of days' worth of any prescription medications you take, a bee-sting kit if you have a known allergy, your eyeglasses if you are hiking in contact lenses, and other similar items. When hiking in the West from Catoctin region of this guide, a snakebite kit is also recommended.

Animals and Critters

When hiking in the mountains of western Maryland, if you are very lucky you will see a black bear or a rattlesnake. There is no need to be afraid of either if you keep your distance. In general, black bears stay clear of humans, but if cornered or hungry their behavior can be unpredictable. If you happen upon a bear, make sure you leave it an escape route so that it will not feel threatened. Back away slowly and it will go about its business. For an excellent, short book on bear behavior, read FalconGuide's *Bear Aware*.

Rattlesnakes are most often seen sunning themselves on rocks or stretched out across a trail where the sun is poking through the trees. Give the snake plenty of room when you walk by. When hiking in the mountains, make a habit of stepping onto rocks or logs and then over them. Do not stretch to put your foot down just beyond the rock or log where you cannot see the ground. The two most common snakebite incidents involve reaching around a rock or tree or stepping into rocky crevices where you cannot see. Watch your step.

Rather than describe every critter, hazard, and remedy in this book, again we refer you to two comprehensive resources: *Wild Country Companion* and *Wilderness First Aid*. Carry the latter in your day pack.

A Word about Water

Your best bet is to assume that no stream or spring you encounter is safe to drink from without treatment, with the exception of protected springs emerging from the ground or pipe before your eyes. In both the West of the Chesapeake Bay and Susquehanna River and the Land between the Bays regions, agricultural runoff and suburban nonpoint-source pollution compromise water safety. In the agricultural areas, the problem is a parasite called *Giardia lamblia,* a protozoan that when ingested can cause "backpacker's diarrhea," a mild name for the intense abdominal cramps brought on by the illness.

In the West from Catoctin region, in addition to the *Giardia* from farm and wild animals, streams in the Allegheny Mountains suffer from the presence of heavy metals leaching into the waterways from mining operations.

Because this book consists primarily of day hikes, let us assume that you will either bring your water with you or get it at the trailhead. In the introduction to each hike, there is a heading called **Trailhead facilities.** If water is available at the trailhead, it is noted there.

Now a word about how much to drink. Without getting too technical, drink a lot, especially in summer. In the heat and humidity of Maryland and Delaware summers, plan for about a quart for every ninety minutes you will be on the trail—assuming you have downed at least that much just before hitting the trail. *Wild Country Companion* will give you the precise details about figuring your body's need for water at various altitudes and temperatures, but here is an easy guideline for the day hikes in this book.

1. Drink a lot of water during the day leading up to your hike; take every opportunity to stop at a water fountain or force an extra glass down while standing in the kitchen. Do not make coffee the only beverage you consume before starting out on a summer hike.

2. Pack at least two quart-size water bottles, and make sure they are full when you start hiking.

3. Have an extra quart bottle or more in the car with you to drink while lacing up your boots and checking your gear. Just before you start your hike, drink whatever is left in the bottle. The best way to avoid thirst-related problems is to drink before your body is crying for it.

4. Invest in a simple water purification system, and carry it with you just in case. A bottle of iodine tablets stowed in your day pack will usually get you through a one-day water emergency.

Trail Etiquette

Courtesy on the trail is contagious. Here are some guidelines.

Go gently. Observe the Zero Impact Hiking guidelines outlined on page 11.

Go courteously. Because most of the trails in Maryland and Delaware are used by hikers and bicyclists—and many by equestrians as well—a few rules of the trails help ensure enjoyment by everyone. Hikers should yield to horses. Yes, horses are big and their dung is dropped right on the trail, but they have to deal with you, too. Bicyclists are supposed to yield to hikers, but there are times when it is easier for hikers to step aside. Work it out courteously. In Maryland most of the trails open only to hikers are designated as such because of a wildlands designation or the fragility of the ecology. Report trail use violations to park officials.

Being courteous also means not hogging the scenery. If you have made it to the top and there is limited space from which to enjoy the view, do not bring a crowd to spend a day in the way of everyone else trying to get a look. Get there, savor it, and then let others enjoy it. It is annoying to hike a few miles to a popular feature and then be made to feel like you are an intruder.

Go quietly. If you can be heard from more than a few feet away when hiking, you are talking too loudly. Not only are you destroying the quiet for other hikers, but you are scaring off the deer, the owls, and all the other wildlife that are seen only by those who go quietly.

Seasons and Weather

Bug Season

If you live in Delaware or east of Allegany County, Maryland, you know that summer means heat and humidity. It also means mosquitoes in the woods and marshlands. In the section that introduces each hike in this guide, there is an entry called **Season.** You will notice that a number of hikes omit summertime from their season. In general, this is an effort to spare you the misery of mosquitoes. If you are prepared for the annoyance or have a high tolerance for these pests, take the necessary precautions (use repellent) and hike away.

By far the most treacherous creature on Delaware or Maryland trails is the deer tick. The best precaution against ticks is to hike in long pants with the cuffs tucked in. A pair of polyester-nylon blend pants will protect you from the elements without making you uncomfortably hot. After the hike, be sure to check your legs, torso, and head for these little arachnids.

Unfortunately for naturalists, nothing else is as effective for repelling mosquitoes and ticks as the chemical compound DEET, found in most insect repellants. Never put DEET directly on your skin, and never put it on the skin of a child. If you use a DEET-based product, apply it to your clothing, especially around the ankles and wrists. Some hikers spray a little on the outside of their hats.

There are now many products on the market that contain no DEET. Instead they contain everything from citronella oil to complex concoctions of other organic compounds. These are the ones to use on your skin.

Stormy Weather

Another summer phenomenon in most of the United States is the afternoon thunderstorm. Always check local weather forecasts before heading out, and think twice about starting a hike when electrical storms are forecast. If you are caught in an electrical storm, here are a few basic precautions:

Find shelter in a low-lying area, preferably amid the shorter trees and shrubs in the area. If you are hiking on a ridge when the storm hits, move off the ridge into a hollow. If possible, move to the side of the ridge opposite the side from which the storm is approaching.

Do not run for cover under tall trees; they act as huge lightning rods. The lightning that strikes any tree in the area causes a charge known as ground current that momentarily electrifies the very ground where you are standing. In fact, most people who are killed by lightning are not actually struck by lightning; they are electrocuted by ground current.

If you are carrying a pack constructed with a metal frame, ditch it at least 50 yards away and seek the low ground. Avoid standing water or getting too close to a water source. In short, do not be on the high ground and do not be in the water.

Just hunker down. Thankfully, most afternoon storms do not last long. And if you can find adequate shelter, a storm on the trail can be beautiful.

Let It Snow

Western Maryland is blessed with snowy winters. This is great for hikers. Because the Maryland mountains are not prone to avalanches and the trails covered in this book travel fairly moderate terrain, snow time is a great time for hiking on snowshoes.

Snowshoe hiking is one of the fastest-growing outdoor pursuits. And for good reason. Hiking in snowshoes can take you into winter wonderlands you have never been able to access. The popularity of snowshoeing, along with several technological advances in the materials used in the construction of snowshoes, has resulted in much lower prices for the gear.

However, one note of caution: Snowshoes are not magical antigravity devices. Walking on a narrow snowpacked ledge on a trail you are not intimately familiar with should be left to the experts. A good guideline for beginner snowshoe hikers is to snowshoe on trails you have already hiked in snow-free months. In the Trail Finder there is a heading for hikes where snowshoes can provide winter access without traversing questionable terrain. For example, the hike through Green Ridge Forest's Fifteenmile Creek Canyon may be suitable for experienced snowshoe hikers, but the terrain will present special challenges to novice snowshoers. Therefore, it is not a highlighted snowshoe hike in this book.

A few hikes in this book are on trails managed for cross-country skiing or snowmobiling. Those are noted in each hike under the **Special considerations** heading.

Backcountry Essentials

Many of the hiking areas in Maryland and Delaware are managed primarily for day use. For these areas, the only permitting requirement may be an entrance fee payable at a contact station. However, some of the state parks do provide developed campsites for tent camping and recreational vehicles. The fees and facilities vary widely. Check with the appropriate managing agency listed in Appendix A.

Most of the hikes in the West from Catoctin region allow backcountry camping. They are listed as day hikes in this guide because they are short enough to be hiked in a day. Camping is permitted in Maryland state forests, provided a backcountry permit is received from the area's managing agency. Information on these agencies can be found in Appendix A. Primitive camping also is permitted on Assateague Island.

Zero Impact Hiking

The increased popularity of hiking has put added pressure on the natural resources that draw us to the trail. Many new hikers, bicyclists, and others have taken to the trail without learning how to protect the natural environment. You can help protect trails and become a knowledgeable steward of the land. To begin, here are seven basic steps. These are only an introduction, however. Consult the FalconGuide *Leave No Trace* for further information.

1. Plan ahead, prepare well, and prevent problems before they occur.
2. Keep noise to a minimum, and strive to be inconspicuous.
3. Pack it in, pack it out.
4. Properly dispose of anything that cannot be packed out.
5. Leave the land as you found it.
6. In popular places, concentrate use.
7. Avoid places that are lightly worn or just beginning to show signs of use.

If you can become an evangelist for only one example that encapsulates the Zero Impact ethic, perhaps it should be the care with which you hike along streams, marshes, and shorelines. Everyone loves a water feature. We want to get as close as we can, to dip our hot feet into cool waters, to see the shorebirds dancing and feeding their chicks. Responsible hikers always resist the urge to get too close.

The trees along these streams play an important role in the health of a stream, not the least of which is to prevent erosion of the fragile stream banks that are the habitat for riparian life. The forest cover over the Maryland and Delaware streams began to disappear long ago when the landscape was cleared for farming and timber. Unwitting hikers can do more damage by stomping down the vegetation around streams and ponds. In the marshlands in southern Maryland and Delaware, shorebirds and aquatic animals mate and inhabit these riparian zones. Stand clear and observe from a distance.

Hiking with Children

Courtesy of the gentle terrain over the two eastern regions covered by this guide, Delaware and Maryland are wonderful places for hiking with children. Kids enjoy the world differently than do adults. Many adults expect their kids to like the same things about hiking that they do. You may enjoy getting to the wide-open view of a valley. Well, that may be your mission, but it may not be your kids'. Young hikers are often more smitten with the idea of lingering to play in creeks and springs, watching the antics of insects, or just hanging out. Take along a hand lens, so that they can see things up close, and a picture book that identifies the plants and bugs they see.

If you are planning a three-hour hike, pack a light blanket or sleeping bag so that you can all enjoy a postlunch siesta. Also, there are a number of quality "kid packs" on the market that enable you to carry a child in a special backpack. For your own enjoyment, when you first start hiking with kids, start with short outings and work up to longer day hikes.

Trail Finder

Use the following table for a quick glance at the special features of each hike.

Water features: has a waterfall, significant contact with creeks and streams, or nice views of water.

Open vistas: has either an open view from a summit or hill or a broad open view of the landscape—not just a view across a field.

Primitive camping: allows you to find a place to camp along the trail.

Campground or cabin: has developed campsites, car camping, or cabins available for rent; may require you to drive from trailhead to campground.

Snowshoeing: places where annual snowfall is above average for the region and where snowshoe hiking is permitted and safe for novices. Nearly every hike in both the West of the Chesapeake Bay and Susquehanna River and the Land between the Bays regions is open to, and safe for, snowshoe hiking; however, snowfalls here tend to be only a few inches at a time.

Suggested for kids: hikes of short to moderate distance, with a minimal degree of difficulty.

Autumn colors: has nice views of deciduous trees displaying foliage, even if the views are across a field; more than just a quick glance from one place.

Little or no car sounds: except at the beginning of a hike, where the trail may be near a roadway, or when crossing a road. In general, these are hikes in which the sounds of cars do not intrude on a quarter or more of the hike.

Trail Finder

Number	Hike	Water Features	Open Vistas	Primitive Camping	Campground or Cabin	Snowshoeing	Suggested for Kids	Autumn Colors	No Car Sounds
1	Herrington Manor SP Loop	●	●		●	●	●		●
2	Swallow Falls SP Loop	●					●		●
3	Deep Creek Vista, Deep Creek Lake SP	●	●		●	●		●	
4	Poplar Lick Run, New Germany SP	●			●	●	●		
5	Monroe Run Trail, Savage River SF	●		●		●			●
6	Lostland Run Loop, Potomac SF	●	●		●	●			
7	Rocky Gap Canyon to Evitts Summit, Rocky Gap SP		●						
8	Twin Oaks Trail, Green Ridge SF	●	●	●	●	●	●	●	●
9	Fifteenmile Creek, Green Ridge SF	●		●		●		●	●
10	C&O Canal Towpath—Paw Paw Tunnel			●	●	●	●	●	●
11	Fort Frederick SP Nature Trail				●	●	●		●
12	Snavely Ford Trail, Antietam National Battlefield	●				●			●
13	Blue Ridge Summit—Hog Rock, Catoctin Mt. Park		●	●	●	●	●	●	
14	Wolf Rock—Chimney Rock Loop, Catoctin Mt. Park		●	●	●	●		●	
15	High Knob—Catoctin Mt. Loop, Gambrill SP		●	●		●		●	
16	Hashawha Loop, Hashawha Env. App. Area		●				●	●	●
17	Beetree Preserve	●	●				●	●	
18	Northern Central Railroad Trail	●	●				●	●	●
19	Gunpowder Falls North and South Loop, Gunpowder Falls SP	●					●	●	●
20	Sweet Air Loop, Gunpowder Falls SP	●	●				●	●	●
21	Susquehanna SP Loop	●			●		●	●	●
22	Wildlands Loop, Gunpowder Falls SP	●	●						●
23	Oregon Ridge Park Loop	●	●				●	●	

Number	Hike	Water Features	Open Vistas	Primitive Camping	Campground or Cabin	Snowshoeing	Suggested for Kids	Autumn Colors	No Car Sounds
24	Morgan Run Natural Environment Area		•			•		•	
25	Soldier's Delight East Loop, Soldier's Delight NEA						•		•
26	Soldier's Delight West Loop, Soldier's Delight NEA		•				•		•
27	Little Bennett Loop, Little Bennett RP	•	•		•		•	•	
28	Schaeffer Farm Trail, Seneca Creek SP						•	•	
29	Sawmill Branch Trail, Patapsco Valley SP; Hilton Area	•			•		•	•	•
30	McKeldin Area Loop, Patapsco Valley SP	•	•				•		
31	Wincopin—Quarry Run Loop, Savage Park	•	•				•		
32	Savage Park River Trail		•				•		
33	Cash Lake Loop, Patuxent Research Refuge								
34	Cedarville State Forest Loop		•				•	•	•
35	Parkers Creek Loop, American Chestnut Land Trust	•	•				•		•
36	American Chestnut Land Trust Loop		•		•		•	•	•
37	Calvert Cliffs SP	•	•				•	•	•
38	Greenwell SP	•	•				•		•
39	Judge Morris Estate, White Clay Creek SP						•	•	
40	Lenape Loop South, Middle Run Natural Area					•			•
41	White Clay Creek Preserve Loop, White Clay Creek SP		•				•	•	
42	Whitetail Trail, White Clay Creek SP	•					•	•	•
43	Carousel Park	•					•		
44	Creek Road Trail, Brandywine Creek SP	•				•	•	•	
45	Swamp Forest Trail, Lums Pond SP	•	•	•	•			•	•

Number	Hike	Water Features	Open Vistas	Primitive Camping	Campground or Cabin	Snowshoeing	Suggested for Kids	Autumn Colors	No Car Sounds
46	Blackbird State Forest Loop, Tybout Tract						●	●	●*
47	Bombay Hook National Wildlife Refuge Loop	●	●	●					
48	Norman G. Wilder Wildlife Area Loop	●	●						●*
49	Killens Pond Loop, Killens Pond SP	●	●				●	●	●*
50	Prime Hook National Wildlife Refuge Loop	●	●				●	●	●
51	Redden State Forest Loop								●
52	Gordons Pond, Cape Henlopen SP	●	●		●		●		●
53	Junction and Breakwater Trail, Cape Henlopen SP	●	●				●		●*
54	Burton's Island Loop, Delware Seashore SP	●	●	●			●		●
55	Seahawk Nature Trail, Holts Landing SP	●	●	●	●		●	●	●
56	Paul Leifer Nature Trail, Furnace Town Historic Site						●	●	●
57	Pocomoke State Forest Hiking Trail, Milburn Landing				●		●	●	●
58	Milburn Cypress Nature Trail, Milburn Landing SP	●			●		●	●	●
59	Trap Pond SP Loop	●	●	●	●		●	●	●*
60	Nanticoke Wildlife Area Loop		●				●	●	●
61	Old School—Holly Tree Loop, Wye Island	●	●		●		●	●	●
62	Tuckahoe Creek Loop, Tuckahoe SP	●			●		●		●

* Denotes some road walking, but otherwise quiet

Map Legend

Boundaries

▨▨▨▨	State Park
▨▨▨▨	State Forest
▨▨▨▨	Environmental/ Preserve/Land Trust
▨▨▨▨	National Rec. Area
— - — - -	State Line

Transportation

=〈70〉=	Interstate
—〈40〉—	U.S. Highway
■—〈9〉—■	State Highway
————	Primary Roads
—〈709〉—	Other Roads
=〈709〉=	Unpaved Road
= = = = =	Unimproved Road
═ ═ ═ ═	Featured Unimproved Trail
▬ ▬ ▬ ▬	Featured Trail
ᴵᴵᴵᴵᴵᴵᴵᴵᴵᴵᴵᴵ	Boardwalk
- - - - - - - -	Other Trail
—→—⊢—⊢—	Tunnel
⊢⊢⊢⊢⊢⊢	Railroad
———■———■—	Powerlines
— — — — —	Gaslines

Hydrology

∿	River/Creek
⫽	Falls
⬤	Lake
~ ~ ~	Marsh/Swamp

Symbols

🚶	Trailhead
❷	Trail Locator
↺	Trail Turnaround
🅿	Parking
🚻	Restroom/Toilet
⛺	Campground
⬆	Cabin/Building
†	Cemetery
🅰	Picnic Table
○	Town
◉	Viewpoint
■	Point of Interest
⚒	Mine
●—●	Gate
⤙	Bridge
🅸	Fire tower
⊏	Shelter
🅱	Ranger Station
❓	Information
⛵	Marina
⛴	Boat Launch
⊡	Ruins
⊙⊙⊙	Tree Line

Physiography

×	Spot Elevation
)(	Pass
▲	Peak

West from
Catoctin

Swallow Falls is an easy hike, even for children. PHOTO COURTESY OF MARYLAND DNR

1 Herrington Manor State Park Loop

A woodland stroll through a pine grove, a forgotten cemetery, and the mixed hardwood forest surrounding Herrington Lake. The hike finishes at the lake's beach.

Location: Herrington Manor State Park is located in Garrett County, Maryland, near the West Virginia border. It is about 200 miles west of Washington, D.C.
Type of hike: 4.2-mile loop.
Difficulty: Moderate.
Season: April through October.
Fees and permits: Entrance fee: Memorial Day to Labor Day, $2.00 per person, in-state; $3.00 per person, out-of-state. Rest of year: $2.00 per car.

Maps: USGS Oakland, Maryland.
Special considerations: When snow is on the ground, plan to visit these trails only on skis. The hike passes through areas managed for hunting; inquire at the park office.
Camping: Cabins are available for a fee with advance registration.
For more information: Swallow Falls State Park.
Trailhead facilities: Snack bar, water, restrooms.

Finding the trailhead: From Interstate 68, take exit 14A and drive 19 miles south on U.S. Highway 219, passing Deep Creek Lake; turn right onto Mayhew Inn Road. Drive 4.3 miles north, and then turn left onto Sang Run Road. In 0.25 mile turn right onto Swallow Falls Road (County Road 20), which becomes Herrington Manor Road and leads west to the park entrance in 8.7 miles (4 miles past entrance to Swallow Falls State Park).

The Hike

This leisurely walk follows ski trails near Herrington Lake. The beach, concession, and kayak rentals make the park an ideal spot to spend the day hiking and enjoying the lake.

Start the hike by walking back up the park road 0.3 mile. Go left, following the yellow blazes; the trail here is identifiable largely by mowing. Enter the woods, and go right at the fork near a giant oak.

Begin circling a pine grove at 0.4 mile. The straight, evenly spaced trunks here are wonderfully reminiscent of Ansel Adams's photography. Enter a clearing at an old family cemetery at 0.7 mile. Of particular interest is a series of markers for Uphold, the spelling of which is modified over three successive generations and illustrated by adjacent headstones.

To continue, return to the point at which you first entered the cemetery clearing and go left, following the yellow blazes. Through the grove, especially where hemlocks are clustered to the east, there is the strong scent of conifers. In May and June, bluets carpet the pathway in places, shimmering all around. At the junction go right to retrace your steps to the park road; cross here and stay with the yellow blazes.

Stay with the yellow blazes until a T intersection with the green trail. Go right and walk below black oak and blue spruce with an understory of American hornbeam. At

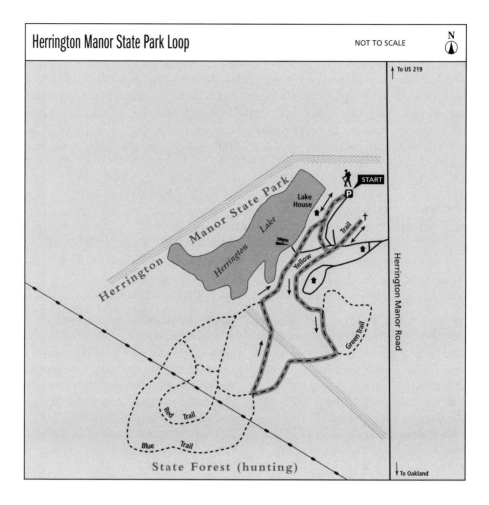

NOT TO SCALE

N

To US 219

Lake House

Herrington Manor State Park

Herrington Lake

START

P

Trail

Yellow

Herrington Manor Road

Green Trail

Red Trail

Blue Trail

State Forest (hunting)

To Oakland

2.0 miles, go right at the T intersection with an unblazed trail; a small spring flows to the right of the trail. Continue straight at the clearing, where a sign marks the beginning of the managed hunting area; enter the woods.

At the next junction go right (power lines will be visible 100 yards to the left). This is the blue-blazed trail, but you may not see a blaze for the first 100 yards or so.

At the next junction the blue and red trails go left. Turn right and follow a narrower footpath, with the lake on your left. At 3.5 miles emerge from the woods at the boat launch; follow the paths beside the lake back to the trailhead.

Miles and Directions

- **0.0** Start at trailhead.
- **0.4** Begin circling a pine grove.
- **0.7** Enter clearing at old cemetery.
- **2.0** Reach junction with unblazed trail.

3.5 Emerge from the woods at Herrington Lake boat launch.

4.2 Arrive back at trailhead.

Options: For an additional 1.5 miles of meandering, go left at the blue–red junction, continuing on the blue trail at the next fork. Turn left at the next junction onto the red trail, and follow it on a loop that circles back to the blue–red junction. Continue straight, with the lake on your left, and emerge at the boat launch.

The trails in the state park are designed for cross-country skiing. There are several color-coded trails in the park.

2 Swallow Falls State Park Loop

An easy circuit hike in Swallow Falls State Park through a mature hemlock forest along the scenic Youghiogheny River to Maryland's tallest waterfall.

Location: Swallow Falls State Park is located in Garrett County, Maryland, near Deep Creek Lake, about 200 miles west of Baltimore.
Type of hike: 1.0-mile loop.
Difficulty: Easy.
Trailhead elevation: 2,300 feet.
Season: April through November.
Fees and permits: Entrance fee: $2.00 per person in-state, $3.00 per person out-of-state, Memorial Day to Labor Day; $2.00 per car at other times.
Maps: USGS Sang Run, Oakland, Maryland–West Virginia.

Special considerations: This is a terrific winter hike in snowshoes.
Camping: The park has a developed campground; permits and information are available from the park office. For reservations call Maryland's statewide reservations line for state parks and forests: (888) 432-2267.
For more information: Swallow Falls State Park.
Trailhead facilities: Restrooms, water fountain, soft drink vending machine, picnic pavilions and tables.

Finding the trailhead: From Interstate 68, take exit 14A and drive 19 miles south on U.S. Highway 219, passing Deep Creek Lake; turn right onto Mayhew Inn Road. Drive 4.3 miles north, and then turn left onto Sang Run Road. In 0.25 mile turn right onto Swallow Falls Road (County Road 20), which leads west to the park entrance in 4.7 miles.

The Hike

This delightful short hike packs into a small package some of the outstanding features of hiking the Allegheny Front, including a stretch along one of the eastern United States' most notable white-water rivers, the Youghiogheny. It is also a perfect

The Youghiogheny River flows north through Garrett County, Maryland. PHOTO COURTESY OF MARYLAND DNR

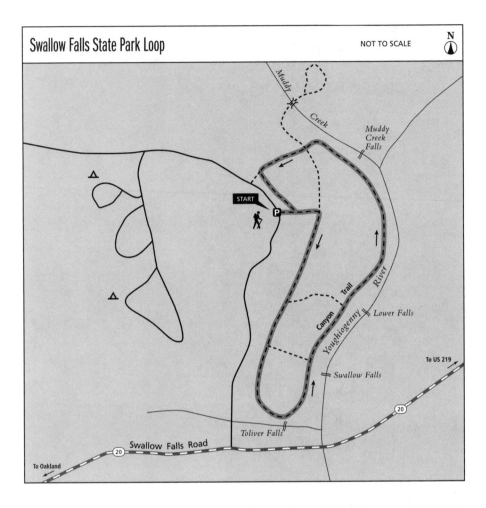

NOT TO SCALE

N

Muddy

Creek

Muddy
Creek
Falls

START

P

Canyon   Trail

Youghiogeny   River

Lower Falls

To US 219

Swallow Falls

20

Toliver Falls

20   Swallow Falls Road

To Oakland

hike for getting an outdoor fix when traveling with small children or with friends or family who take the outdoors in small doses. There are picnic tables and a pavilion, so a prehike picnic makes for a real kid pleaser.

The trailhead is just beyond the comfort station and kiosk at the north end of the parking area. Traveling southeast (right) from the kiosk, immediately find yourself in a stand of huge, ancient hemlocks and white pines. To protect these 300-year-old trees and their ecosystem, the forty-acre grove is designated a Sensitive Management Area, which means the grove is managed as a wilderness. Trees are allowed to fall or burn as nature wills; only trees blocking trail access are cleared.

At 0.4 mile descend east to the first of four waterfalls on the hike, Toliver Falls on Toliver Run. Here the hemlock boughs slant nearly into the run, creating a dense shade over a low cascade—a nice spot to spend time splashing about in the ripples 100 yards above Toliver Run's confluence with the north-flowing Youghiogheny or, as it is known to white-water runners everywhere, the "Yough."

Scampering over wet boulders to the mossy Canyon Trail, heading north along the Yough, you will be just out of earshot of Toliver Falls when Swallow Falls appears on your right—the second falls on the hike. The hemlock and pine are accompanied by mountain laurel and rhododendron, and the granite outcrops in and near the water call out for further exploration. As a point of Zero Impact Hiking ethics, follow the established passages to the river. So many enthusiastic hikers have trammeled new paths to the water that in places the bank is losing its protective trees. The trees keep the waters clean and cool enough for trout and other cold water–loving fish.

Another 200 yards downriver is Swallow Rock and the Lower Falls, popular spots to capture this scenic hike on camera. Below the falls, boulders strewn into the river provide access for getting a great angle on the cascade from the middle of the river. At 0.7 mile, Muddy Creek drops into the Yough to create a rare type of river confluence. Muddy Creek flows southeast, anticipating a wash into a south-flowing river. But with the Yough flowing north, Muddy Creek seems to be headed in the wrong direction when it spills into the river. Instead of a smooth junction, the clash creates quite a stir of water and mist.

Just beyond the confluence is Muddy Creek Falls, at 63 feet the highest waterfall in Maryland. To the left, steps lead to the top of the falls; you will want to take plenty of time to explore it from every angle. Prime photography opportunities here are during midday, when the sun is high.

From the top of the falls, follow Muddy Creek to a junction with a footpath leading over the creek and into the forest. For an additional ramble of less than half a mile through dense rhododendron, go right at the junction and over the footbridge. On the other side of the creek, the trail makes a circuit.

From this junction it is 0.2 mile back to the car. On the way, be sure to stop at the overlook and historical marker commemorating a camping trip of four notable Americans: Henry Ford, Thomas Edison, John Burrows, and Harvey Firestone.

Miles and Directions

0.0 Start at trailhead just beyond comfort station.

0.4 Descend to Toliver Falls on Toliver Run.

0.6 Begin views of Swallow Falls; Swallow Rock and Lower Falls.

0.7 Arrive at Muddy Creek Falls.

0.8 Reach bridge; junction with short loop trail.

0.9 Pass historic marker.

1.0 Arrive back at trailhead.

3 Deep Creek Vista, Deep Creek Lake State Park

The trail climbs to the flattop ridge of Meadow Mountain for a stunning view of Deep Creek Lake. On the way down, stop at an abandoned mine site for an insight into mountain cultural history.

Location: Deep Creek Lake State Park in Garrett County in western Maryland, 200 miles northwest of Washington, D.C.
Type of hike: 2.9-mile out-and-back.
Difficulty: Moderate.
Elevation gain: 400 feet.
Season: April through May, October through November.
Fees and permits: No fees or permits required.
Maps: USGS McHenry, Maryland.

Special considerations: For those seeking quiet enjoyment of the natural setting, this hike should be avoided Memorial Day to Labor Day. The continuous sounds of outboard motors on the lake may be a distraction.
Camping: Developed campsites are available in the park; registration and a fee are required.
For more information: Deep Creek Lake Recreation Area.
Trailhead facilities: Water and privy inside park.

Finding the trailhead: From Frederick, Maryland, drive west on Interstate 70 to Interstate 68 West in Hancock. Go 69 miles and then exit south on U.S. Highway 219 to Deep Creek Lake. After crossing the lake on US 219, pass through the Thayerville commercial area and turn left onto Glendale Road. After crossing the next bridge, take an immediate left onto State Park Road. Cross a small bridge and turn left at the T junction, following signs for the beach area. Proceed past the entrance station and look for trailhead on the right.

The Hike

Most of the people who hike in the park never get a good view of Deep Creek Lake; they content themselves with a terribly obstructed peep from the fire tower. Too bad. The view from the wooden platform specially constructed for the purpose is the main objective of this hike.

From the parking area, cross State Park Road and ascend the 0.1-mile connecting path. Turn left onto the white-blazed Meadow Mountain Trail, an 11-mile trail that follows the ridgeline. Hiking west in a slow ascent, see striped maple saplings that dot the understory, easily identifiable by the dark green stripes on a smooth, olive-green bark.

At 0.4 mile pass the red-blazed Old Brant Mine Trail on the right, which will be used for the descent at the end of the hike. Then switchback east for a steep climb of 200 feet over a quarter of a mile. Just as the climb becomes a chore, the trail levels off at the top end of Old Brant Mine, at 0.9 mile. You could take Old Brant Mine Trail directly to this spot, but it is a much steeper climb.

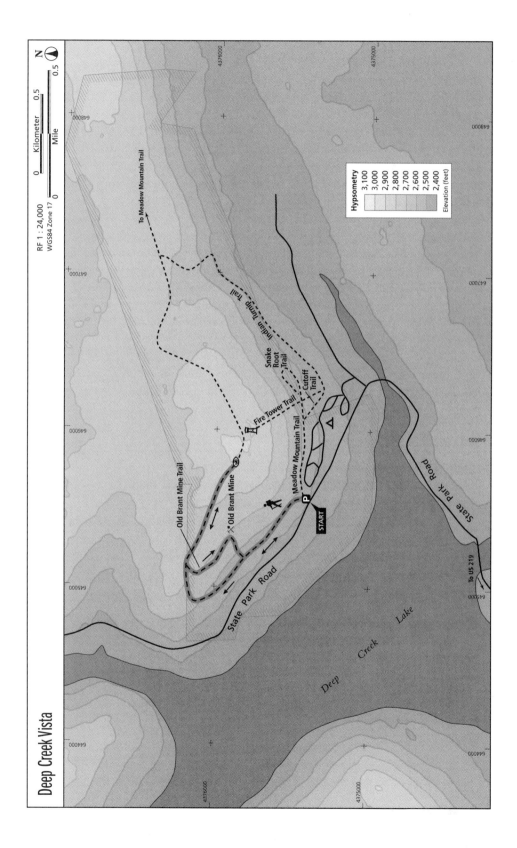

Deep Creek Vista

RF 1 : 24,000
WGS84 Zone 17

N

0   Kilometer   0.5

0   Mile   0.5

Hypsometry
3,100
3,000
2,900
2,800
2,700
2,600
2,500
2,400
Elevation (feet)

To Meadow Mountain Trail

Indian Tump Trail

Snake Root Trail

Fire Tower Trail

Cutoff Trail

Old Brant Mine Trail

Old Brant Mine

Meadow Mountain Trail

START

P

State Park Road

State Park Road

Deep Creek Lake

To US 219

Continue east along the ridge. Here it is apparent why this ridge is called Meadow Mountain. Its flat, wide top holds water like a rimmed plate. The ground is carpeted in ferns and mushrooms. Wildflowers typically found in bottomlands flourish in small pockets.

At 1.5 miles turn right at the vista access trail; a sign marks the way. The vista is about 175 yards south of the main trail. From the platform there is a dramatic view south over the lake and into the West Virginia Alleghenies. In summer the sound of motorboats makes its way to the top of Meadow Mountain, so you might want to save this hike for late September. Then the leaves have already fallen from the ridge-line trees, but the lower reaches are ablaze in color.

Return to Meadow Mountain Trail by retracing your steps, and turn left back onto the white-blazed trail (at 1.7 miles, including the jaunt to the vista). At 2.3 miles turn left onto the red-blazed Old Brant Mine Trail; the blazes may disappear for a hundred yards or so. At the mine site, take some time to examine the fine reconstructed camp there. The mine operated for only a few years in the 1920s, when Garrett County was practically still a frontier. Unfortunately for the mine's owners, both contracted illness caused by their work and were forced to abandon the mine.

Continue descending on the red-blazed trail to a junction with Meadow Mountain Trail at 2.5 miles. Turn left and follow the white blazes to the access trail; turn right to return to the trailhead.

Miles and Directions

- **0.0** Start at trailhead, across State Park Road from parking lot.
- **0.4** Pass junction with end of Old Brant Mine Trail.
- **0.9** Reach junction with beginning of Old Brant Mine Trail.
- **1.5** Turn right at vista access trail junction; after drinking your fill of the view, start back by retracing your steps.
- **2.3** Junction with beginning of Old Brant Mine Trail (on return); turn left.
- **2.5** Reach Meadow Mountain Trail junction; turn left.
- **2.9** Arrive back at trailhead.

Options: For a loop of 3.9 miles, continue east on Meadow Mountain Trail after visiting the vista. In 0.9 mile, or 2.4 miles from the trailhead, turn right onto Indian Turnip Trail and descend. At Fire Tower Trail, 3.2 miles from the trailhead, turn right and then immediately left onto Meadow Mountain Cutoff Trail, which ascends 150 yards to Meadow Mountain Trail. The starting trailhead is 0.5 mile farther west.

4 Poplar Lick Run, New Germany State Park

Following wide, color-coded cross-country ski trails, this is a pleasant walk along Poplar Lick Run, a babbling stream offering many opportunities to stop and enjoy the woods. There is an interlude to a cool pine grove. Because the hike covers mostly wooded areas, there are few opportunities for long views of the landscape.

Location: New Germany State Park in Garrett County, 180 miles west of Washington, D.C.
Type of hike: 5.0-mile loop.
Difficulty: Moderate.
Elevation gain: Minimal.
Season: April through November.
Fees and permits: $2.00-per-person entrance fee on weekends, June through August.
Maps: USGS Bittinger, Barton, Frostburg, Grantsville, Maryland.
Special considerations: Pets are not allowed on the New Germany trails. Trails are designated for cross-country skiing when snow is present.
Camping: Cabins are available within the

park; advance registration and a fee are required. In the forest surrounding the park, there are developed sites and backpacking opportunities. Registration is required for both; there is a fee for the developed sites. For reservations, call Maryland's statewide reservations line for state parks and forests: (888) 432-2267.
For more information: New Germany State Park.
Trailhead facilities: Water is available from a spigot used by campers, located just past the turnoff to Lot 5. There are restrooms at the park meeting facility, which is walking distance from the trailhead.

Finding the trailhead: From Frederick, Maryland, drive west on Interstate 70 to Hancock. Then go 65 miles west on Interstate 68 to Grantsville, Maryland, and take exit 19 north onto Bittinger Road. In 0.5 mile turn right (east) onto Alternate U.S. Highway 40. In 3 miles turn south (right) onto Chestnut Ridge Road, which will end in 2 miles at New Germany Road. Turn left. In 2 miles proceed past the Savage River Complex headquarters on the right. Just beyond, turn left into New Germany State Park. Proceed to Lot 5; the trailhead is at the far end of the lot behind the information board. (*Note:* Directions are from the Grantsville exit to provide an opportunity to obtain provisions; you can also exit directly from I-68 onto Chestnut Ridge Road at exit 22.)

The Hike

Hemlocks, mountain laurel, azaleas, and the sound of tumbling water await you on this woodland hike. From the information board, follow the green blazes on the park road for 150 yards; then turn right (west), following the yellow blazes. Cross the bridge and stay left with the blazes. Rhododendrons and ferns form the understory beneath the hemlocks shading the stream on your left.

Pass through an old picnic area and water treatment facility, and then duck into woods and climb a small knob, with Poplar Lick Run on your left. Continue past

Maryland's western parks and forests are ideal for winter snowshoeing and skiing. PHOTO COURTESY OF MARYLAND DNR

the yellow spur that breaks west at 0.6 mile, and move along a wooded ledge; a wooded knoll rises to the right, and the landscape drops left toward the stream.

At 0.9 mile enter a garden area planted with native species. A bench and small waterfall make for an inviting rest stop. Cross the bridge and turn right onto the green-blazed Three Bridges Trail. In 150 yards stay right, now following the blue blazes. Over the next 0.8 mile the trail weaves near and over the stream and into and out of small patches of sunlight. A small waterfall near the third bridge (not counting the one in the garden area) drops into a small pool teeming with small fish that will hypnotize young hikers.

Reaching the gate at Poplar Lick Trail, at 1.7 miles, turn left and cross the creek. Poplar Lick Trail descends toward the Savage River. Although the trail is open to motorized trail use, there are several quiet places to camp near the stream. Ascend on Three Bridges Trail, a wide ski trail that is steep in places. Climb almost 400 feet over the next half a mile, pausing for rests to look behind you to Meadow Mountain. These are the only open views on the hike. Reaching a stand of hemlock and cedar on your left, at 2.6 miles, watch for the purple blazes leading right just as the trail reaches the top of the hill.

The pine grove is a short detour into a dark, swampy world. It offers a striking difference from the lush vegetation only half a mile back. There is almost no ground

Poplar Lick Run

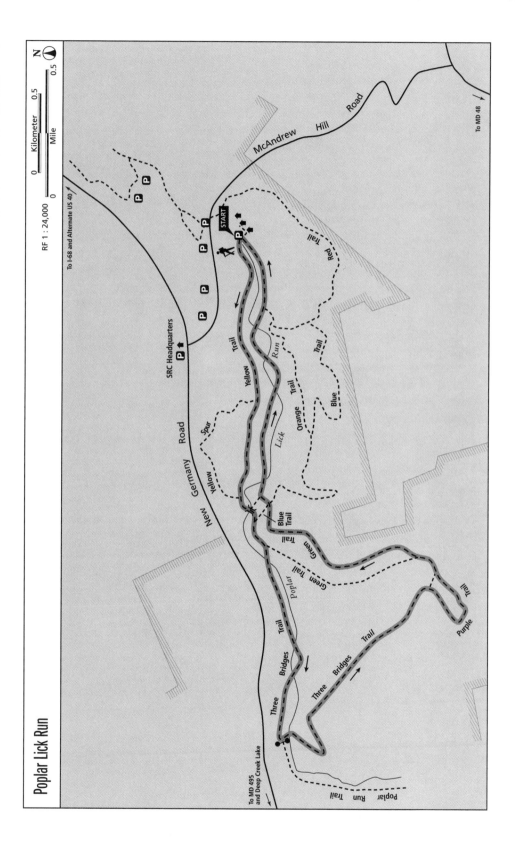

RF 1 : 24,000

To I-68 and Alternate US 40

SRC Headquarters

New Germany Road

McAndrew Hill Road

To MD 48

To MD 495 and Deep Creek Lake

START

Yellow Trail

Yellow Spur

Blue Trail

Green Trail

Poplar Trail

Three Bridges Trail

Three Bridges Trail

Purple Trail

Poplar Run Trail

Poplar Lick Run

Orange Trail

Blue Trail

Red Trail

cover or understory—only straight, fragrant conifers living in a soupy soil created by the small bowl at the top of this knoll.

Emerging from the pine grove, go straight at the junction to rejoin the blue trail. This is a tricky spot. The trail to the left is the blue trail you ascended on; the gated trail to the right descends into the forest. You will actually see the gated trail first, so the junction with the blue trail will feel like a left turn. Stay straight on the blue trail. Just below, at 3.1 miles, reach the top of the green trail loop. Go right, but either spur will lead to Poplar Lick. (If you want to spend a little more time following the stream, despite having to retrace your steps for a few hundreds yards covered earlier in the hike, go left at the fork.)

Taking the right fork, descend to a junction with the blue trail, just above the stream. Take the soft left (the hard left leads back to Three Bridges Trail) and reach the stream, at 3.6 miles, just northeast of the garden area that you passed at 0.9 mile. Follow the green trail as it crosses Poplar Lick Run four times over the next mile on its route back to the trailhead. Watch for wildlife, especially deer, near the stream in the late afternoon hours.

Miles and Directions

- **0.0** Start at trailhead at the information board.
- **0.6** Continue past fork at yellow spur.
- **0.9** Cross bridge to Three Bridges Trail.
- **1.7** Reach gate at Poplar Lick Trail; turn left and cross creek.
- **2.6** Follow purple blazes for pine grove loop.
- **3.6** Reach stream.
- **5.0** Arrive back at trailhead.

Options: The color-coded trails offer many options for shorter and longer hikes through the woods, including backpacking down Poplar Lick Trail. For a 2.0-mile stroll along Poplar Lick Run, turn left onto the green trail after crossing the bridge at 0.9 mile.

5 Monroe Run Trail, Savage River State Forest

A creekside hike into a very remote, wild stream valley covered in a canopy of hard-woods and hemlocks. There are twenty-two stream crossings, some on bridges, many by rock hopping. On an autumn weekday in late afternoon, you are as likely to see a black bear as another person.

Location: Monroe Run Trail is located in Savage River State Forest in Garrett County, Maryland, about 185 miles west of Washington, D.C. The trail begins in the state forest and ends in Big Run State Park.

Type of hike: 4.6-mile one-way shuttle or 9.2-mile out-and-back.

Difficulty: Moderate due to stream crossings; 1,100-foot descent.

Season: April through November; winter on snowshoes.

Fees and permits: No fees and permits required.

Maps: USGS Bittinger, Maryland.

Special considerations: This trail has many stream crossings that are subject to flooding, and there are no constructed bridges (there are a few simple log bridges). Most of the time, all the crossings can be managed with the only consequence being an occasional wet boot. In high water, especially in spring, a few crossings may require wading in shallow water. Fast-moving water, even knee deep, should be crossed only by or with the assistance of experienced hikers.

Camping: Camping is permitted; a permit is required for primitive camping, and a fee is required for developed sites at the bottom of the trail. For reservations call Maryland's statewide reservations line for state parks and forests: (888) 432-2267.

For more information: Savage River Complex.

Trailhead facilities: None.

Finding the trailhead: From Frederick, Maryland, drive west on Interstate 70 to Hancock. Then go 65 miles west on Interstate 68 to Grantsville, Maryland, and take exit 19 north onto Bittinger Road. In 0.5 mile, turn right (east) onto Alternate U.S. Highway 40. In 3 miles, turn south (right) onto Chestnut Ridge Road, which will end in 2 miles at New Germany Road. Turn left. In 5 miles reach the Monroe Run overlook and trailhead on the left. (*Note:* Directions are from the Grantsville exit to provide an opportunity to obtain provisions; you can also exit directly from I-68 onto Chestnut Ridge Road at exit 22.)

The Hike

With the casual terrain of the trail, this hike can be covered in a couple of hours of walking. To truly enjoy it, however, plan on at least twice that long. This is one of the wildest stream canyons in Maryland, and because it offers no loop options without a road walk, one of the quietest. Because the trail descends into the canyon, there is no intrusion of noise from outside activity.

This hike is especially suited for an overnight hike, either by creating a loop (see Options) or by hiking in to a favorite spot along the stream and then out the same way. Before hiking, take a few minutes to gaze at the canyon from the overlook.

Morning mist rises from a stream valley in western Maryland. PHOTO COURTESY OF MARYLAND DNR

Begin by descending on a wide path, remnants of an old road built by the Civilian Conservation Corps (CCC) in the 1930s as a connector between camps atop and below Meadow Mountain. The wooden guardrails at sharp turns on the downhill side were placed by the CCC crews. There are a few openings in the canopy near the top, with views west up the mountain and south toward Savage River Reservoir.

The terrain eases as the trail approaches Monroe Run; at 1.1 miles come to the first of more than twenty crossings (the precise number depends on the weather). Near the stream here are several good campsites, back under tall oaks and tulip poplars. The understory leading from the trail is dense with rhododendron, at times so thick that even on sunny days it is nearly nighttime on the ground.

At 2.0 miles reach a large hemlock grove. The temperature here seems to drop by several degrees. In fact, it is the cooling effect of hemlock groves that stave off evaporation on headwater streams like Monroe Run. Scientists are battling a blight that threatens to destroy the hemlocks of the southern Appalachians, a potentially calamitous event that would alter the entire ecosystem of these mountains.

Several stream crossings farther on, beginning at about 2.6 miles, is a series of secluded campsites. If you plan to camp along Monroe Run, use one of the sites that

Monroe Run Trail

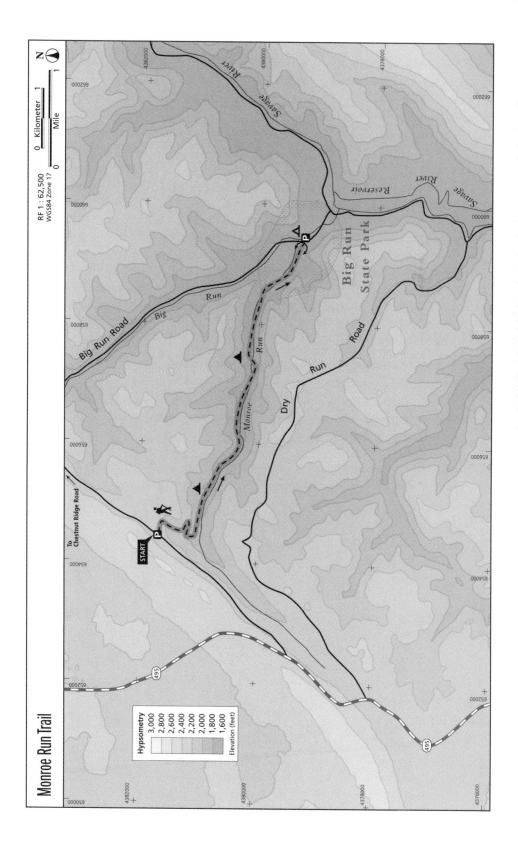

RF 1 : 62,500
WGS84 Zone 17

0   Kilometer   1

0   Mile   1

N

Hypsometry

3,000
2,800
2,600
2,400
2,200
2,000
1,800
1,600

Elevation (feet)

To
Chestnut Ridge Road

START

495

Monroe

Run

Big   Run   Road

Big

Run

Dry

Run

Road

Big Run
State Park

Reservoir

Savage   River

Savage
River

495

have already been tended. There are enough sites along the run to provide solitude, but any more such sites would threaten the wild experience of the canyon. If forced to camp in a new site, be sure to exercise Zero Impact camping by eliminating any sign of your presence before leaving.

The canyon narrows to barely wider than Monroe Run at 3.2 miles and stays that way for about half a mile. Then, in a wider flatland, the run divides into two, and at times three, streams, creating small isolated islands. In rainy periods these areas form a washed-out delta of alternately fast-moving and stalled water. Take great care if crossing in these conditions.

The final crossing comes at 3.9 miles, where the run reaches wide bottomland. As you approach the bottom, you are more likely to encounter hikers venturing uphill from the developed campsites near Big Run Road. Still, except on weekends in summer, a lonesome, remote feeling dominates the trail.

At 4.6 miles reach Big Run Road. Car camping at the developed sites through this area affords a quiet spot for launching day hikes to the surrounding mountains.

Miles and Directions

0.0 Start at trailhead after enjoying the view from the overlook.

1.1 Cross Monroe Run for the first time.

2.6 Reach series of secluded campsites.

3.9 Cross Monroe Run for the last time; there are developed campsites nearby.

4.6 Reach Big Run Road, your shuttle or turnaround point.

Options: You can make a loop hike by turning left onto Big Run Road at the bottom of the trail and then turning left onto New Germany Road, for a round-trip of 8.0 miles. Although this is a road walk, it is very scenic and sees little automobile traffic.

6 Lostland Run Loop, Potomac State Forest

A hike through a hemlock-laurel canyon, following Lostland Run en route to the Potomac. There are stream crossings on footbridges, a waterfall, and many opportunities to view wildlife.

Location: Potomac State Forest is in Garrett County in western Maryland.
Type of hike: 7.4-mile loop.
Difficulty: Moderate.
Elevation gain: Lose 650 feet and then gain 650 feet on road walk.
Season: April through November.
Fees and permits: No fees or permits required.
Maps: USGS Gorman, Maryland–West Virginia; Deer Park, Maryland; Mt. Storm, West Virginia.
Special considerations: In the first mile of the hike, there are two sections of rough and rocky terrain. They are passable by hikers of

most abilities, but they make for slow going for a time.
Camping: The gravel Lostland Run Road serves primitive car campsites, which may be reserved for a fee through forest headquarters. Despite the fact that some of the campsites are literally adjacent to the road, the place has a remote quality. For reservations call Maryland's statewide reservations line for state parks and forests: (888) 432-2267.
For more information: Potomac State Forest.
Trailhead facilities: There is a water spigot behind the headquarters office.

Finding the trailhead: From Frederick, Maryland, drive west on Interstate 70 to Interstate 68 West in Hancock. Go 69 miles on I-68, exit south on U.S. Highway 219 toward Deep Creek Lake, and go 26 miles to Oakland, Maryland. Stay on US 219 when it turns left in Oakland; when US 219 turns right outside of town, go straight onto Maryland Highway 135. In about 2 miles, turn right onto Maryland Highway 560 just outside Mountain Lake Park. In 2 miles turn left onto Bethlehem Road (staying right at the fork at 2 miles). In 1.4 miles turn left onto Combination Road; in 0.5 mile turn left onto Potomac Camp Road. The forest headquarters is about a mile farther on the left. To find the trailhead from the parking area, cross the road and walk 75 feet back up the road; look for a wooden marker.

The Hike

You can lose your cares amid the hemlock and laurel along the swift Lostland Run and forget the time gazing at Cascade Falls deep in the gorge. The trail crosses the run several times, and there are several scenic falls.

There are a few areas of rough and rocky terrain and a couple of places where the trail seems to disappear, but with little effort you will steer the course toward the cliffs of the Potomac River at the bottom of the run. The river is reached at 4.0 miles, after a hike that is largely downhill. The return to the trailhead is via the gravel Lostland Run Road, which serves the camping area. It is mostly uphill from the river, but the grade is not overly challenging and is plenty wide enough to walk side by side with a companion.

Maryland's rugged western mountains have many miles of short rambles for hikers of all abilities.
PHOTO COURTESY OF MARYLAND DNR

From the trailhead the path and white blazes are easy to follow, tracing the drainage of a seasonal run on the north side of South Prong Lostland Run (you will follow the South Prong until its confluence with the North Prong at 2.1 miles). At 0.6 mile the trail passes close to the creek and the road. The intermittent clanging of steel you will hear is a lime dozer; these are installed on several streams in western Maryland to restore the pH balance after the destruction left by mining operations. Just beyond is a rocky section, followed by the footbridge to the south side at 0.9 mile.

Turning immediately after the bridge, follow a footpath above the run, with hemlocks and red pine overhead and rhododendron below the ledge. A steep stairway of carved logs drops to the run at 1.3 miles, where the trail crosses back to the north side on a log bridge forged from a tree that happened to fall in the perfect place.

At 1.5 miles cross the South Prong Lostland Run on a nifty swinging bridge constructed by the Maryland Conservation Corps, a youth program responsible for many good works in Maryland forests. Ascend to the ledge above the run, which now enters a steep gorge. Watch for blazes here—the trail is not always obvious, and it is easy to get distracted by beautiful foliage in the cool, dark gorge.

At 2.1 miles the trail breaks left away from the run and crosses North Prong Lostland Run just before the confluence of the two prongs. If you miss the break, the path will end at the confluence. From there you will see the bridge 100 feet to the left.

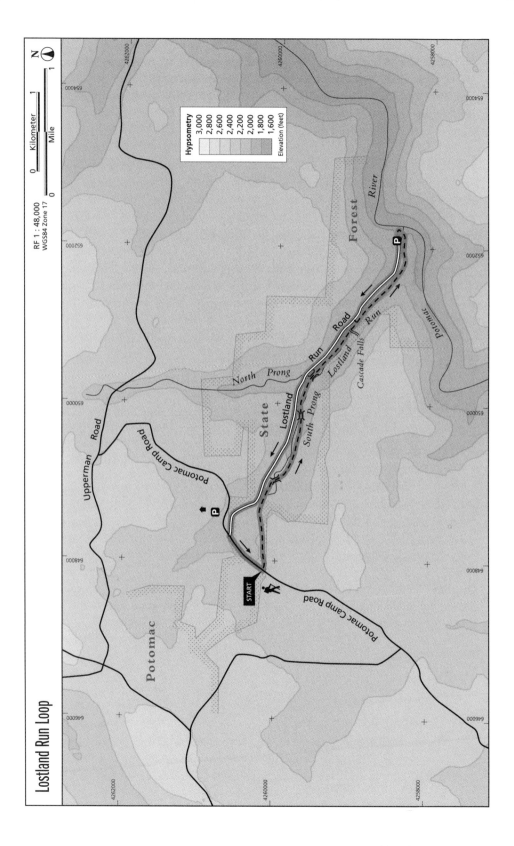

Lostland Run Loop

RF 1 : 48,000
WGS84 Zone 17

Hypsometry

	3,000
	2,800
	2,600
	2,400
	2,200
	2,000
	1,800
	1,600

Elevation (feet)

N

Potomac State Forest

Potomac

Upperman Road

Potomac Camp Road

Potomac Camp Road

North Prong

Lostland Run Road

South Prong

Lostland Run

Cascade Falls

Potomac River

START

P

P

Follow a wide cart path that keeps to the high road as the run drops to the right. A quarter of a mile later, watch for a switchback descending right—a false trail continues straight ahead. The next 0.5 mile is a delightful stroll down in the gorge, up close to the fast-flowing water. This is prime habitat for black bears and nocturnal hunters such as bobcats and owls.

Hugging a narrow ledge at stream level, the trail passes under a dense canopy, dark even at midday. Cross several small knobs and then reach Cascade Falls at 3.0 miles. A viewing platform provides an excellent prospect. If you are lucky enough to have the falls all to yourself, you will want to linger here. Then climb wooden stairs following blue blazes that lead to a trailhead serving the falls. At the top of the bluff, follow the white blazes right; the blue blazes continue straight to Lostland Run Road.

The final mile below the falls is the most remote and solitary. The path alternates from ledge walking on the bluffs above to close, intimate contact with the stream. Just before the trail emerges at the Potomac River parking area at 4.0 miles, a footbridge leads across the run.

Before heading up Lostland Run Road for the return walk, follow the path at the end of the parking area to the cliffs above the Potomac and take in the splendid views.

Miles and Directions

0.0 Start at the trailhead at a wooden marker.

0.9 Cross footbridge to south side of South Prong.

1.3 Descend steep log steps to log bridge; cross back to north side.

1.5 Cross South Prong on swinging bridge.

2.1 Cross North Prong on a footbridge.

3.0 Reach Cascade Falls.

4.0 Emerge from trail at Potomac River parking area.

7.4 Arrive back at trailhead.

Options: With a second car stashed at the bottom of the trail, you can shorten the hike to 4.0 miles, eliminating a 3.4-mile walk along the gravel camping road.

7 Rocky Gap Canyon to Evitts Summit, Rocky Gap State Park

A challenging walk through the dark and lush Rocky Gap Canyon followed by an ascent over an old woods road to a monument marking the Mason-Dixon Line high atop Evitts Mountain, where there are expansive views. Along the way, visit the historic homestead of the first white settler in the rugged Allegheny Mountains.

Location: Rocky Gap State Park in Allegany County, Maryland, is 12 miles east of Cumberland, Maryland.

Type of hike: 5.2-mile out-and-back.

Difficulty: Moderate.

Elevation gain: 1,200 feet.

Season: Year-round.

Fees and permits: No fees or permits required.

Maps: USGS Evitts Creek, Maryland–Pennsylvania–West Virginia.

Special considerations: The wide dirt road of Evitts Homesite Trail makes an especially fine trail for snowshoe hiking.

Camping: A developed campground is available in the park. For reservations call Maryland's statewide reservations line for state parks and forests: (888) 432-2267.

For more information: Rocky Gap State Park.

Trailhead facilities: Water, restrooms at park headquarters at park entrance, other refreshments at lodge.

Finding the trailhead: From the junction of Interstates 70 and 68 in Hancock, Maryland, drive 30 miles west on I-68 to exit 50, Rocky Gap State Park. Go straight at the junction with the park road, following directions to the lodge. Bear left at the lodge and continue past it 1 mile to the trailhead parking on the left.

The Hike

This hike begins with a visit to an enchanting hemlock canyon and climbs to the summit of Evitts Mountain, where there are endless views of the Allegheny Mountains and a Mason-Dixon Line marker that is placed, as most were, in the middle of nowhere. From Rocky Gap Run in the canyon, you will climb 1,200 feet over 2 miles, but the majority of the ascent is over a wide dirt road that provides a stable surface and plenty of rest spots. The 0.5-mile walk through the canyon is rocky and steep at times, but hikers comfortable sliding down a couple of boulders on their backsides will fare just fine.

From the nature trail parking area, walk through the gate on the paved road; do not follow the gate onto the gravel road at the left. One hundred yards beyond a trailhead for Canyon Overlook Trail, at 0.2 mile, follow a footpath left into the woods at a sign marking the Evitts Homesite Trail. Immediately you will forget you are in a resort area only 400 yards from the lodge. Rhododendron and azalea abound under a dense canopy.

A trail system circles Lake Habib at Rocky Gap State Park. PHOTO COURTESY OF MARYLAND DNR

Follow the white blazes left at the fork at 0.3 mile; the trail straight ahead leads to the dam. Descend for 75 feet over boulders and outcrops, only a couple of which require hand maneuvers. In the canyon the trail follows a ledge on a narrow footpath surrounded by hemlock, table mountain pine, giant oaks, and pignut hickory.

Just as the trail begins a final dip into the canyon, a side trail leads 50 feet straight ahead to a view of Rocky Gap Run below. Towering above are scarlet oaks, marked by their smooth vertical stripes on the bark. Below, a thicket of rhododendron leans over the creek. To the left, the canyon walls reveal the layered shale of the Alleghenies.

Descend into the canyon, and at 0.5 mile, cross Rocky Gap Run on a footbridge. Then begin a steep ascent that pauses enough to catch a breath. Emerge onto an old farm road at 0.9 mile, which is Evitts Homesite Trail. Follow the trail left and ascend. The pleasant walk under many white oaks, Maryland's state tree, is marred only by the sounds of trucks rising on the wind from a mile away on the highway. But as the trail slabs around the hill, you will leave the noise behind. The climb to the top from here is steady but offers plenty of pauses in its bends, where the road is level for a short stretch.

A short trail at 2.0 miles leads 75 yards right to the Evitts Homesite. A man whose first name seems forgotten by all, Mr. "Everts" (the spelling varies among local sources) escaped to these rugged mountains in 1801 to live out his life as a hermit.

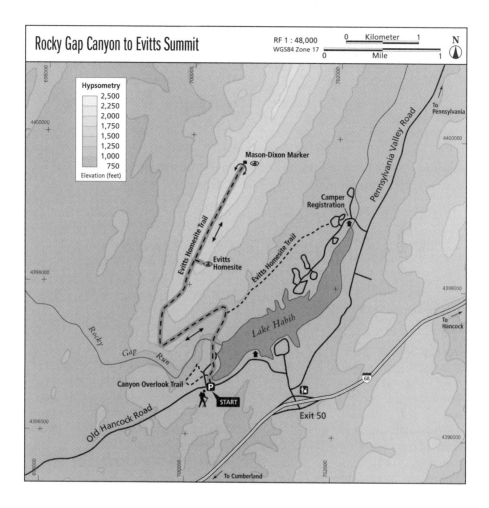

Rocky Gap Canyon to Evitts Summit

RF 1 : 48,000
WGS84 Zone 17

Hypsometry
2,500
2,250
2,000
1,750
1,500
1,250
1,000
750
Elevation (feet)

Mason-Dixon Marker

Camper Registration

Evitts Homesite Trail

Evitts Homesite

Evitts Homesite Trail

To Pennsylvania

Pennsylvania Valley Road

To Hancock

Rocky Gap Run

Lake Habib

Canyon Overlook Trail

START

68

Exit 50

Old Hancock Road

To Cumberland

Some accounts cite bad business deals; others, failure at love. Only a stone well and a few stone fences remain.

Back on the trail, climb steadily on the woods road another 0.6 mile to an aviation signal tower. The Mason-Dixon marker is a dozen steps farther on the left; the views another dozen steps are farther into Pennsylvania. The wonderful view of the rugged Allegheny Mountains reveals why, to this day, the area remains rather remote, except for the city of Cumberland a short distance west.

Return to the trailhead by retracing your steps. At the bottom, just before the trailhead, a side trip onto the 0.25-mile Canyon Overlook Trail is recommended.

Miles and Directions

0.0   Start at nature trail parking area; walk through gate onto paved road.

0.2   Reach junction with Canyon Overlook Trail.

0.3	Turn left at fork.
0.5	Cross Rocky Gap Run on a footbridge.
0.9	Reach Evitts Homesite Trail junction; go left.
2.0	Follow short trail right to Evitts Homesite.
2.6	Reach signal tower and Mason-Dixon Line marker. Enjoy the views before retracing your steps to the trailhead.
5.2	Arrive back at trailhead.

Options: After visiting the canyon and reaching Evitts Homesite Trail, you can turn northeast for a mile-long stroll along Lake Habib.

8 Twin Oaks Trail, Green Ridge State Forest

A pleasant, sometimes challenging hike featuring more than a dozen stream crossings, a few rugged ascents through pine forest, and mountain views.

Location: Green Ridge State Forest is in Allegany County, Maryland, just off Interstate 68, about 140 miles northwest of Washington, D.C.
Type of hike: 4.0-mile loop; overnight or day hike.
Difficulty: Moderate.
Elevation gain: Several steep climbs, none more than 150 feet.
Season: April through November.
Fees and permits: Camping registration required.

Maps: USGS Artemas, Maryland.
Special considerations: During spring, be prepared for muddy conditions along Pine Lick. The area is managed for hunting; check with rangers for season dates.
Camping: Camping is available; self-registration is required at the forest office.
For more information: Green Ridge State Forest.
Trailhead facilities: None.

Finding the trailhead: From the junction of Interstates 68 and 70 in western Maryland, go west on I-68. Take exit 62 to Fifteenmile Creek Road/Maryland Highway 40 and travel northeast. At a fork at 0.5 mile, bear left to follow unpaved Fifteenmile Creek Road. Proceed 1 mile to Double Pine Road and turn left. Follow this road for 2.5 miles past several campsites to the end of the road at Old Cumberland Road. Park here, where Twin Oak Trail crosses.

The Hike

This is a fine hike for introducing a young person (or someone not so young) to backpacking. Or you can enjoy it all in a day. The hike offers a blend of streamside rambling, rock-hop creek crossings, and deep woods walking. Although there are several ascents that will get even a fit hiker heaving, none are sustained for more than a few hundred yards. Nor do they climb more than a couple hundred feet. At about 45,000 acres, Green Ridge State Forest is Maryland's largest contiguous public land

Green Ridge State Forest is one of Maryland's largest state lands. PHOTO COURTESY OF MARY-LAND DNR

area. It is also a land of incredible biodiveristy: There are more species of trees and shrubs in this forest than in all of Europe.

From the trailhead, facing south (away from Old Cumberland Road) turn right to follow Twin Oaks Trail as it gradually ascends through new pines to the junction with Pine Lick Trail. Turn left. Continue a casual climb through hardwood groves mixed with Virginia pines. Pass campsite number 5 on the left at 0.4 mile; if the camp is empty you can take a break at the picnic site there.

In another 300 yards the terrain levels as you enter a grassy dale. The unlikely clearing in the forest is a managed "edge," the type of habitat favored by small game and deer. Green Ridge State Forest is managed for multiple use; these small clearings enable managers to concentrate the impacts of game management to specific zones (be sure to check the forest Web site or office for hunting schedule).

Begin a long and sometimes steep descent into the hollow of Pine Lick, a shallow creek that alternates between meandering curves and headlong rushes toward Fifteenmile Creek. Following the creek, the trail crosses on stepping-stones a dozen

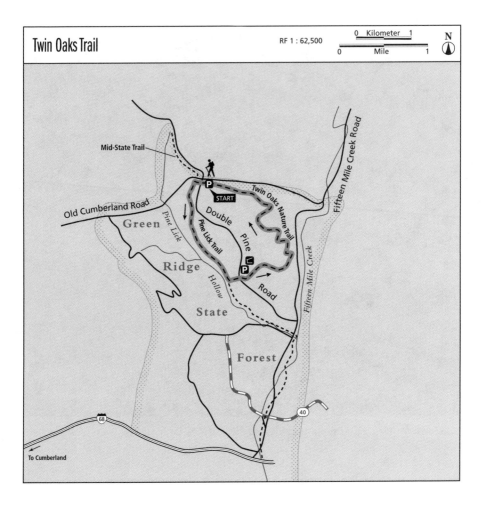

times in little more than a mile. In high water, the trip is not one to take with small children, unless they are on your back. In warm weather the worse thing that will happen is wet sneakers—although the whole bottomland can be muddy the day after a big rain. Whatever the weather, Pine Lick Hollow is a kid's paradise, full of wildflowers and tadpoles in vernal pools in spring.

Reach Pine Lick camping shelter at 1.7 miles, a three-sided primitive outpost facing the creek, and a meadow visited by deer, turkey, and hawks—a nice place to watch the mountains grow dark on a summer evening.

Just beyond the shelter, turn left onto Twin Oaks Nature Trail and climb through the woods to the crossing of Double Pine Road at 1.9 miles. Look for the white blazes across the road, just uphill. The path on this side of the road is little subtler, but trust the white blazes as the trail descends into a hollow. Note the many folds and depressions in the land. At the top of the hill, turn left onto an old woods road. After descending, turn left at the T junction with the Mid-State Trail at 2.4 miles.

There are wonderful views of Green Ridge straight ahead, and the trail is wide enough for kids to run amidst the new-growth woodlands. At the bottom of this hill, cross a small stream and turn right into the woods. After crossing the stream again, ascend on switchbacks for the longest climb of the hike. If you stop for a breath, there are wonderful views behind you.

At 2.9 miles, at the top of the hill, pass through a pine plantation on flat ground, then into a clearing managed for wildlife. About 150 yards beyond the clearing, watch for blazes breaking right—the wide road will continue straight, but you will turn right. Continue through dense woods, then descend steeply on switchbacks to cross a bridgeless creek at 3.7 miles. Cross back to the other side 200 yards later and start a long ascent. At the top of the hill is an open forest lush with ferns and colorful with dogwoods in spring.

Emerge from the woods on wide level path maintained for accessible hunting. Reach Double Pine Road and the end of the hike at 4.0 miles.

Miles and Directions

0.0 Start at trailhead; junction of trail and Old Cumberland Road.
1.7 Reach Pine Lick camping shelter.
1.9 Cross Double Pine Road.
2.4 Turn left at T junction, and enjoy the views of Green Ridge.
2.9 Pass through pine plantation into a meadow, then take a sharp right turn.
3.7 Cross a bridgeless creek.
4.0 Arrive back at trailhead.

Options: To walk the second half of the loop on a wide, lightly traveled dirt road, turn left onto Double Pine Road at 1.9 miles.

9 Fifteenmile Creek, Green Ridge State Forest

One of Maryland's best hikes for getting away from it all, this is a circuit hike in and above the remote canyon of Fifteenmile Creek.

Location: This trail is in Green Ridge State Forest in Allegany County, Maryland, 140 miles northwest of Washington, D.C.

Type of hike: 5.4-mile loop.

Difficulty: Moderate.

Elevation gain: 380 feet.

Season: April through November; wildflowers abundant in May and June.

Fees and permits: No fees or permits required.

Maps: USGS Artemas, Maryland–Pennsylvania–West Virginia.

Special considerations: The forest is open to hunting November through February; check with the state forest headquarters for details.

The trail is well maintained for foot travel and is passable by hikers of most abilities, with two minor exceptions on the circuit hike: In two places the trail follows a narrow ledge that requires careful going with young children or novice hikers. There is no bridge crossing

Fifteenmile Creek at 4.2 miles, where "high water" usually means about 24 inches at a moderate flow. Consider bringing an old pair of sneakers for this crossing.

If there has been heavy rain in the days before your hike, drive down to the creek crossing before setting out on your hike. That way, you will know long before reaching the final crossing whether your return to the visitor center will be an uneventful uphill road walk or a return by the way you came.

Camping: Primitive sites are available along the river; contact the visitor center for information on developed campsites in the forest. For reservations call Maryland's statewide reservations line for state parks and forests: (888) 432-2267.

For more information: Green Ridge State Forest.

Trailhead facilities: Water, restrooms at comfort station; visitor center has displays.

Finding the trailhead: From the junction of Interstates 70 and 270 near Frederick, Maryland, drive west 29 miles to I-68 in Hancock, Maryland. Take I-68 26 miles west to exit 64, Flintstone. Go south (right) at the end of the exit ramp. Cross over I-68 and in 0.3 mile, turn right into the state forest headquarters. The trailhead, marked with a white diamond, is beside the restrooms.

The Hike

Fifteenmile Creek slices a 200-foot gorge between Green Ridge and Town Hill on its way to the Potomac River. The 45,000-acre Green Ridge State Forest provides a sense of the wild backcountry, only two-and-a-half hours from Washington, D.C. Considering the hike begins only a few hundred yards from the interstate and then spends the first 0.3 mile in proximity to it, this ramble offers surprising solitude. It also presents a nice opportunity to combine hiking with fly fishing in one of several shaded holes down in the gorge. The hike travels south on Green Ridge Hiking Trail, spending about 3.0 miles within sight and sound of tumbling water.

Fifteenmile Creek cuts a steep gorge through Green Ridge. PHOTO COURTESY OF MARYLAND DNR

Starting at the state forest visitor center, the first 0.5 mile is an unremarkable scamper through conifer and maple as the trail makes its escape from the intrusion of I–68, sitting practically astride the trail. Completed in the 1980s to provide a high-speed route west over the rugged Allegheny Front, the highway has succeeded in bisecting key forests and hiking lands. After the trail breaks south away from the road at 0.5 mile, it ascends into eastern cedar and pine along an old forest road. Soon the highway is easily forgotten.

Following the ridgeline at about 1,000 feet, the trail enters a stand of towering chestnut oaks and scattered eastern hemlock, signaling a more mature forest of more hardwoods and fewer pines that the trail will follow along the creek. Just beyond a remnant pine grove, the trail passes the ruins of an old cabin, unremarkable except for the tin shard implanted deep into the trunk of an ash tree and, high above the ruins, another sign of the hardwoods reclaiming a forest stripped clean a century ago for charcoal and tanning bark.

The pathway ends at a T intersection with Green Ridge Hiking Trail North Spur at 1.1 miles, the high point on the hike at 1,060 feet. To the north (right) it is 6.3 miles to the Pennsylvania border and the southern terminus of the Mid-State Trail,

Fifteenmile Creek

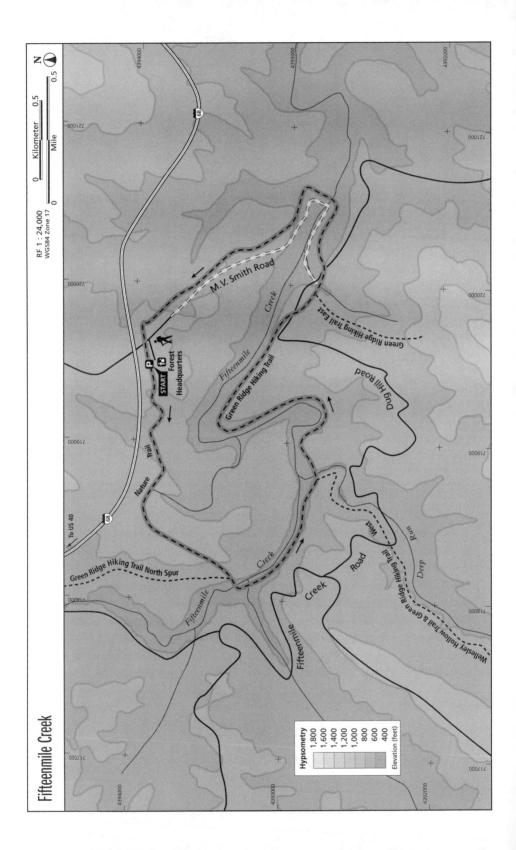

RF 1 : 24,000
WGS84 Zone 17

N

Kilometer
0   0.5

Mile
0   0.5

M.V. Smith Road

Forest Headquarters

START

P

Fifteenmile Creek

Green Ridge Hiking Trail

Green Ridge Hiking Trail East

Dug Hill Road

Nature Trail

To US 40

Green Ridge Hiking Trail North Spur

Fifteenmile Creek

Fifteenmile Creek

Creek Road

West

Deep Run

Wellesley Hollow Trail & Green Ridge Hiking Trail

Hypsometry

1,800
1,600
1,400
1,200
1,000
800
600
400

Elevation (feet)

4394000
4393000
4392000

717000
718000
719000
720000
721000

a 187-mile path through the heart of the Keystone State. To the south it is 13.7 miles to the Potomac. Looking in that direction, in the leafless months you can catch a revealing view of the regional topography with the view to the left of Town Hill.

The descent to Fifteenmile Creek, at 690 feet, is steep but not overly challenging. It is made more enjoyable by the rock formations lining the trail, reminders of the volcanic activity that built the mountains. At 1.3 miles cross Fifteenmile Creek on a beautiful wooden footbridge. After a big rain, when the creek is roaring, you can watch an hour float by just sitting on the bridge above the torrent.

Following the crossing, the trail cuts sharply left and then travels 0.5 mile of up and down, but none of the climbs are challenging for more than 50 yards. The sound of falling water and songbirds, coupled with sightings of deer and wild turkey, will be remembered long after the climbs. In its 3.0 miles along the river—at times down in the gorge astride the river and at times a hundred feet above—the trail passes one of the more wild, remote landscapes in Maryland.

If you have brought rod and reel along, Deep Run, at 1.9 miles, is the place to find a spot where the water runs fast and cool. This is the end of the Green Ridge Hiking Trail North Spur as well as the junction with the main Green Ridge Hiking Trail. To the south (right), Wellesley Hollow and Green Ridge Hiking Trails climb a saddle of Town Hill up the headwaters of Deep Run and then descend along Big Run to the Chesapeake & Ohio Canal. Straight ahead, the Green Ridge Hiking Trail heads east.

Crossing Deep Run, Green Ridge Hiking Trail stays left of the hill for about a hundred yards and then veers subtly right up the ridge on an old woods road. Follow the markings carefully through the next 0.5 mile—a couple of false trails and old roads veer from the trail. With the sandstone cliffs and the hemlock stands capturing your attention, it would be easy to stray down a dead end. After crossing an unnamed run, the trail enters a long, lazy curve where the bottomlands offer prime campsites and swimming holes. Even during the summer months, it is possible to move downstream and find an out-of-the-way spot for a quiet lunch and a dip. The best swimming hole, but one you will not enjoy alone, is at about 3 miles, just before the middle of the creek bend. It sits beneath sandstone towering a hundred feet from the gorge.

From here the trail climbs amid oak and hemlock, offering occasional views of the gorge and back to Green Ridge, until passing under a sparkling cool cascade at 3.4 miles. The waterfall seems to emerge from the side of the rock face, a fine place to shower off the early miles of the hike if you can stand the chill. The climb from here takes the trail away from Fifteenmile Creek and then through oak and hickory stands, where there are remnant American chestnut trees—they will grow to a dozen feet or more before succumbing to the chestnut blight that decimated this once all-American species early in the twentieth century.

The trail emerges onto the dirt-and-gravel Dug Hill Road at 3.6 miles and goes left. There is no sign here. Follow the road 350 yards and turn left onto M.V. Smith Road at 3.8 miles, which is marked by a gate. (Green Ridge Hiking Trail continues on Dug Hill Road.) The road is public, but the property along it is private, so hikers should stick to the road as it passes old hunting camps en route to a creek crossing at 4.2 miles. Exercise judgment here, and know your own skills. When the water is a foot or more deep, it can be surprisingly swift. If it looks too challenging for your level of experience you can retrace your steps and enjoy a return along the creek.

From the other side of the creek, you are 1.2 miles from the visitor center via M.V. Smith Road.

Miles and Directions

0.0 Start at the trailhead at visitor center.

1.1 Reach junction with Green Ridge Hiking Trail North Spur. Begin descent to Fifteenmile Creek.

1.3 Cross Fifteenmile Creek on a footbridge.

1.9 Reach Deep Run and junction with Wellesley Hollow Trail.

3.6 Emerge onto Dug Hill Road; turn left.

3.8 Turn left onto M. V. Smith Road.

4.2 Carefully cross creek and return to visitor center via M. V. Smith Road.

5.4 Arrive back at trailhead.

10 C&O Canal Towpath–Paw Paw Tunnel

A walk along the Chesapeake & Ohio Canal Towpath through a tunnel more than half a mile long, followed by a scenic walk near a remote stretch of the Potomac. The return hike is over a shoulder of the mountain on the Potomac side, offering stunning views of the West Virginia mountain landscape.

Location: Paw Paw Tunnel on the C&O Canal is about 100 miles northwest of Washington, D.C., and 15 miles southeast of Cumberland, Maryland, just across the Potomac River from Paw Paw, West Virginia.
Type of hike: 3.1-mile lollipop.
Difficulty: Moderate.
Elevation gain: 360 feet.
Season: April and May for flowering trees and wildflowers.
Fees and permits: No fees or permits required.

Maps: USGS Paw Paw, West Virginia. Map and guide available from C&O National Historical Park (see Appendix A).
Camping: There is a campsite on the trail 1.0 mile north of the tunnel; registration with the National Park Service is required.
Special considerations: Bring a flashlight for walking through the tunnel.
For more information: C&O National Historical Park.
Trailhead facilities: Portable privy and water pump at trailhead.

Finding the trailhead: From the Capital Beltway, go north on Interstate 270 to Interstate 70 West. At Hancock, Maryland, take Interstate 68 West to Cumberland, exiting onto Maryland Highway 51 south. Follow MD 51 about 25 miles to the tunnel trailhead on the left. The trailhead is at the far end of the parking area.

The Hike

You could take longer getting to the trailhead than hiking this delightful section of the C&O Canal Towpath, but you will find you want to savor every moment out there. Take a flashlight along to better explore the tunnel walls and the several places where brick courses have been removed back to stone.

To get on the towpath, which passes through the parking area, follow the signs to the tunnel. Black cherry, serviceberry, and redbud line the path, putting on quite a flower show in late April and early May. To the right is the former "section house," which served as home and office for the tunnel's area superintendent.

The tunnel entrance is at 0.5 mile (the pathway emerging from the right just before the entrance is the overmountain return route). Note the natural arch of the shale above the tunnel opening, a contributing factor in the choice of this location for the tunnel. Climbing the stairs to examine the exterior tunnel closely, you will see water dripping ceaselessly through the shale. If you have ever stood by a river and wondered how the water just keeps flowing, the answer is revealed here. All over the mountain, gravity is slowly pulling water through the earth and toward its drainage.

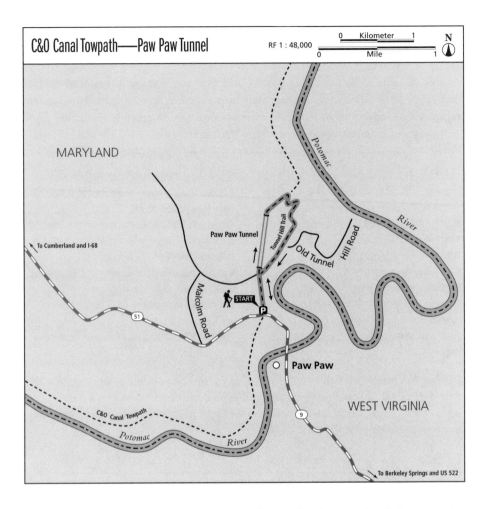

Enter the tunnel, and for the next 0.5 mile wander through the darkness on the 4-foot-wide path. The only light inside comes from the openings at either end of the tunnel. You can rely on the handrail for support and guidance; it is the same rail followed by canal men and mules until the canal's closing in 1924. The rail is as smooth as a wood floor from the action of the tow ropes gliding over it between mule and barge for so many years.

Most people prefer to hike through with flashlights off, except to examine features here and there, but you may find the surface too uneven for that. In either case, two points of Zero Impact Hiking apply: (1) Keep your flashlight to the floor, except when exploring features, so as not to disturb the darkness for others; and (2) keep your conversation to a whisper because part of the experience is the utter silence of the tunnel.

Exit the tunnel at 1.1 miles and continue north, first on a boardwalk and then back on the towpath. In spring, at your feet you will find wild pink. Above, water cascading over the shale walls of the tunnel gorge splashes into the canal channel. To head back over the mountain, watch for a trail sign on the right at 1.4 miles. The trail breaks to a hard right switchback. Before ascending, take as much time as you can to wander down the canal. You will find the remains of three canal locks, once used to raise and lower the water level for barge passage. You also may see signs of beaver plying their trade in the canal waters or at the Potomac River shoreline.

At the cutoff trail for the return hike, begin a steady ascent on a woods road, staying with the orange or red blazes (both are called orange, but some appear red). You will climb for nearly half a mile, gaining more than 350 feet, but there are several places to stop and enjoy the landscape. Two hundred yards into the ascent is a wonderful view west of Green Ridge Mountain, the eastern shoulder through which the tunnel passes.

At 2.1 miles reach the upper prominence and junction with another woods road. One path makes a hard left back behind you, one goes straight, and another is a soft left. Take the soft left and descend. The trail becomes a narrow footpath that slabs around the shoulder of the hill and then descends on switchbacks. Stay on the trail here; the switchbacks protect the hillside ecology.

Still a hundred feet above the river, at about 2.4 miles, is an open spot offering long views of the Potomac, the town of Paw Paw, and West Virginia. From here you can see the wide bends in the river, known as Paw Paw Bends, that prompted canal builders to blast a tunnel through Green Ridge rather than build the canal around so many curves.

Reach the towpath at the tunnel's south end at 2.6 miles, and continue south back toward the trailhead. Just before the trailhead, a footpath diverges left to lead past the old section house, allowing a close-up view of the structure.

Miles and Directions

- **0.0** Start at trailhead, far side of parking lot.
- **0.5** Reach south tunnel entrance.
- **1.1** Exit tunnel; continue north.
- **1.4** Reach junction with Tunnel Hill Trail; make a hard right onto switchback.
- **2.1** Arrive at junction with footpath; turn left and begin descent.
- **2.4** Enjoy views of Potomac River, Paw Paw, and West Virginia.
- **2.6** Reach junction with towpath at south end of tunnel; continue south.
- **3.1** Arrive back at trailhead.

11 Fort Frederick State Park Nature Trail

An easy walk through a young forest in an area that was previously logged. A good hike for children on a family outing to the park or for a field study of forest succession.

Location: Fort Frederick State Park is located in Washington County, Maryland, about 80 miles northwest of Washington, D.C., and 12 miles southeast of Hancock, Maryland.
Type of hike: 1.2-mile loop.
Difficulty: Easy.
Season: April through November.
Fees and permits: No fees or permits required.

Maps: USGS Clear Spring, Maryland.
Special considerations: Pets are not permitted at Fort Frederick State Park.
Camping: Camping is available, at the park's riverfront campground.
For more information: Park Manager, Fort Frederick State Park.
Trailhead facilities: Water; restrooms at the park visitor center.

Finding the trailhead: From Interstate 70 in western Maryland, take exit 12 (Big Pool–Indian Springs) and travel 1.1 miles east on Maryland Highway 56 to the entrance of Fort Frederick State Park. Turn right into the park; bear left in 0.1 mile and follow the road 0.4 mile to Fort Frederick National Historic Monument. Turn left just past the fort, and travel 0.5 mile to the parking at the picnic area.

The Hike

Because it is very short and not entirely pristine, Fort Frederick State Park Nature Trail is not a "destination hike." Nevertheless, a walk on the 1.2-mile loop could be a nice part of a family outing to the park or a field study of forest succession. In addition to the nature trail, the park boasts Fort Frederick, the national historic monument that played a role in the French and Indian, Revolutionary, and Civil Wars. The historic Chesapeake & Ohio Canal Towpath passes through the park, as does, of course, the Potomac River. With the picnic area by the trailhead, it is a great place to spend a day exploring the human and natural history of the area.

On the white-blazed nature trail, climb a hill from the parking area, passing through the dense thickets and saplings common to recovering forests, and then bend into an older forest of pines and mixed hardwoods. The pine duff path descends to a wash, crossing the narrow stream on a primitive log footbridge, and then switchbacks up a hillside. At the crest of the hill, cross another small clearing overgrown with thickets. Leaving the clearing, reenter the woods—a mix of pines and the young oaks, hickories, and black walnuts that will one day succeed the conifers.

Already you will have a sense of why this part of the park is called the pine plantation area. The marks of logging are everywhere, but so are the signs of recovery. As

Fort Frederick on the Potomac River was part of the western defensive front during the French and Indian War. PHOTO COURTESY OF MARYLAND DNR

you walk the woods here, note the different stages a forest passes through on its way from clearing to thicket to pine forest to an ever-increasing mix of hardwoods.

Continuing through the woods, follow the trail as it bends to the left and then cuts through a clearing and back into the woods by a stone pile on the right. The navigating gets a little tricky here. Though an Eagle Scout is making preparations to repair and maintain the trail, there are places on the path where its thin log borders can be hard to see. This is one of those areas. Turn right into the woods by the stone pile, then quickly left, and follow the trail for 25 yards to the next clearing. At the clearing, look downhill and to the right for a post marked with the number 6. Cut through the clearing to the post and then turn left, following a white blaze into the woods.

The trail now travels through a more mature woodland. Still young by forest standards, there are nevertheless some big pines along with sturdy oaks, maples, and sweet gums. There are also grassy meadows where deer browse. After passing through the meadows, turn left into even bigger hardwoods—mostly tall, straight tulip trees on their way to being stately giants. In the shade of the poplars, the trail bends

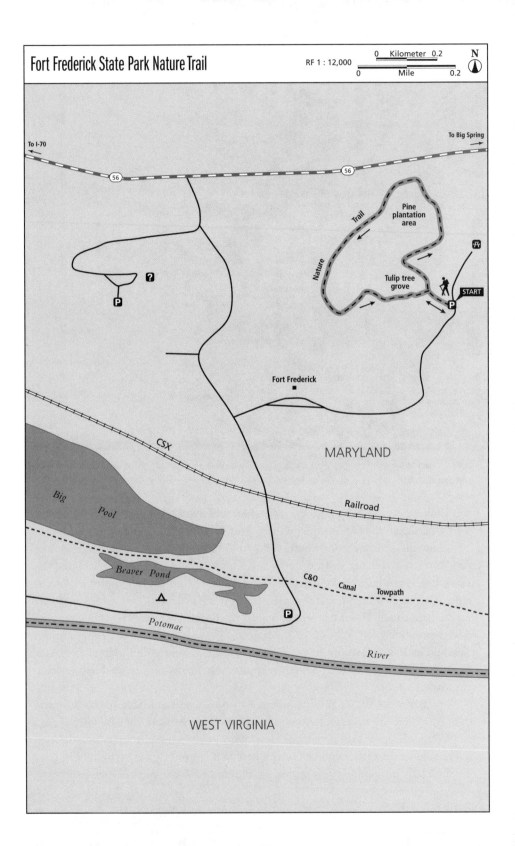

Fort Frederick State Park Nature Trail

RF 1 : 12,000

0 Kilometer 0.2

0 Mile 0.2

N

To I-70

To Big Spring

56

56

Pine plantation area

Trail

Nature

Tulip tree grove

START

P

?

P

Fort Frederick

CSX

MARYLAND

Big Pool

Beaver Pond

C&O Canal Towpath

Railroad

Potomac

River

WEST VIRGINIA

through another meadow—first right, then sharply left—and continues through a stand of pines back to the trailhead.

Miles and Directions

0.0 Start at trailhead.
0.3 Enter pine plantation area.
1.0 Turn left onto tulip tree grove.
1.2 Arrive back at trailhead.

Options: You can also hike on the C&O Canal Towpath or the park's other short nature trail, the Wetlands Trail.

12 Snavely Ford Trail, Antietam National Battlefield

A pleasant circuit walk along the surprisingly wild Antietam Creek, one of three fronts in the Battle of Antietam, the bloodiest day of the Civil War. Wild turkey, beaver, barred owls, and other wildlife inhabit the stream valley. Cows can often be seen grazing on the other side of the creek.

Location: The hike is in Antietam National Battlefield, located in Washington County, Maryland, about 75 miles northwest of Washington, D.C.
Type of hike: 2.2-mile loop.
Difficulty: Easy.
Season: October through May.
Fees and permits: No fees or permits required.
Maps: USGS Keedysville, Maryland.

Special considerations: The creek is stocked with trout in spring; licenses are available at a store near the park. The rest of the battlefield and the charming town of Sharpsburg make a fine conclusion to the hike. A hiking ritual: Stop at Nutters in Sharpsburg for ice cream.
Camping: No camping is available.
For more information: Antietam National Battlefield.
Trailhead facilities: None; water and restrooms are available at the visitor center.

Finding the trailhead: From the Capital Beltway, drive north on Interstate 270 to Interstate 70 West. In 25 miles, exit onto Maryland Highway 65 South. The Antietam National Battlefield visitor center is 10 miles on the left. To reach the trailhead, continue 1 mile to the town of Sharpsburg and turn left onto Maryland Highway 34. In about 0.5 mile, descend from a hill and turn right into the park. At the bottom of the next hill, just after crossing a road bridge, turn left. (Turning right leads to Harpers Ferry Road, the route you will take to exit the park.) Parking for Burnside Bridge is at the end of the road. The hike begins at the bottom of the steps leading to the bridge.

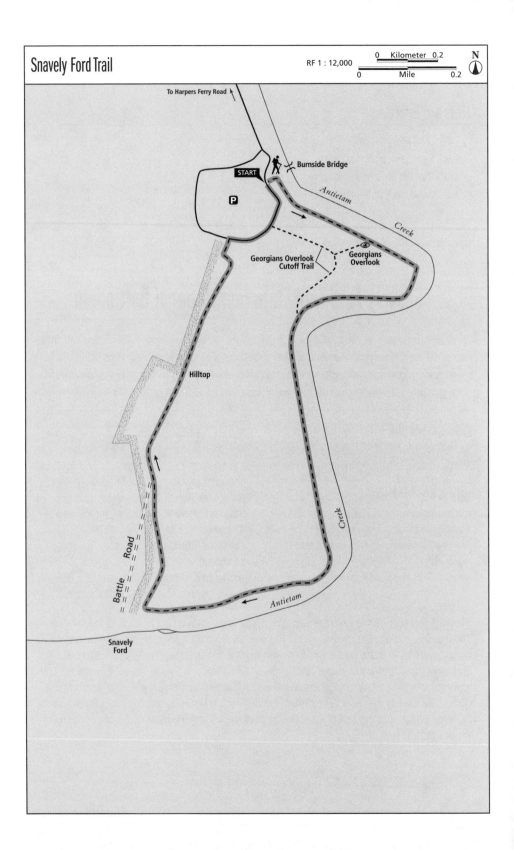

Snavely Ford Trail

RF 1 : 12,000

0   Kilometer   0.2

0   Mile   0.2

N

To Harpers Ferry Road

Burnside Bridge

START

P

Antietam

Creek

Georgians Overlook
Cutoff Trail

Georgians
Overlook

Hilltop

Battle   Road

Creek

Antietam

Snavely
Ford

The Hike

The lovely bucolic countryside belies the carnage that took place along the creek on September 17, 1862. The Battle of Antietam (also known as the Battle of Sharpsburg) took place in three phases over 12 square miles. Down by the creek, Union general Burnside tried to move his army over the bridge and into Sharpsburg. The streamside trail preserves the landscape that saw the death of thousands. Now it is alive with towering oaks and maples, blackberries on the edges, and the scent of pawpaws by the bank.

From the parking area, descend the steps and follow Georgians Overlook Trail. Take some time to enjoy the overlook, from which Southern troops trained their rifles on Federal troops approaching the bridge. From the overlook descend to the creek and turn right.

Ancient beech trees line the creek and uplands, while the bottomland is still thick with the lower story of second-generation forest. The hillside to the right is home to wild turkeys, barred owls, and deer. In spring there are Dutchman's-breeches flapping in the breeze; in fall the pawpaws give the forest a banana smell.

At 1.2 miles reach Snavely Ford, the crossing point for several divisions of Union soldiers on a flanking maneuver. They made their way up the hill toward Sharpsburg here; the road they traveled is still visible to the left beginning at about 1.3 miles. Uphill, the forest cover changes to thick red cedar. On early evening hikes, you may see several deer leaving the cedar cover to follow the trail down to the creek.

At the top of the hill, at 1.8 miles, a dirt road to the right leads to an old homestead. To the left, the parking area is 0.5 mile down a dirt cart path.

Miles and Directions

0.0 Start at trailhead at bottom of steps.

0.1 Reach Georgians Overlook cutoff.

1.2 Reach Snavely Ford.

1.4 Views of battle road begin.

1.8 At top of hill, turn left on cart path to return to trailhead.

2.2 Arrive back at trailhead.

Options: For a shorter hike of 1.6 miles, walk the route in reverse and take the Georgians Overlook cutoff trail. It is not marked, but it will be the only trail leading left from the creek.

Snowy days at Antietam National Battlefield mean solitude for snowshoers and cross-country skiers. PHOTO COURTESY OF MARYLAND DNR

13 Blue Ridge Summit–Hog Rock, Catoctin Mountain Park

A ramble through hardwood forests and over ridges of Catoctin Mountain, with views of the Blue Ridge and the Monocacy Valley. In spring, dogwoods and other flowering trees are abundant.

Location: Catoctin Mountain Park, a unit of the National Park Service, is located in Frederick County, Maryland, about 50 miles northwest of Washington, D.C.

Type of hike: 5.1-mile loop.

Difficulty: Moderate.

Elevation gain: 700 feet.

Season: September through May.

Fees and permits: No fees or permits required.

Maps: USGS Blue Ridge Summit, Pennsylvania; "Catoctin Mountains," National Park Service; and topo map sold in National Park Service visitor center.

Special considerations: This hike is described as moderate because most of the climbing is done in two short stretches: the first 0.25 mile

and the 0.3 mile approaching Blue Ridge Summit Overlook. Most of the rest of the hike is a mixture of level ground and gradual ascents and descents. This is a beautiful hike in winter, especially in snowshoes after a winter storm.

Camping: In Catoctin Mountain Park and adjacent Cunningham Falls State Park, camping is available in campgrounds only; several locations have multiple sites. Cabins are also available.

For more information: Catoctin Mountain Park and Cunningham Falls State Park.

Trailhead facilities: Water fountain outside visitor center; bookstore, museum, restrooms, and water fountain inside visitor center.

Finding the trailhead: From the Capital Beltway, drive north on Interstate 270 about 32 miles and exit onto U.S. Highway 15 North. In 17 miles, head west on Maryland Highway 77 (at Thurmont). Catoctin Mountain Park Visitor Center is 3 miles on the right. The trailhead is at the far end of the lot.

The Hike

In about two hours, you can visit a splendid waterfall, enjoy a spectacular view of the Monocacy watershed, and find an intimate cross ridge at Catoctin's summit and South Mountain, all while wandering through a second-growth, almost-old-growth-again, hardwood forest. But what is the rush? The hike is short enough that extended stays are in order at each highlight.

Starting at the trailhead at the visitor center, begin ascending toward Hog Rock and Thurmont Vista. The first 0.25 mile is a rude start to automobile-weary legs, but leveler ground is found soon enough. The dogwoods and spicebush, scattered here and there with mountain laurel, are reason enough to take it slow and get your lungs working. This is a scenic hike any time of year, but spring on Catoctin Mountain is a world of flowering trees.

Blue Ridge Summit–Hog Rock; Wolf Rock–Chimney Rock Loop

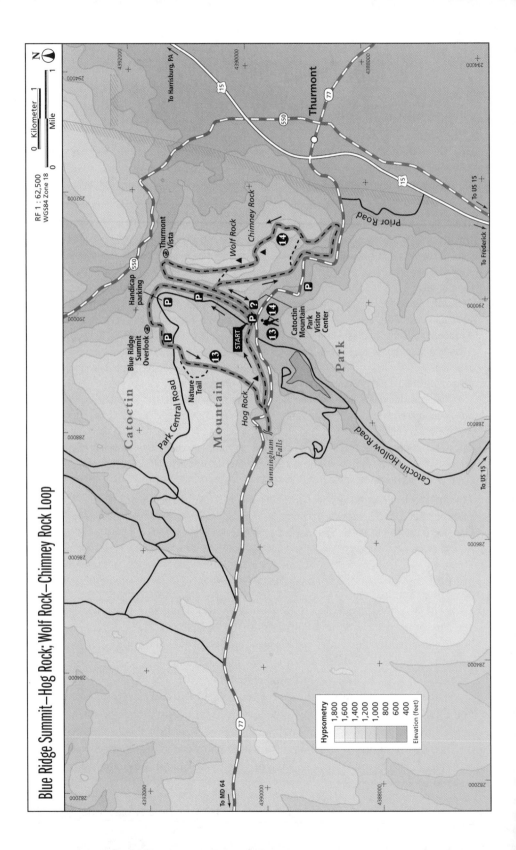

RF 1 : 62,500
WGS84 Zone 18

N

0   Kilometer   1
0   Mile   1

Hypsometry
1,800
1,600
1,400
1,200
1,000
800
600
400
Elevation (feet)

To Harrisburg, PA

Thurmont

Catoctin   Mountain   Park

Thurmont Vista

Wolf Rock

Chimney Rock

Blue Ridge Summit Overlook

Handicap parking

Park Central Road

Nature Trail

Hog Rock

Cunningham Falls

Catoctin Mountain Park Visitor Center

Prior Road

Catoctin Hollow Road

START

To MD 64

To US 15

To Frederick

To US 15

At 0.6 mile Wolf Rock Trail leads east to Wolf Rock, a formation of Weverton quartzite named for its resemblance to the snout and mane of a wolf. You can detour to Wolf Rock without backtracking to this junction: From Wolf Rock hike north past Thurmont Vista to rejoin this hike at the 1.0-mile point (Thurmont Vista Trail junction). It will add about 1.6 miles to the hike and a fair amount of up and down.

Following the ridgeline north from the junction with Wolf Rock Trail, to the left is Charcoal Trail, which tells the story of the charcoal industry that, along with leather tanning, supported the mountain settlers in the nineteenth century. The bark was gathered and sold to leather tanners, and the trees were felled to make charcoal as a fuel for nearby iron furnaces. The mountain people effectively worked themselves out of an existence, however, because their livelihoods were hardly sustainable once they had denuded Catoctin Mountain of every tree. The story is true for many of the nearby mountains of the Blue Ridge. Still, the process of charcoal production is fascinating, worthy of a detour to Charcoal Trail.

At 1.0 mile is a junction with the Thurmont Vista Trail, leading right. The left trail leads 250 yards to a trailhead. Go straight toward Hog Rock and descend into a small hollow. Pass through a boulder field of Catoctin greenstone, a basalt rock formed from compressed lava flows. Then begin a long, slow ascent toward Blue Ridge Summit Overlook, passing another boulder field where rock has tumbled down the mountainside. A section of level ground prepares you for a short, intense rise of about 100 feet over only 200 yards.

Another brief respite from ascending follows, then a quick final ascent to Blue Ridge Summit Overlook at 1.7 miles. A short trail leads to the view over the ledge. From here you can almost reach out and touch Catoctin's summit, at 1,880 feet about a half mile away on the other side of a narrow hollow. On a clear day you can also spy South Mountain between the ridges, part of the jumbled collection of peaks and hollows that make up the Blue Ridge. In some places the Blue Ridge runs southwest to northwest in one clearly defined ridge. In many others, the naming of one mountain as a separate summit seems almost arbitrary.

From here follow the ridge and gently descend amid mature chestnut oak and beech. On a damp day particularly, the scent of sassafras fills the air. At the Hog Rock Nature Trail junction, at 2.1 miles, there are picnic tables and privies. Crossing Park Central Road, follow Hog Rock Nature Trail on a casual ascent. Mature sugar maples and basswood line the trail. The crosscut wounds on the maples that resemble closed lips are the handiwork of woodpeckers and other insect-loving birds. They cut a horizontal gash in the trunk, which gets the sap running. When insects come to feed on the sap, the birds arrive for their own feeding.

Several interesting rock formations of Catoctin greenstone abut the trail; shagbark hickory rise above them. The nuts, once favored by swine turned loose to roam the woods, now attract legions of squirrels and chipmunks. To this day, hickory is a choice wood for tool handles. Before the mountain was cut for bark and charcoal, the hickory here was prized for hammer mauls.

Hog Rock, at 2.5 miles, is a fine rest stop. A huge, flat outcrop of greenstone, it is also the place for a nap—especially on weekdays, when you stand a good chance of having the place to yourself. As was the custom throughout much of the Blue Ridge, mountain farmers let their swine run wild through the woods, allowing them to graze on nuts and seeds and whatever else they could find. In autumn, the hogs typically ended up at the base of this rock, feasting on hickory and chestnuts. The farmers would retrieve the fattened animals here at Hog Rock.

From Hog Rock begin a slow 1.0-mile descent toward Cunningham Falls. There are a few stream crossings and boulder fields amid the towering, misnamed tulip poplars and the occasional, aptly named musclewood tree. The tulip poplar, known by its excellent upright posture, light-gray bark, and distinctive mitten-shaped leaves, actually is not a poplar at all. It is a member of the magnolia family. The musclewood's small stature belies its strength, so tough it was once used to make ox yokes.

Descend more steeply for the final 200 yards to reach the junction with the short trail to Cunningham Falls, at 3.5 miles. Viewing the falls requires a short detour. Cross MD 77 into Cunningham Falls State Park, and follow the boardwalk another hundred yards to the falls. Early morning and late afternoon are the best times to find some solitude there—winter is a great time to visit. The 0.1-mile detour to the falls puts you back at the main trail at 3.7 miles.

On the main trail, the final 1.4 miles is an easy ramble under tulip poplars and beech, with two short ascents over low knobs. The bookstore and museum inside the visitor center make a good finish to this hike.

Miles and Directions

0.0 Start at trailhead at visitor center.

0.6 Reach junction with Wolf Rock Trail.

1.0 Reach junction with Thurmont Vista Trail; go straight.

1.7 Arrive at Blue Ridge Summit Overlook.

2.1 Reach junction with Hog Rock Nature Trail.

2.2 Cross Park Central Road and follow nature trail.

2.5 Arrive at Hog Rock, a good rest stop.

3.5 Reach junction with short trail to Cunningham Falls.

3.7 Arrive back at main trail.

5.1 Arrive back at visitor center.

Options: For a short hike to Cunningham Falls, start at the visitor center and hike west, reversing the final 1.6 miles of this hike.

14 Wolf Rock–Chimney Rock Loop, Catoctin Mountain Park

This is a somewhat rugged hike to two outstanding vistas and a fascinating rock formation known as Wolf Rock, traveling through immense stands of hardwoods and abundant mountain laurel.

See map on page 62
Location: Catoctin Mountain Park, a unit of the National Park Service, is located in Frederick County, Maryland, about 50 miles northwest of Washington, D.C.
Type of hike: 4.8-mile loop.
Difficulty: Strenuous.
Elevation gain: 500 feet overall, a lot of up and down.
Season: April through November.
Fees and permits: No fees or permits required.

Maps: USGS Blue Ridge Summit, Pennsylvania; Cunningham Falls State Park map.
Special considerations: With two outstanding vistas, add plenty of time to your itinerary for enjoying the views.
Camping: Camping is available; registration and a fee are required.
For more information: Catoctin Mountain Park.
Trailhead facilities: Water and restrooms are in the Catoctin Mountain Park Visitor Center; books on local natural history are for sale.

Finding the trailhead: From the Capital Beltway, drive north on Interstate 270 about 32 miles and exit onto U.S. Highway 15 North. In 17 miles head west on Maryland Highway 77 (at Thurmont). Catoctin Mountain Park Visitor Center is 3 miles on the right. The trailhead is at the far end of the lot.

The Hike

Starting at the trailhead at the visitor center, begin ascending toward Hog Rock and Thurmont Vista through dogwoods and spicebush. In spring these blooming trees team with mountain laurel and rhododendron to create quite a flower show.

At 0.6 mile turn right (east), following the sign to Wolf Rock. Ascend by switchback to a junction at 0.8 mile. Go right, toward Chimney Rock. Begin a long descent, steeply at times, amid a field of huge boulders. Stay left when, at 1.7 miles, the trail drops right to the national park headquarters. Ascend again below Chimney Rock, a huge outcropping composed of Weverton quartzite.

The trail levels off and slabs north, keeping Chimney Rock on the left, then makes a final quick ascent to an access trail to Chimney Rock at 2.2 miles. The peak to the southeast is 1,500-foot Cat Rock, accessible from the trailhead across from the National Park Service headquarters. Reaching it requires an ascent of 700 feet in less than a mile.

Back on the main trail, turn left and continue north toward Wolf Rock—a formation of Weverton quartzite named for its resemblance to the snout and mane of a wolf—reached at 2.7 miles.

Hike north from Wolf Rock, passing a trail junction at 2.8 miles; the path leads 1.0 mile back to the visitor center. The next 0.8 mile en route to Thurmont Vista can offer surprising solitude in this popular hiking area. Many more hikers will take the short route to Wolf and Chimney Rocks without making the circuit. And while the vistas get top billing on this hike, the huge old growth through this section is memorable.

Reach Thurmont Vista at 3.6 miles. The view to the east at the beginning of the twenty-first century is vastly different than it was at the start of the previous century. The fertile farmland of the Monocacy Valley is giving way to houses. Intense efforts are under way to preserve the valley's historic farmland.

Hiking north, pass an old cart path descending east and then reach a junction at 3.8 miles. Turn left and descend the mountain toward the trailhead. Along the way, an interpretive trail parallels the path 100 yards west. It tells the story of the charcoal enterprise that clear-cut the entire mountain in the nineteenth century. It adds little time, but some informative enrichment, to the hike.

Miles and Directions

- **0.0** Start at trailhead at visitor center.
- **0.8** Reach fork to Chimney Rock; go right.
- **1.7** Stay left where trail drops right to park headquarters.
- **2.2** Arrive at Chimney Rock.
- **2.7** Reach Wolf Rock.
- **3.6** Arrive at Thurmont Vista.
- **3.8** Come to junction; turn left to begin descent toward trailhead.
- **4.8** Arrive back at trailhead.

Options: For a shorter, much easier hike, go left at the cutoff to Chimney Rock (Milepoint 0.8 above). At the next junction turn right to visit Wolf Rock, then hike north to Thurmont Vista as described above. You can also press on to Chimney Rock from Wolf Rock and then retrace your steps to Wolf Rock. From there, continue as described above.

15 High Knob–Catoctin Mountain Loop, Gambrill State Park

A circuit along and beside the ridge of Catoctin Mountain through mature hardwood forest, offering excellent views east and west.

Location: The hike is in Gambrill State Park, located 45 miles northwest of Washington, D.C.
Type of hike: 5.0-mile loop.
Difficulty: Moderate.
Elevation gain: Minimal.
Season: Year-round.
Fees and permits: No fees or permits required.

Maps: USGS Frederick, Maryland.
Camping: Camping is available; a permit and fee are required.
For more information: Gambrill State Park.
Trailhead facilities: None; water is available from fountains at 0.5 mile.

Finding the trailhead: From the Capital Beltway, drive north on Interstate 270 to Interstate 70 West. In 2.5 miles exit onto Alternate U.S. Highway 40 West. At the top of the hill, turn right onto Ridge Road, which ends at U.S. Highway 40. Turn right (east) onto US 40. In 1 mile turn left (north) onto Gambrill Park Road (staying right at the fork to Rock Run Area). In 1.2 miles turn right into the trail system parking area.

The Hike

This hike along Catoctin Mountain offers plentiful, sweeping views north and west of South Mountain, home of the Appalachian Trail. On the hike's return on the east side of the ridge are scenes of the Monocacy River watershed. The views west are slightly marred by the distant sounds of I–70, which passes below about 3 miles to the west. But the sounds on the east side of the ridge are more likely to be those of woodpeckers and barred owls.

Begin the hike at the message board. A 5-foot relief map of the trail system gives a bird's-eye view of the hike and the southern end of Catoctin Mountain. Crossing Gambrill Park Road, follow the trail marked with yellow, black, red, and green blazes into the woods; go right at the fork following the yellow and green blazes, where the black trail goes straight ahead. The black trail, which will rejoin the route at 0.7 mile, offers a quieter woodland walk away from the people at High Knob but at the expense of excellent views.

Ascend steeply for 200 yards, then, in the level clearing, follow the green and yellow blazes sharply left. After another short ascent, just before a picnic pavilion, follow the yellow trail left. The green blazes continue straight ahead.

Follow the ridgeline below the "tearoom," a park building open to the public and available for public functions (mentioned here because the view from the terrace is memorable). At High Knob, at 0.4 mile, pass below a limestone outcropping.

Catoctin Mountain Park is part of a 20,000-acre forest preserve in Frederick County. PHOTO COURTESY OF MARYLAND DNR

It is worth a few minutes to scale to the top for the views of Sugar Loaf Mountain. Another 100 feet down the trail is an overlook with expansive views of South Mountain to the west and north. In another 200 feet is an overlook constructed of stone, perched on the ledge. Picnic tables are nearby.

Follow a descent in a tunnel of mountain laurel and white pine to the junction with the black trail, reentering from the left at 0.7 mile. Two hundred yards later, at 0.8 mile, watch for a side trail to the left that leads to an open ledge with the last sweeping view on this hike. Just beyond this point, the black trail breaks east toward the road, offering a quick return option to the trailhead by crossing the road, rejoining the yellow trail, and then turning south.

From the junction the yellow trail follows a rocky path for a while and then again finds soft trail, for the next 1.3 miles never venturing more than a hundred yards from Gambrill Park Road. The road is not a distraction. This is a nice, casual walk under a hardwood canopy, with mountain laurel ever present.

After crossing an old cart path, cross Gambrill Park Road at 2.2 miles and enter woods on a dirt road, where locust trees are dying out and giving way to oaks and

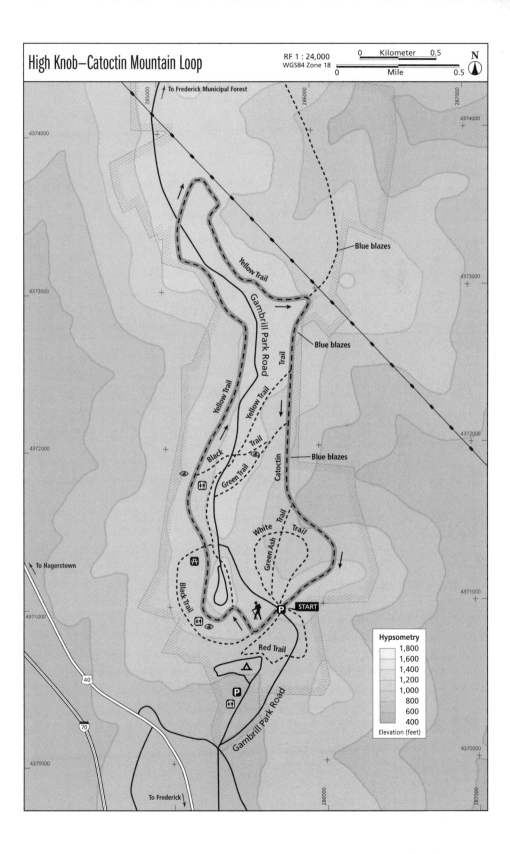

High Knob–Catoctin Mountain Loop

RF 1 : 24,000
WGS84 Zone 18

0 Kilometer 0.5

0 Mile 0.5

N

To Frederick Municipal Forest

Blue blazes

Yellow Trail

Gambrill Park Road

Blue blazes

Yellow Trail

Yellow Trail

Blue blazes

Black Trail

Catoctin Trail

Green Trail

White Trail

Green Ash Trail

To Hagerstown

Black Trail

START

P

Red Trail

40

70

Gambrill Park Road

To Frederick

Hypsometry

	1,800
	1,600
	1,400
	1,200
	1,000
	800
	600
	400

Elevation (feet)

maples. At the power line go right and follow the utility corridor for 150 yards before ducking back into the forest cover. Over a small knob, the trail descends into a hollow with a steep rise to the right and a small pond to the left. Except in summer, when the pond is a mosquito haven, the pond is an excellent place to sit back and await deer in search of a drink. Two hundred feet beyond the pond, watch for yellow blazes breaking right, uphill. Do not go straight; if you come to the power line, you have gone too far.

Ascend through mature oaks and hickory. The landscape uphill is open forest. The upper story is so dense that little sunlight reaches the floor in summer, the mark of a mature forest. Pass a flat seam of limestone—another great rest area—and cross a gravel road into the woods. Staying left, cross under power lines and follow the trail into a cutout dirt road.

Just beyond, at 3.3 miles, is the junction with the blue-blazed Catoctin Trail, a 27-mile backpacking trail that begins at the same trailhead as this hike. It reaches this junction by traversing the east side of the ridge. From here the Catoctin Trail heads north on the dirt road through Frederick City Municipal Forest, Cunningham Falls State Park, and Catoctin Mountain Park.

Turn right and follow the yellow-and-blue-blazed Catoctin Trail south. Along here are wonderful views east through the trees of the Monocacy Valley and Braddock Heights. At 3.4 miles the yellow trail breaks right, climbing southwest toward the trailhead. Stay left on the blue trail. For the next 0.5 mile the blue trail descends the east ridge. To the left the mountain gives way to a steep drop into a dark hollow; to the right is a steep rise into white pine.

At 3.8 miles an old road enters from the right, descending the knob. This is the black and green trail. The old road crosses the trail and disappears into the hollow, where many maps show a water source called Bootjack Spring (do not rely on it). The black and green blazes continue the descent now with the blue-blazed Catoctin Trail.

The trail bottoms out at yet another old wagon path, a remnant of the farming that once took place on the mountains here, and begins the long but gentle climb up the ridgeline. At 4.4 miles the green trail makes a steep ascent toward the trailhead, offering a challenging shortcut. Follow the blue and black blazes, and ascend on a wide path beneath birch, maple, and scattered white pine.

At the top of the climb, just as the trail levels off and settles into a soft, wide dirt path, note a subtle trail to the left that forms a kind of cul-de-sac. This is a short path over a small knob to several quiet napping spots. From here follow the level path past the junction with the red trail at 5.0 miles and to the trailhead.

Miles and Directions

0.0 Start at trailhead at message board.

0.4 Pass below limestone outcropping at High Knob.

0.8 Watch for side trail to left leading to view from an outcrop.

2.2 Cross Gambrill Park Road and enter woods on dirt road.

3.3 Reach junction with Catoctin Trail; turn right.

3.4 Yellow trail breaks right to trailhead; stay left on blue-blazed trail.

3.8 Come to junction with black and green trail, which now follows the blue-blazed Catoctin Trail.

4.4 Stay on blue-and-black-blazed trail as green trail breaks off.

5.0 Arrive back at trailhead.

West of the Chesapeake Bay and Susquehanna River

16 Hashawha Loop, Hashawha Environmental Appreciation Area

A fine walk through surprisingly deep woods in a county park. There are views of Pars Ridge, the principal geologic feature of Carroll County, and passages through open meadows and cultivated fields. Watch for blue herons and other waterfowl from the boardwalk across tiny Lake Hashawha.

Location: Hashawha Environmental Appreciation Area is located in Carroll County, Maryland, about 30 miles northwest of Baltimore and 5 miles north of Westminster.
Type of hike: 4.5-mile loop.
Difficulty: Easy.
Season: Year-round.
Fees and permits: No fees or permits required.
Maps: USGS Finksburg, Maryland.
Special considerations: When the nature cen-

ter is closed, no water is available.
Camping: No camping is available.
For more information: Bear Branch Nature Center.
Trailhead facilities: Water and restrooms are available at Bear Branch Nature Center. The facility, which houses wildlife exhibits and offers a wide array of programming, is open Wednesday through Saturday 10 A.M. to 5 P.M. and Sunday noon to 5 P.M.

Finding the trailhead: Follow Maryland Highway 97 north from Westminster 5 miles to John Owings Road. Turn right and go 2 miles to Hashawha Environmental Appreciation Area on the left. Proceed past the lake and up the hill to Bear Branch Nature Center. The trailhead is at the far end of the parking area.

The Hike

Carroll County is not known as a hiking destination. But the quiet woods, the opportunity to see a fox or hawk hunting in a cornfield or beaver plying the stream, and the extensive variety of wildflowers in the stream bottomland all combine to make this an outing worth traveling for—especially when combined with a visit to Westminster's Main Street or other Carroll County attractions.

Following the blue blazes from the rear of the nature center parking area, descend the path to a picnic pavilion. Turn right with the blazes, and follow a wide path 250 yards to a fork in the blue trail. Go left into woods, ascending a small knob through oak and dogwood and then passing a trail leading left back to the picnic area. Ascend easily through a white pine grove, with a nice view of farmland on the right and a meadow on the left. In the distance is the scenic wooded hillside of Pars Ridge, a narrow crest running from Washington, D.C., into southern Pennsylvania and the feature that gives the region its famous rolling countryside.

At 0.8 mile the woods open at the raptor center, which houses birds of prey that are brought here following life-threatening injuries. Take the green- and yellow-

Hashawha Loop

RF 1 : 12,000

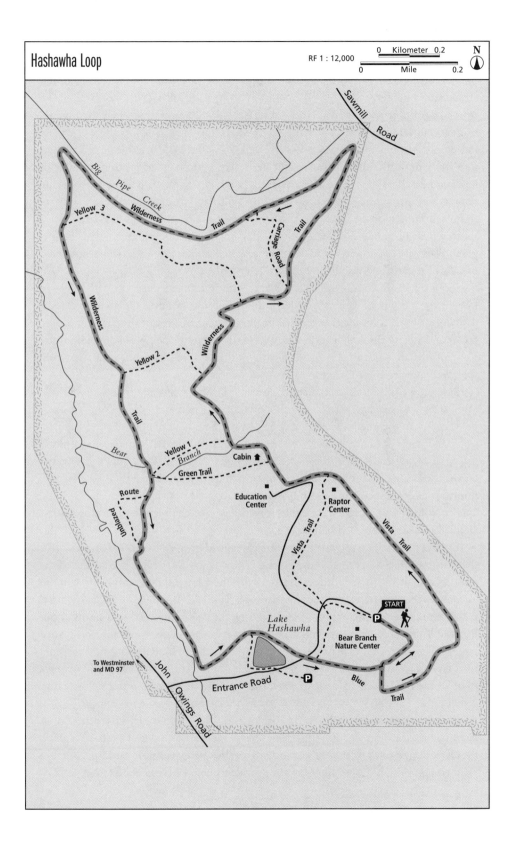

blazed trail right along the park road leading to the education center (closed to the public). Blue blazes continue intermittently, but the blue-blazed Vista Trail turns left at the raptor center.

Go right onto an old farm road. Quiet hikers will be rewarded here with views of deer and rabbits, which favor the edge where the farm fields to the right meet the woods just beyond. At 1.1 miles the yellow-blazed Wilderness Trail skirts right into the woods. Before you turn right here, take a moment to examine the 1800s log cabin. In the 1990s the cabin was entirely reconstructed. It is now open during festivals and for group programs. Now you will have to content yourself with an outside examination because vandals have forced a closure of the building. (For a shorter hike of about 2 miles, continue past the cabin on the green trail. Follow green blazes through new woodlands and seasonal wetland down in the bottomland of a small stream, and rejoin the hike as described below at 3.3 miles.)

From the cabin, follow the yellow blazes leading right on a narrow path between low shrubs and wildflowers, a veritable butterfly alley in summer. On an early August day, you may see a hundred butterflies in this 40 feet of green tunnel. Enter a pine grove, and ascend through a cool, sweet-scented canopy. If the pines here seem more plantation than wild, it is because farmers often planted pines as a fast-growing source of lumber and firewood.

Pass an unblazed trail on the right; do not follow it. Continue following the yellow blazes, and descend into a deep hollow; then ascend and emerge into an open field. The corn or other crop that may be planted here is a common feature in many Maryland parks, where the park and agricultural uses coexist. It makes for a pleasurable hike, especially for those remembering childhood hikes through nearby farms. Turn right, and follow the line of trees for 50 yards. Enter the woods again, this time under mixed hardwoods, passing the Yellow Loop 1 junction at 1.3 miles. The loop forms a shorter, woodland loop that rejoins the main trail of this hike at about 3 miles, as described below.

Enter a field with a splendid view straight ahead of the extending Pars Ridge—the quintessential Carroll County scene. If you reach this scene late in the afternoon, pause at the woods' edge and scan the field for wildlife activity. If you are lucky, you may see a coyote ambling through the field. If you are especially lucky, it will be in pursuit of a rabbit. Continue straight across the field to a point about halfway to the trees and turn left, following a narrow, subtle rut in the tread. Your target is the edge of a row of trees extending into the field. Reaching the treeline, turn right and follow a path toward the trees; a subtle variation between two sections of the field marks your path. Descend into the trees, passing the Yellow Loop 2 marker at 1.5 miles.

Begin a long descent on a wide path, passing two yellow-blazed shortcut trails en route to the bottom. Emerge from the woods onto a gravel path in a wide meadow. Thirty yards to the right is a gated trailhead at Sawmill Road. Turn left and walk through the meadow hugging the woods to your left. Big Pipe Creek, one of the largest streams entirely within Carroll County, is 75 yards to the right beneath the birches and a few cottonwoods. Watch for deer and smaller denizens, such as gophers, scattering at the sound of you.

At 2.1 miles, just after passing a second yellow-blazed shortcut to the left, enter the woods and begin ascending on a wide path. The path to the right of the trees provides stream access to Big Pipe Creek. Ascending, the hillside suddenly drops right dramatically and the creek is 50 feet below you. The next 0.5 mile is as lovely a walk as you will find anywhere in Maryland. With the ridge rising steeply to your left and the stream splashing far below, this is a place to walk slowly and savor your time.

After a gentle descent back to stream level, turn sharply left away from the creek and ascend at 2.6 miles. The trail that continues straight ahead is open to hikers but is managed for hunting in season. Check with the park office for information when hiking from September through March. Fifty yards after turning left here, be sure to stay right at the fork, following the yellow blazes.

Climb steeply for about a hundred yards and then find level ground. Over the next 0.5 mile follow the yellow blazes past junctions with Yellow Loops 2 and 1, rambling over knobs and descending into hollows. From time to time, the trail emerges into small meadows, lush with blackberries and wildlife-viewing opportunities.

At 3.3 miles descend to a small stream and cross on a footbridge. Continue straight in the meadow for 20 yards to reach a junction. The cabin you passed at 1.1 miles is now 200 yards to the left. Turn right at this junction, following the blue blazes in and out of the woods. You have the option of taking the high trail or low trail at 3.4 miles. The high trail takes a direct route through the field, while the low trail ducks into the woods—the distance is about the same, and the two rejoin as the trail enters another field in 200 yards. In this field watch for the green blazes on a post. You will walk into the field, then turn right into its center, then left about 60 yards from the woods. If you come to the stream and a swinging rope, you have gone too far.

At 3.9 miles reach a clearing at Bear Branch Creek. (A wooden bridge over the stream leads to an equestrian trail system.) Follow the green blazes, taking the middle left. Walk around the top of the Lake Hashawha, and follow the boardwalk across the water. Blue herons, red-winged blackbirds, and other birds are a common sight, as is the occasional snake sunning itself on the boards.

Cross the park road at 4.2 miles and turn left. Turn right onto the blue trail, and follow it about 0.25 mile back to the trailhead.

Miles and Directions

0.0 Start at trailhead at rear of nature center parking area.

0.8 Arrive at the raptor center; go right, following green and yellow blazes.

1.1 Reach junction with Wilderness Trail; examine cabin before turning right onto Wilderness Trail.

1.3 Pass Yellow Loop 1 junction.

1.5 Pass marker for Yellow Loop 2 junction.

2.1 Pass carriage road to the left.

2.6 Turn sharply left at Big Pipe Creek and ascend.

3.3 Descend to small stream and cross on footbridge.

3.4 At split in trail, follow either route.

3.9 Reach clearing at Bear Branch Creek.

4.2 Cross park road and turn left. Then turn right onto blue trail.

4.5 Arrive back at trailhead.

Options: You can create a 2.0-mile loop by following the green trail at 1.1 miles instead of taking the yellow-blazed Wilderness Trail as described. You also can use Yellow Loop 1 or 2 for a shorter hike. The blue-blazed Vista Trail makes a 1.2-mile loop back to Bear Branch, leaving from the raptor area at 0.8 mile.

17 Beetree Preserve

This hike combines views of the open rural Baltimore County countryside with a circuit through the woods.

Location: Beetree Preserve is along the Northern Central Railroad Trail, 18 miles north of Cockeysville, Maryland.

Type of hike: 3.7-mile loop.

Difficulty: Moderate.

Elevation gain: 100 feet.

Season: Spring.

Fees and permits: No fees or permits required.

Maps: USGA New Freedom, Pennsylvania

Special considerations: Beetree Preserve is privately owned by the Towson Presbyterian Church; please respect any trail closures related to church-sponsored events. Calling in advance of your hike is recommended.

Camping: Camping is available for organized groups under church sponsorship.

For more information: Towson Presbyterian Church; (410) 823-6500.

Trailhead facilities: Pay phone and privy.

Finding the trailhead: From the Baltimore Beltway (Interstate 695), travel north 17 miles on Interstate 83 to exit 33, York Road. Go north on York Road (Maryland Highway 45) for 1 mile, and turn left onto Kaufman Road. In about 0.7 mile turn left onto Bentley Road, and proceed 0.7 mile to the parking area on the right.

The Hike

This hike offers one of the few circuit hikes along the Northern Central Railroad Trail, allowing you to hike a little on the wide flat path of the famous NCRR through the rolling countryside, then duck into the woods for a ramble around a

Dogwood, azaleas, and other wildflowers abound in the pockets of woodland along the Northern Central Railroad Trail. PHOTO COURTESY OF MARYLAND DNR ▶

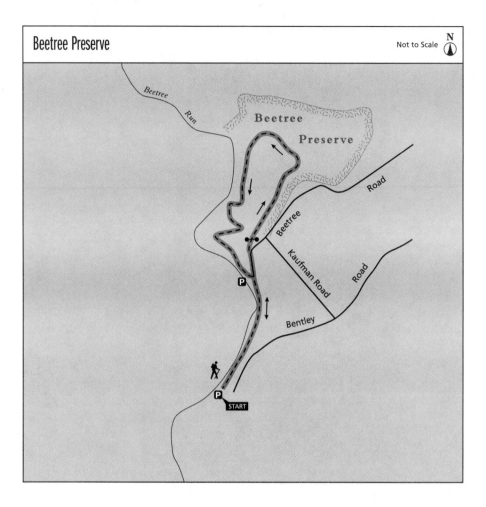

hilltop nature preserve. The hike's main attraction is the varied experiences that it packs into a short hike—the NCRR, recovering forestland, the babbling of Beetree Run, and passage above a scenic stream hollow. This is a particularly enjoyable short ramble in spring, when you will see the varied blooms of flowers and trees in the woods and under the NCRR's open skies.

Walk north with the parking area on your right. If you've never hiked or biked the NCRR before, this will be enough to entice you to walk and bike its length. In places the landscape surrounding this former rail line still resembles the countryside of long ago, when the morning milk was sent south to Baltimore by train. Beginning in the 1950s the line began sending commuters down and back, then closed altogether.

Turn right onto Beetree Road at 0.8 mile, and walk straight to the sharp bend in the road a few hundred yards ahead. At the bend go straight to leave the road and enter the trail behind a gate. Climb a steep hill into the woods for 200 yards. It levels off in a small clearing. Stay right for a pleasant walk through recovering woods for 0.5 mile. At a clearing at 1.3 miles, take the soft left (the middle trail, not the extreme left) into the woods.

After a long, gradual descent, reach a T at the bottom of the hill, at 1.6 miles. Turn left and walk with Beetree Run on your right. There are a few excellent kid-size pools for wading and splashing. At the next T junction, turn left to leave the stream and ascend on an old roadbed while slabbing around the hill. To your right, a wide hollow opens up. In spring the wildflowers, redbud, and dogwood are abundant here.

Continue to climb gradually. At 2.3 miles return to a small clearing visited earlier. Take the first right into the woods and follow the yellow blazes across a flat, wide ridge. Pass through a collection of camping shelters, following the yellow-blazed trail out of camp 175 yards to another T junction. Go left and descend steeply to a clearing to rejoin the Northern Central Railroad Trail at 2.7 miles. Turn left.

Traveling south, cross Beetree Run on a bridge, then cross Beetree Road at 2.9 miles (this is where you left the NCRR earlier). Continue down the NCRR back to the trailhead.

Miles and Directions

0.0 Start at trailhead on Bentley Road.

0.8 Turn right onto Beetree Road.

1.3 Take soft left at clearing.

2.3 Return to clearing; take first right, following yellow blazes.

2.7 Rejoin Northern Central Railroad Trail.

2.9 Cross Beetree Road.

3.7 Arrive back at trailhead.

Options: Park at Beetree Road and hike the woods circuit only, picking up the route at Milepoint 0.8.

18 Northern Central Railroad Trail

A walk along 8 miles of the 20-mile Maryland section of the Northern Central Railroad Trail, a converted rail-trail through the rolling countryside of northern Baltimore County. Stow a bicycle at the south end for a 16-mile hike-bike excursion.

Location: The trail, part of the Gunpowder Falls State Park system, is located in Baltimore County and stretches from the Pennsylvania line to Cockeysville, Maryland, about 5 miles north of the Baltimore Beltway. The trailhead for this hike is in Bentley Springs, 17 miles north of the Baltimore Beltway.

Type of hike: 16.0-mile out-and-back.

Difficulty: Easy.

Season: Year-round.

Fees and permits: No fees or permits required.

Maps: USGS New Freedom, Pennsylvania; Hereford, Cockeysville, Maryland.

Special considerations: The trail is 10 feet wide, composed of crushed limestone. At the northern section there is plenty of solitude. As you approach Monkton, weekend bicycle traffic can be substantial. If you want the Monkton section all to yourself, travel midweek or, best of all, in winter.

Camping: No camping is available.

For more information: Gunpowder Falls State Park.

Trailhead facilities: At Bentley Springs there is a pay phone and a privy. The station at Monkton has been restored as an administrative office for the state park. The building also houses a museum and meeting rooms. Restrooms and water are available. Across the trail, refreshments and provisions are available at the store in the Old Monkton Hotel. There is also an outdoors store that sells hiking and biking accessories.

Finding the trailhead: From the Baltimore Beltway (Interstate 695), travel north 17 miles on Interstate 83 to exit 33, York Road. Go north on York Road (Maryland Highway 45) for 1 mile, and turn left onto Kaufman Road. In about 0.7 mile turn left onto Bentley Road and proceed 0.7 mile to the parking area on the right.

The Hike

The trail follows the railbed of one of the oldest railroads in America—the Northern Central, completed in 1838. It operated as a milk train, taking daily early-morning runs into Baltimore. The passenger line carried Civil War wounded from Gettysburg to Baltimore, then carried the body of President Abraham Lincoln north en route to his burial in Illinois. It later become a commuter rail, with daily service to Baltimore until 1959.

Monkton, the southern trailhead for this hike, is a happening spot on weekends. People of all ages congregate there, awaiting or finishing their time on the trail. The bike shop is a gathering place, the vegetarian deli dishes up an assortment of sandwiches and sweets, and Lycra-clad cyclists chat it up with safari-shirted birders. The hike from Bentley Springs to Monkton is an easy three hours; what's hard is pulling yourself away to walk back.

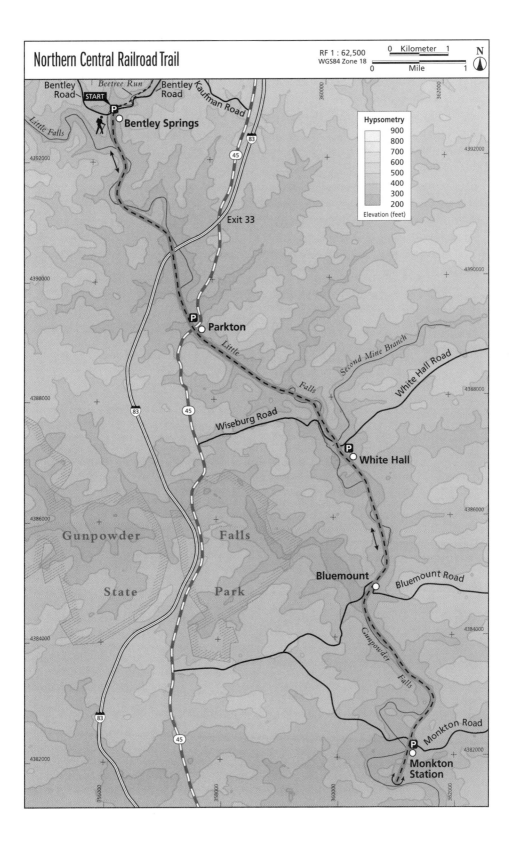

Northern Central Railroad Trail

RF 1 : 62,500
WGS84 Zone 18

0 Kilometer 1

0 Mile 1

N

Bentley Road
Beetree Run
Bentley Road
Kaufman Road
START
Little Falls
Bentley Springs
83
45
Exit 33

Hypsometry
900
800
700
600
500
400
300
200
Elevation (feet)

4392000
4392000
4390000
4390000

Parkton
Little
Falls
Second Mine Branch
White Hall Road

4388000
4388000

83
45
Wiseburg Road
White Hall

4386000
4386000

Gunpowder   Falls

State   Park

Bluemount
Bluemount Road

Gunpowder
Falls

4384000
4384000

83
45
Monkton Road

4382000
Monkton Station
4382000

300000
302000
356000
358000
360000
362000

From the Bentley Springs trailhead, walk south along Beetree Run. Bentley Springs is a town of old homes and farmland. It is a former resort, hosting legions of Baltimoreans trying to escape the summer heat. Little Falls joins the trail from the west, and for nearly 0.5 mile Beetree Run and Little Falls are in view. The confluence of the two streams, at 0.5 mile, offers some of the best trout fishing around, as well as some of the more picturesque views of the surrounding countryside. After the confluence, Little Falls leaves the trail for a time.

The trail enters Parkton at 2.7 miles. The section south of Parkton boasts some of the trail's most dramatic views of Little Falls. Then the landscape rises sharply on both sides, leaving only the stream and the trail in a narrow cut in the landscape. There is trailhead parking in Parkton.

The swiftly moving Little Falls disappears to the east, then reappears a mile later as it emerges sluggishly from a broad bend just above White Hall, at 4.6 miles. Here, Second Mine Branch drains into Little Falls, which disappears behind the tiny village. The subtle changes in the character of the stream valley and trail become more evident in this section. The valley is wider and the woods are denser than in the north. There are farms in the area, but the sense of history here is more of mills than milk. White Hall is a former paper mill town, and the look of the old as well as the new architecture ties the area more closely to the city of Baltimore than to the other villages in the area.

Just after the trail crosses Bluemount Road, at 6.0 miles, cross Little Falls for the final time. It disappears west and empties into Gunpowder Falls. Moving south, just above Monkton Station, the stone remains of the town of Pleasant Valley can be seen. Only a cross section of a two-story structure marks the old town from the trail. Gunpowder Falls moves behind a hill to the east, and the trail descends along a rock face into Monkton, one of a dozen historic towns along the old line. If you left your vehicle back at Bentley Springs, this is your turnaround point.

Miles and Directions

0.0 Start at Bentley Springs trailhead.

0.5 Reach the confluence of Beetree Run and Little Falls.

2.7 Enter Parkton.

4.6 Reach the village of White Hall.

6.0 Cross Bluemount Road.

8.0 Reach Monkton, your turnaround point.

16.0 Arrive back at Bentley Springs.

Options: There is trailhead parking at each of the historic towns visited on the hike. You can make a shorter trip by walking as far as you like and then returning. Or you can shuttle by leaving a car at a second location. For a truly remarkable day, plant a bicycle at the Monkton Station and make the return by bike.

19 Gunpowder Falls North and South Loop, Gunpowder Falls State Park

A walk through mixed hardwood and conifer woodlands along and above scenic Gunpowder Falls.

Location: The Hereford area of Gunpowder Falls State Park is 20 miles north of Baltimore in Baltimore County.
Type of hike: 9.6-mile figure-eight loop.
Difficulty: Moderate.
Season: Year-round.
Fees and permits: No fees or permits required.
Maps: USGS Hereford, Maryland.

Special considerations: Gunpowder Falls is a stocked trout stream; licenses are required. Check at the trailhead in the fall for information on hunting season. If you stay on the trail, you will not enter hunting lands.
Camping: No camping is available.
For more information: Gunpowder Falls State Park.
Trailhead facilities: None. There is a comfort station, open in summer, at Bunker Hill Road.

Finding the trailhead: From the Baltimore Beltway (Interstate 695), travel north 12 miles on Interstate 83 to the Hereford exit. Go west on Maryland Highway 137 (Mount Carmel Road) 1 mile, and turn right (north) onto Masemore Road. Trailhead parking is 2.4 miles ahead on the right, on the south side of Gunpowder Falls.

The Hike

You can make a day of hiking in the wooded stream valley of Gunpowder Falls and the ridges above it, or you can take one of several shorter loop hikes. Raven Rock Falls, the stone ruins along Panther Branch, and views of hemlocks clinging to the canyon above Mingo Branch are just a few of the sights along the way. You might also encounter red fox, beaver, and wild turkey.

From the trailhead follow the white blazes over a small footbridge and walk east downstream, entering the woods. This is the only bridge over the many feeder creeks along the route, but the other crossings can be made with a few steps or a long hop over stones.

Trout stocked in Gunpowder Falls favor the bend in the river here, where beaver have created standing pools. In spring they can also be seen in great numbers in the shallows another hundred yards downstream. The hillsides and cliffs along the river are steep enough to provide the cool temperatures and drainage favored by mountain laurel.

Stay with the white blazes as the trail breaks away from the river at about 0.5 mile and climbs through a stand of mature hemlock. Cross a seasonal stream, passable even in wet weather, and continue climbing with the stream now on the right. This is the steepest ascent of the hike, but it lasts only 250 yards and climbs only 150

Gunpowder Falls North and South Loop

feet, leveling off in a clearing at the junction with the blue-blazed Mingo Forks Trail, leading south at 0.7 mile. (Mingo Forks and Bunker Hill Trails create a 3.0-mile loop back to this spot.)

Staying left at the fork, descend into ash and maple, with views between the trees to the north slope of Gunpowder Falls. A managed hunting area comes within 50 yards of the trail on the right. A long switchback descends steeply to the crossing, at 1.0 mile, of Mingo Branch, a 12-foot-wide creek offering plenty of stepping-stones, except in high water when it presents a shin-deep wade.

Ascend amid white pine and black walnut to the blue-blazed Bunker Hill Trail, which leads right to Mingo Forks Trail and left to a comfort station and a picnic area. A hundred yards farther, emerge from the woods to the Bunker Hill trailhead parking and Bunker Hill Road at 1.3 miles. Fifty yards north is the old road bridge crossing. Formerly, the bridge enabled a roadway through the park. But when a flood removed the bridge, the state chose not to rebuild it, thereby preserving the wild, remote setting. Instead of a throughway, Bunker Hill Road now serves as a quiet trailhead on both sides of the river.

Cross the road and stay left of the amphitheater below a limestone knob where finches and hummingbirds buzz beneath the pines, then rejoin the river. Stay with the white blazes, breaking from the river and climbing along a sunken road surrounded by laurel. At the top of the hill, stay to the left of a stand of white pine, taking care not to wander right at the fork with a blue-blazed trail.

For the next mile the trail hugs the ridgeline until descending via two switchbacks to cross under I–83, at 2.8 miles, and then emerging from the woods to cross York Road, at 3.0 miles. Just east of York Road is a junction with the blue-blazed Panther Branch Trail, which heads south, uphill. In another 100 yards, search for white blazes climbing right, taking care not to follow a false trail that continues along Gunpowder Falls. If you lose the blazes and come to an eroded section of path immediately adjacent to the river, turn back to find the white blazes, which ascend the ridgeline where it seems a cool breeze is constantly blowing.

Along the trail over the next 0.5 mile, there are a few spots to step off and enjoy the views of the canyon and, especially in winter, the hillside northwest of the river. Descending on a long switchback, the trail rejoins the river and enters a steep wooded canyon. At twilight, the trail through the canyon is a thoroughfare for white-tailed deer and other animals making their way to water. For deer as well as people, there is no easy way up the south slope. Startled animals may make a break across the river, which is deeper and swifter here, forcing an otherwise graceful creature into awkward maneuvers.

At 4.0 miles, pass Raven Rock Falls on the north side. A popular fishing and picnicking spot, the falls are accessible via Gunpowder North Trail, 1.0 mile east of York Road. But the best view of the falls is on this side of the river.

For the next mile, the trail follows river bottomland, punctuated here and there with jaunts over small knobs. In summer the brush invades the path in places but creates an abundance of blackberries within arm's reach of the trail. Pass Sandy Lane Trail at 4.4 miles. This trail offers a 0.8-mile shortcut back to York Road.

The junction with the blue-blazed Panther Branch Trail is at 5.0 miles. Here, the white-blazed Gunpowder South Trail continues east 0.5 mile to Big Falls Road. (One option for the return hike is to continue on to Falls Road, cross the road bridge, and then head west on Gunpowder North Trail to York Road. From there the trail follows the same route as this hike, which will arrive at York Road via the upland route.)

Follow Panther Branch Trail west (right), moving upstream through a low canyon draped by laurel on the west with black walnut and other "recovery species" on the north. The crowded stand of the fast-growing walnut and pine above the dense underbrush is evidence that this side of the stream was at one time cleared for agriculture or settlement. Perhaps because of the steep slope, the mature forest on the other side of the stream was left relatively untouched.

Ruins of earlier settlement are still evident as the trail passes the remains of a kiln and a stone foundation. At about 5.8 miles, there is a junction. The trail continuing straight ahead over a stream is a horse trail that follows Panther Branch from the other side. Stay right; the blazes may be scant for the next 0.25 mile. Keep the stream on your left, and continue uphill until Panther Branch disappears and the trail enters an open field.

Crossing the field, see the ruins of a farmhouse and buildings to the right in the distance. Back in the woods, go right on an old road and follow it until the blue blazes duck right onto a narrow footpath. Watch for the sign, which is easy to miss.

It is also easy to get confused at the west junction with Sandy Lane Trail, at 6.7 miles. This junction is only about 0.25 mile west of the first (east) junction at 4.4 miles. Follow the blue blazes left; then watch for an immediate blue blaze left onto a narrow footpath, which comes to an old cart path in 25 yards. Go right on the cart path; in 20 yards another easy-to-miss left turn takes the trail back onto a narrow path, which follows a narrow ridge and descends, reaching York Road at 7.2 miles, at the same spot you passed earlier on this hike at 3.0 miles.

Cross York Road, and follow the shoulder north over the bridge 175 yards until the blue blazes of Gunpowder North Trail are visible on the trees to the left. Climb over the road barrier, and follow the blue blazes west along the north bank. The remaining 2.3 miles trace along the north bank the same territory covered in the first leg of the hike. However, on this side the trail closely follows at river level with no elevation change—you can coast for the last 2.3 miles.

Even though you are covering what is by now familiar ground, the view and experience are quite different. There are two highlights: crossing a cascading stream just before Bunker Hill Road at 8.3 miles, and a stunning look up the hemlock-covered canyon walls at about 8.8 miles. In early evening you may be treated to the sights of turkey roosting in the maples above the ridge and the sounds of barred owl setting out for the hunt.

Miles and Directions

0.0 Start at trailhead off Masemore Road.

0.7 Reach Mingo Forks Trail junction; stay left at fork.

1.0 Cross Mingo Branch.

1.3 Emerge from woods to Bunker Hill Road and picnic area.

3.0 Cross York Road.

4.0 Pass Raven Rock Falls.

4.4 Pass junction with Sandy Lane Trail (east end).

5.0 Reach junction with Panther Branch Trail; turn right (west).

6.7 Reach Sandy Lane Trail junction (west end). Follow blue blazes left, then left again.

7.2 Cross York Road for the second time.

8.3 Cross stream just before Bunker Hill Road.

9.6 Cross bridge to trailhead.

Options: A 5.6-mile circuit can be made by crossing the river at York Road and heading west on Gunpowder North Trail, skipping the middle 4.2 miles. A 10.4-mile circuit is possible by taking Gunpowder South Trail to Big Falls Road and returning on Gunpowder North Trail. A 2.7-mile loop is possible by heading west from the parking area on Gunpowder South Trail for 1.7 miles and then returning via Gunpowder Highland Trail.

20 Sweet Air Loop, Gunpowder Falls State Park

A wonderfully quiet hike offering a diversity of experiences: plentiful contact with Little Gunpowder Falls, a small pond in the woods, farm fields, immense tulip poplars, and small pine groves. In late July and early August, blackberries are plentiful.

Location: This hike, in the Sweet Air Area of Gunpowder Falls State Park, hugs the Baltimore–Harford County line about 15 miles northeast of Baltimore.

Type of hike: 5.5-mile loop.

Difficulty: Easy.

Season: Year-round (July and August for blackberries).

Fees and permits: No fees or permits required.

Maps: USGS Phoenix, Maryland.

Special considerations: Bring along a container of frozen cream laced with sugar for blackberries in late July and August. The

cream will melt while you hike, making a great dessert. The loop described below passes close to private property in one place. Other loops within the park pass close to several houses. The trail also passes through cornfields leased to private farmers. Please respect the privacy and property of all.

Camping: No camping is available.

For more information: Gunpowder Falls State Park.

Trailhead facilities: A small picnic shelter with one table is available; a large map of the entire area appears on the information board.

Finding the trailhead: From the Baltimore Beltway (Interstate 695), drive 7 miles north on Interstate 83 to the Shawan Road East exit. In 1 mile turn right onto York Road (Maryland Highway 45); in 0.5 mile turn left onto Ashland Road (Maryland Highway 145, which becomes Paper Mill Road). Continue straight through the intersection with Maryland Highway 146, after which Paper Mill Road changes to Sweet Air Road. In 8.5 miles from I-83, turn left onto Green Road. In 1.7 miles turn left onto Moore's Road; about a quarter of a mile farther, turn left onto Dalton Bevard Road, the park access road. Proceed to the trailhead parking area.

The Hike

The hike begins from the small picnic shelter at the west end of the parking area. Facing the shelter, locate the white-blazed trail at the far right (north end) of the clearing; a sign reads BARLEY POND LOOP. Enter the woods, following a wide tractor path; watch for blackberries in season.

Beyond a row of pine trees, enter a cornfield, where the yellow-blazed loop goes left. Continue straight, and walk between two sections of the field. When the corn is high, you will walk in a green tunnel scented sweetly with corn; when the corn is low or not yet planted, there is a picturesque view west.

Follow the yellow-blazed trail left as it leaves the white blazes. Enter the woods, and follow a wide path under large poplars. The understory is white with dogwoods and alive with redbud in spring. Reach Barley Pond at 0.5 mile, a quiet rest stop in a shady place. To continue, retrace your steps to where you first encountered the

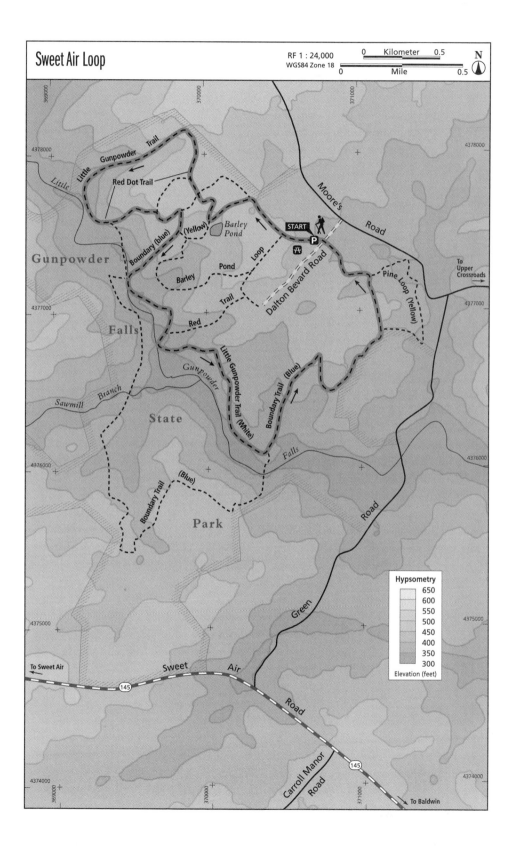

Sweet Air Loop

RF 1 : 24,000
WGS84 Zone 18

0   Kilometer   0.5

0   Mile   0.5

N

Little Gunpowder Trail

Red Dot Trail

Boundary (blue)

(Yellow)

Barley Pond

START

Moore's Road

Gunpowder

Barley

Pond

Loop

To Upper Crossroads

Pine Loop (Yellow)

Falls

Red

Trail

Dalton Bevard Road

Gunpowder

Little Gunpowder Trail (White)

Boundary Trail (Blue)

Sawmill   Branch

State

Falls

Boundary Trail (Blue)

Park

Green

Road

Road

To Sweet Air

Sweet   Air

145

Road

Carroll Manor   Road

145

To Baldwin

Hypsometry

650
600
550
500
450
400
350
300

Elevation (feet)

pond; then retreat back up the trail 75 feet from the pond and turn left onto an unmarked trail, which leads up the slope of a small hollow to the white-blazed Little Gunpowder Trail, at 0.6 mile. Turn left onto Little Gunpowder Trail; in about 160 yards, turn right onto a connecting red-blazed trail, at 0.7 mile.

Reach a junction with the blue-blazed Boundary Trail at 0.8 mile; continue straight on the red trail, a quiet footpath that hugs the woods and circles an open meadow. Follow the footpath for 1.0 mile to a junction with Little Gunpowder Trail, at 1.8 miles. Turn left (if you want to trim a little from the hike, you can continue straight because this route will rejoin Little Gunpowder Trail about 0.25 a mile down the trail).

The Boundary Trail joins from the left at 2.0 miles. Follow it parallel to the white-blazed trail for 150 yards, and then break right to follow a footpath above a narrow stream valley. Ferns carpet the ground rising uphill to the right, and in spring wildflowers surround the small stream. Cross a small stream just before entering a clearing, taking care to follow the established footpath so as not to add to an erosion problem caused by inappropriate travel through this section. Turn right at the clearing onto Boundary Trail, and reach Little Gunpowder Falls at 2.3 miles. Boundary Trail continues across the unbridged stream, which is fine for horses, but most hikers will find it a little deeper than they care to ford.

Turn left onto the white-blazed Little Gunpowder Trail, and follow the river downstream. The woods here are quiet and old, with tulip poplars and silver maples towering 80 to 100 feet. Anglers will find several large pools and a few small falls for plying the waters (check with park authorities for season and license requirements). At about 2.8 miles stay left with the white trail as it ascends away from the river, leaving the equestrian trail to follow the stream.

Climb steeply, but briefly, to a ledge that moves downstream above a small hollow, and then climb gently. Pass a junction with a red-blazed connecting trail at 3.0 miles. (You can take a shortcut back to the trailhead by going left here, then left at the next junction, then right onto the yellow-blazed Barley Pond Loop. A quarter of a mile farther, reach the white trail at the spot at which you first entered the cornfield. The trailhead is 0.2 mile to the right.)

Continuing on the white trail, follow above the river and below giant tulip poplars. Then duck deeper into the woods and cross a small stream on a wooden footbridge, before climbing a gentle rise. When you reach level ground, Little Gunpowder Falls will be 100 feet below, about 75 yards west (right). A right side trail at 3.6 miles leads 100 feet to stream access and a few nice pools.

Descend steeply to a junction with Boundary Trail at 4.2 miles. For a detour to a few very nice pools, you can go right here and follow the blue trail 175 yards. Walk upstream a short distance if you want to play in the water. If watering yourself in the inviting pools just downstream of the river crossing, be aware that horses also use the blue trail to cross. You can also continue over the river here by rock-hopping to explore the western reaches of the park.

Over a few short miles, the terrain of Gunpowder Falls changes from hilly Piedmont to the meadows of the Coastal Plain. PHOTO BY JAYSON KNOTT/MARYLAND DNR

From the junction of the white-blazed Little Gunpowder Trail and the blue-blazed Boundary Trail, turn left (a hard left) and ascend following the blue blazes. Go right when the trail enters an open field at 4.4 miles; watch for abundant blackberries at the woods' edge as you make your way around the field just outside the woods. Just as a house comes into view, watch for the blue blazes turning right into the woods for a brief interlude of 100 yards; emerge again into the field uphill. Continue past the house.

Stay left after passing the house (the pathway to the right is private property; please respect it). Pass through a line of trees, and go right into another field. At the end of this clearing, enter the woods and continue straight ahead to a junction with a second yellow-blazed trail. Go left, and follow under mixed hardwoods and white and red pines. Blackberries are plentiful from here to the trailhead, and the smell of pine through here is sweet and intense.

Pass another junction with the yellow-blazed Pine Loop at 5.2 miles, and ascend a small knoll (staying to the right at a split in the trail). Emerging from the woods at the park access road, cross the road and proceed to the trailhead.

Miles and Directions

0.0 Start from picnic shelter.

0.5 Reach Barley Pond.

0.6 At junction, turn left onto Little Gunpowder Trail.

0.7 Turn right onto connecting trail (red blazes).

0.8 Continue straight on red trail at junction with Boundary Trail.

1.8 Reach junction with Little Gunpowder Trail; turn left.

2.0 Boundary Trail joins from the left.

2.3 Arrive at Little Gunpowder Falls.

2.8 Stay left with white trail, and ascend away from the river.

3.0 Pass junction with red trail. (You can use this trail as a shortcut back to the trailhead.)

4.2 Reach junction with Boundary Trail.

4.4 Go right when trail enters field. FYI: Look for blackberries here in season.

5.2 Pass Pine Loop junction; bear right at split as trail climbs knoll.

5.5 Arrive back at trailhead.

Options: A shorter, 3.7-mile variation of this hike is described above. You can also follow the Boundary Trail for a western loop that leaves this hike at 1.8 miles and rejoins it at Milepoint 4.2. This would add only about 0.5 mile but would require crossing the unbridged Little Gunpowder Falls, which averages about 12 to 18 inches deep at the crossing. A pair of old sneakers in your day pack is all you need.

21 Susquehanna State Park Loop

An easy ramble through hardwood forest with great rewards: expansive views of the Susquehanna River, old farm ruins, and, if you are lucky, bald eagles.

Location: Susquehanna State Park is located in Harford County, Maryland, about 35 miles northeast of Baltimore.
Type of hike: 4.5-mile loop.
Difficulty: Easy.
Season: Year-round.
Fees and permits: No fees or permits required.
Maps: USGS Conowingo Dam, Aberdeen, Maryland.
Special considerations: The blazes in the park tend to be confusing. Old red blazes, no longer functional, still mark trees. The blue route seems to appear and disappear because blue is used both for a park trail and

for the Mason-Dixon Trail, a long-distance trail that passes through the park. Follow the directions provided here closely. The trail passes adjacent hunting lands. Check with the park office for details when hiking during hunting season. The hike described here starts at the historic area, but you can start at the picnic area just as easily.
Camping: Camping is available at the campground; registration and a fee are required.
For more information: Susquehanna State Park.
Trailhead facilities: Nature center, vending machines.

Finding the trailhead: From Baltimore drive north on Interstate 95 for 21 miles to the Maryland Highway 155 exit west to Churchville. In 1.5 miles turn right onto Maryland Highway 161 North; in 0.25 mile turn right onto Rock Run Road. Follow signs for historic sites for 4 miles to the trailhead at the river.

The Hike

This is a fine hike for young hikers. There is plenty to see without great challenge. Plan to spend some time at the ridge overlook, enjoying the view and giving the eagles a chance to appear.

From the historic area trailhead, walk up Rock Run Road away from the river 175 yards; turn right to enter the woods following the red and blue blazes. The trail passes under hardwoods, especially poplar and chestnut oak, making an easy ascent toward the ridgeline. Beginning at about 0.6 mile and continuing for a few hundred yards are views east across the river. Find a comfortable spot, and enjoy the view.

At 1.0 mile bear right onto the Silver Spur Trail. Begin a slow descent through the woods, and turn left onto the Deer Creek Trail. In spring, bluebells color the forest floor, while dogwood and serviceberry paint the understory bright white. Pass through two narrow hollows, one of which contains a giant beech tree, and come to a small pine grove. The pines were planted as a lumber crop in the early nineteenth century; the remnant trees are now dying back as the hardwoods mature and block the sun from the pines.

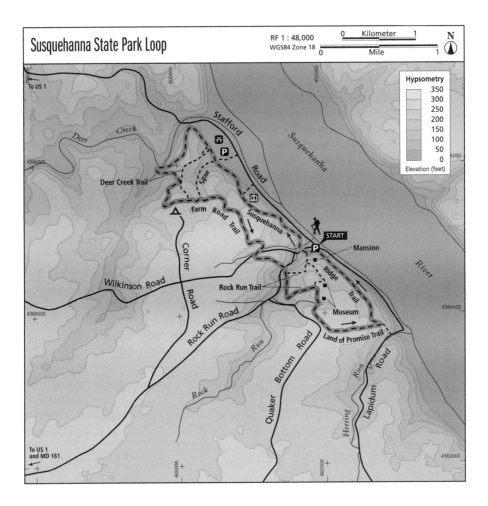

Susquehanna State Park Loop

RF 1 : 48,000
WGS84 Zone 18

Just beyond the pines, enter an open meadow where a post, at 1.5 miles, marks the junction with the blue-blazed Farm Road Trail. The Deer Creek Trail returns to the picnic area from the post straight ahead. Follow the Farm Road Trail into the woods and walk along a small brook. Walk through a narrow hollow, above which poplar and chestnut oak tower on both sides. At 2.0 miles the spur trail to the right leads 0.3 mile to the campground loops. Continue straight on Farm Road Trail.

At the top of the hill, emerge from the woods into a broad field. Following the road, the trail winds around the field under open sky. At 2.5 miles the Silver Spur Trail leads left 100 feet to old farm ruins. These ruins are worth taking the time to explore.

Back on Farm Road Trail, continue around the field another 250 yards; enter the woods and slowly descend. Cross Wilkinson Road at 3.2 miles, then Rock Run Road at a point about 0.5 mile above the trailhead at 3.6 miles. Just beyond Rock Run Road, cross Rock Run and turn left onto the Rock Run Y Trail. For an

The Susquehanna River is a popular weekend spot for anglers and boaters, as well as hikers and bicyclists. PHOTO COURTESY OF MARYLAND DNR

extended hike, you can turn right onto Rock Run Y Trail, taking a left at the fork and doubling back on the Land of Promise Trail.

At 4.2 miles Rock Run Y Trail ends at Land of Promise Trail, an interpretive path that visits the historic sites along the river. Go left, passing a mansion at 4.3 miles and other historic sites, and return to trailhead parking.

Miles and Directions

0.0 Start at historic area trailhead.

0.1 Turn right at the red trail junction, entering the woods.

0.6 Enjoy views of the river.

1.0 Pass Silver Spur Trail on left.

1.5 A post marks junction with Farm Road Trail; turn left. (**FYI:** The trail straight ahead leads to a picnic area.)

2.0 Pass spur trail to campground.

2.5 Reach spur trail to farm ruins—worth the time to explore.

3.2 Cross Wilkinson Road.

3.6 Cross Rock Run Road.

3.7 Cross Rock Run and turn left onto; Rock Run Y Trail.

4.2 Reach Land of Promise Trail junction; turn left.

4.3 Pass mansion and other historic sites.

4.5 Arrive back at trailhead.

Options: You can make this a short 2.5-mile hike by taking the cutoff at the farmstead ruins to return to the red trail and then heading south back to the trailhead, retracing your earlier steps.

22 Wildlands Loop, Gunpowder Falls State Park

This loop follows the upland forests of the fall zone, crossing a few streams and visiting a pleasant waterfall, then meanders downstream along Big Gunpowder Falls as it leaves the piedmont.

Location: This hike is located in Baltimore County, about 12 miles northeast of Baltimore.

Type of hike: 5.2-mile loop.

Difficulty: Moderate.

Season: Year-round.

Fees and permits: No fees or permits required.

Maps: USGS White Marsh, Maryland.

Special considerations: The area is very popular on weekends. Early in the day and late in the afternoon, it is possible to find solitude here. Also, because there are several options for hiking in the park, people tend to disperse.

Camping: No camping is available.

For more information: Gunpowder Falls State Park.

Trailhead facilities: Information board with large map of the area.

Finding the trailhead: From the Baltimore Beltway (Interstate 695), take the Bel Air Road North exit (alternately known as Belair Road, it is U.S. Highway 1). In just under 5.5 miles, cross the bridge over Big Gunpowder Falls, and then take an immediate right into the trailhead parking area. The hike begins behind the information board.

The Hike

Watching Big Gunpowder Falls sliding through several narrow gorges, it is hard to believe that only 5 miles downstream the falls will spread to a deltalike, broad river more than a mile wide. From the information board, descend steps behind the board to a tunnel under the Bel Air Road (US 1) bridge. Continue past the junction with Big Gunpowder Trail, which leads left just beyond the bridge, to a trail junction marking the beginning of the Stocksdale and Wildlands Trails. To the left, Stocksdale Trail follows the former route of the old Stocksdale Road. (This is the return route of the hike.) Turn right into the woods; follow the pink blazes over level ground for about 100 yards, and then ascend.

As you climb, steeply at times, you will see that Big Gunpowder Falls sits at the bottom of a rather narrow ravine. This may seem rather unusual to those accustomed to thinking of Baltimore as more closely linked to Chesapeake Bay and the coastal plain than to the piedmont to the north of town. Here, as the falls pass through the transition known as the fall zone, the landscape is still part piedmont, and the steep grade illustrates the point. Perhaps in a few million years, the uplift that created this ravine will erode to a point where it more closely resembles the landscape of Days Cove, an estuarine flatland only a few miles south.

At 1.9 miles reach the end of Wildlands Trail at the junction of the blue-blazed Stocksdale Trail. To the left, Stocksdale Trail takes a shortcut to return to Big Gun-

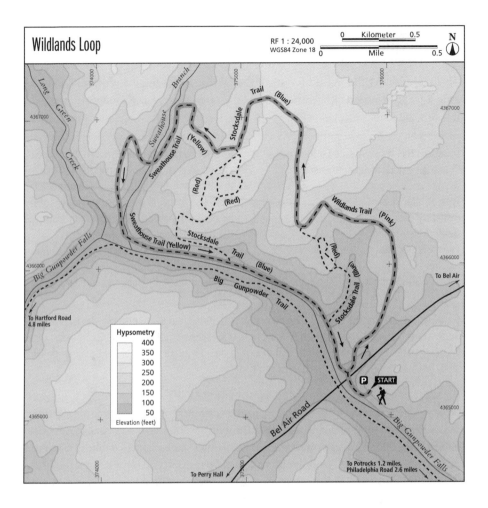

Wildlands Loop

RF 1 : 24,000
WGS84 Zone 18

Kilometer 0.5

Mile 0.5

N

Hypsometry

400
350
300
250
200
150
100
50

Elevation (feet)

powder Falls 0.4 mile upstream from the trailhead. Go right, following the blue blazes, and continue through younger woods and fairly open meadow, remnants of the area's agricultural past. In winter amid the brush you can still see fence posts and other reminders. The pine trees through this area are plantation planted. Some were planted by former farmers for use as firewood; the younger trees were planted by the State of Maryland at the establishment of the park as a way of protecting the falls' watershed from erosion and runoff.

Stocksdale Trail breaks left at the junction with the yellow-blazed Sweathouse Trail at 2.7 miles—Big Gunpowder Falls is 0.9 mile downhill. The trail to the left is the actual right-of-way of the old Stocksdale Road. To the right it continues out of the park. Take the soft right, following the yellow blazes. Ascend a knoll, and begin a casual descent to Sweathouse Branch. Reach the stream, and follow the trail left for 0.5 mile of very pleasant streamside walking; the stream gurgles and in places tumbles toward the falls. Cross Sweathouse Branch; ascend upstream along a tributary of it for 0.25 mile before crossing the tributary and descending.

A side trail at 3.9 miles leads right 180 yards to a picturesque little cascade on Long Green Creek. In addition to offering a pleasant spot for soaking your feet in one of three nearby pools, the cascade is a fine illustration of the Big and Little Gunpowder Falls topography. The "falls" are casual cascades through the fall zone. Back on Sweathouse Trail, cross Sweathouse Branch again and continue east, downstream along Gunpowder Falls. If you see hikers rambling along the other side of river, they are on Big Gunpowder Trail, a 20-plus-mile footpath from the northern part of the county to Days Cove.

Rejoin the blue-blazed Stocksdale Trail at 4.4 miles. There are several places along the way in which the stream valley is more of a steep gorge that drops all the way to the stream, while on the south side of Big Gunpowder Falls there is gentle bottomland. Continue past a fork, at 4.9 miles; to the left Stocksdale Trail leads uphill on a loop that eventually leads back to this spot. Cross a small stream, and walk downstream to the tunnel under Bel Air Road. Pass under the road and return to the trailhead.

Miles and Directions

- **0.0** Start at trailhead at information board.
- **0.1** Wildlands and Stocksdale Trails junction; turn right onto Wildlands Trail.
- **1.9** Go right at junction with Stocksdale Trail.
- **2.7** Reach junction with Sweathouse Trail; take soft right onto this trail.
- **3.9** Side trail leads 180 yards to Long Green Creek.
- **4.4** Rejoin Stocksdale Trail.
- **5.2** Arrive back at trailhead.

Options: For a 3.0-mile loop, go left onto the blue-blazed Stocksdale Trail at Milepoint 1.9 instead of going right. Follow this blue trail 0.7 mile to the opposite end of the loop made by the Stocksdale Trail. Turn left to return to the trailhead. South of the trailhead are other loops, which are illustrated on a map at the trailhead information board.

23 Oregon Ridge Park Loop

A walk along old logging trails under mature second-growth hardwoods in Maryland's horse country, with an interlude along a secluded clear-running brook.

Location: Oregon Ridge Park is located in Baltimore County, about 10 miles north of the Baltimore Beltway.

Type of hike: 4.0-mile loop.

Difficulty: Easy.

Elevation gain: Minimal.

Season: Year-round.

Fees and permits: No fees or permits required.

Maps: USGS Cockeysville, Maryland.

Special considerations: The trails in the park are effectively marked at major trail junctions. The mileage listed on the signs indicates the total length of the trail. For example, S. JAMES

CAMPBELL TRAIL, 1.4 MILES, means that the trail is 1.4 miles long. It does not mean that the trail begins 1.4 miles from the sign. Also, there are several stream crossings without bridges; most are shallow enough to traipse through, and all are narrow enough to rock-hop across. A public beach at Oregon Lake offers a fine finish to a summer hike.

Camping: No camping is available.

For more information: Oregon Ridge Park.

Trailhead facilities: Water and restrooms are available at the nature center, which is open until 5:00 P.M.

Finding the trailhead: From the Baltimore Beltway (Interstate 695), travel 7 miles north on Interstate 83 to exit 20, Shawan Road West. In 1 mile turn left onto Beaver Dam Road, then immediately go right at the fork into the park. Continue past the beach parking area, following signs for nature center parking.

The Hike

People who grow up in central Maryland usually discover at a young age the bucolic beauty of northern Baltimore County, and many are familiar with the beach at Oregon Lake. Sadly, many never discover the lush woods traversed by the park's excellent trail system. What a shame!

The bedrock beneath the trails is some of the oldest rock in Maryland. The rolling ridges are composed of metamorphic rock known as Loch Raven schist. Created three billion years ago by pressurized shale, the rock is easily identified by its shiny quartz, feldspar, and garnet crystals.

The ridge supplied iron ore to smelting furnaces formerly located within what are now park boundaries. Little evidence of the open-pit operations remains today, at least to the casual eye.

From the parking area, locate a set of log steps at the northeast corner of the lot (you passed them as you drove in). Turn right onto the trail; in 100 feet turn left at the fork onto the blue-blazed Laurel Trail. Ascend a gentle grade beneath chestnut oak, accompanied by the mountain laurel that are often found with this tree. The ridge's well-drained soils offer the perfect conditions for chestnut oak, tulip poplar,

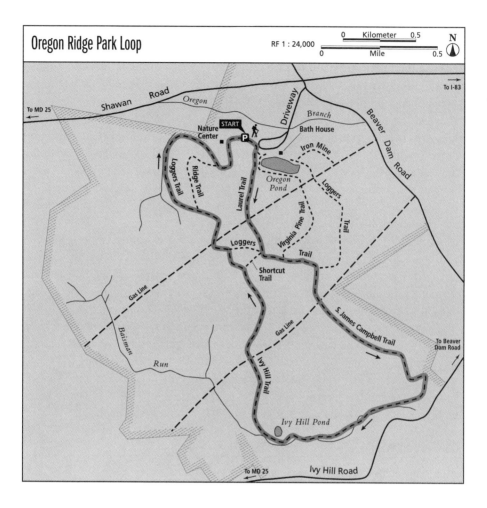

RF 1 : 24,000

0   Kilometer   0.5

0   Mile   0.5

N

To MD 25

Shawan   Road   Oregon

Driveway

Branch

To I-83

Nature Center

START

Bath House

Iron Mine

Beaver Dam Road

Loggers Trail

Ridge Trail

Laurel Trail

Oregon Pond

Loggers

Virginia Pine Trail

Trail

Loggers

Trail

Shortcut Trail

Gas Line

Baisman

Run

Gas Line

S. James Campbell Trail

To Beaver Dam Road

Ivy Hill Trail

Ivy Hill Pond

To MD 25

Ivy Hill Road

and mountain laurel, which dominate the Oregon Ridge forest.

At the top of the ridge, pass into an open meadow, maintained as a gas line right-of-way. It is an unnatural break in the forest cover, but it provides the opportunity for berries to flourish on the woods' edge, drawing deer and other wildlife out for a snack. Back in the woods, at 0.4 mile, turn left onto the red-blazed Loggers Trail and follow a wide path through mature, open forest. The wide path was carved by horse teams hauling timber from the ridge. Then pass the green-blazed Virginia Pine Trail, which breaks left (see Options below).

At 0.7 mile is the junction with the yellow-blazed S. James Campbell Trail, leading southeast to the right. Before turning right onto this trail, continue another 100 feet and follow Loggers Trail left (do not go straight) to an overlook at a ski run.

Back on the S. James Campbell Trail, cross a second gas right-of-way and reenter the woods, walking below some enormous tulip poplars and red oaks. At 1.3

miles begin a descent via switchbacks, where a brush blockade closes off an old trail. At the bottom of the ridge, the trail becomes a much narrower footpath, following Baisman Run upstream. This is a picturesque little stream through a narrow, wooded canyon—an invitation to slow down and enjoy the scenery, especially at one of the several upcoming stream crossings.

Cross the run at 1.7 miles, passing a log bench streamside. Over the next 0.25 mile, cross the run four more times. Coming to a T intersection, go right, staying on the yellow-blazed trail (the trail to the left leads to Ivy Hill Road). Pass beneath Ivy Hill Pond at 2.0 miles and begin ascending on Ivy Hill Trail, a wide logging road. Just past the pond, pass a junction with trails leading left over the run and uphill to the right. The path climbing right is a steep, wooded route reconnecting with Ivy Hill Trail about 400 yards uphill.

At the top of the hill, pass briefly into open field over another right-of-way at 2.4 miles. The trail junction at 3.0 miles creates a shortcut left to the return via Loggers Trail. Follow the white blazes for 0.25 mile to a T intersection and turn left. Passing through the right-of-way a final time, turn right and follow the woods' edge 160 yards before ducking left back into the woods.

The tan-blazed Ridge Trail at 3.3 miles leads right toward the nature center trailhead—a shortcut to be taken if darkness is falling quickly in the woods. But staying left on the red-blazed Loggers Trail will take you for a final stretch along the sound of water, passing near a small creek. At 3.9 miles the tan-blazed trail rejoins Loggers Trail from the right. Just beyond, a wooden bridge to the left leads to the nature center. From there follow the paved driveway 150 feet right to the trailhead.

Miles and Directions

0.0   Start at trailhead near log steps. Turn right onto Laurel Trail.

0.4   Turn left onto red-blazed Loggers Trail.

0.7   Reach S. James Campbell Trail junction. Walk 100 yards to overlook before turning right at junction.

1.7   Cross Baisman Run.

2.0   Pass Ivy Hill Pond, and begin ascending on Ivy Hill Trail.

3.0   Reach Shortcut Trail junction. Follow white blazes 0.25 mile and turn left at T intersection.

3.9   Cross wooden bridge to nature center.

4.0   Arrive back at trailhead.

Options: Several color-coded, intersecting trails make a number of shorter loops possible, some of which are pointed out here. You can create a 1.0-mile or 1.5-mile circuit past the Oregon Lake beach. Following the directions above, turn left at 0.5 mile onto the green-blazed Virginia Pine Trail, or at 0.7 mile continue on the red-blazed Loggers Trail by descending left. Both trails lead to the orange-blazed Lake Trail; turn left and follow that trail west to the nature center trailhead.

24 Morgan Run Natural Environment Area

A hike for birders. You will see a variety of raptors at work as you walk through old fields and young forest, followed by an interlude into a steep creek ravine.

Location: Morgan Run Natural Environment Area is in Carroll County, Maryland, 10 miles south of Westminster.
Type of hike: 4.1-mile loop.
Difficulty: Moderate.
Elevation gain: Many short ups and downs.
Season: Warmer months when raptors are present.
Fees and permits: No fees or permits required.

Maps: USGS Finksburg, Maryland.
Special considerations: The area is open to hunting; check the kiosk for schedules. There is no hunting in Maryland on Sunday. Although the elevation gain is minimal, this hike has many short ups and downs.
Camping: No camping is available.
For more information: Maryland Department of Natural Resources.
Trailhead facilities: None.

Finding the trailhead: From Interstate 70 take Maryland Highway 97 North. About 6.5 miles south of Winchester, make a right turn onto Bartholow Road and then turn left onto Jim Bowers, followed by an immediate left onto Ben Rose Lane to the Morgan Run entrance.

The Hike

This hike is for the birds, especially the raptors. Much of the walk is through old fields and recovering forest. In the fields, red-tailed hawks and kestrels ply their trade with impunity. In the woods, barred owls hoot to alert others downtrail of your presence there. By the hedgerows, even the shrill killdeer cannot drown the songs of indigo buntings and rufous-sided towhees, darting in and out of the thicket. In the woods in spring, you can sit by Morgan Run for an hour listening to the courting wood thrushes.

Except for the wooded sections, the trail system here is a network of mowed paths through and around the fields—some in succession to forest. When you get to know the area, you can wander without regard to orientation. However, the hills, tall thickets, and relative sameness of some of the fields make it possible to lose direction. The hike described below offers specific turns to keep you oriented and provides a little of everything Morgan Run NEA has to offer. If you wander the fields and go astray, walk uphill. From the tree line at the high point is a vista that will reveal your location.

From the trailhead kiosk, walk the path leading straight ahead. In less that 200 yards there is a picnic table in a small clearing. Continue down the path as it hugs the contours of the hill. You are making your way to the first tree line at the top. The slower you go, the better. Hikers often are averse to these types of hikes, wanting big trees and big hills. But these fields and thickets teem with wildlife. If you're

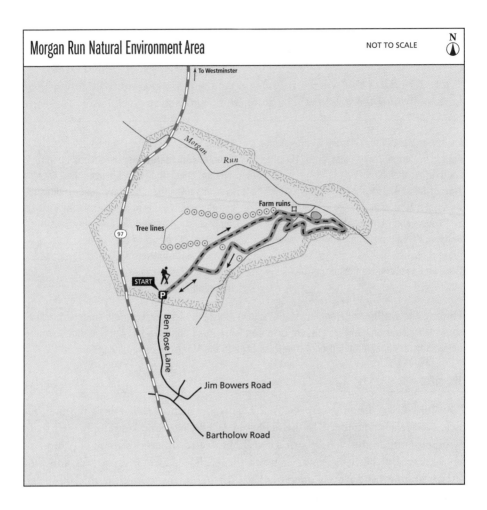

NOT TO SCALE

N

To Westminster

Morgan

Run

Farm ruins

Tree lines

97

START

P

Ben Rose Lane

Jim Bowers Road

Bartholow Road

lucky, you will see a fox cross your path before you even pass through the first line of trees, at 0.5 mile, where you enter the wildland area.

In the wildland the thicket has matured to young woodland, where eastern red cedar, spicebush, and witch hazel sprout amid the white locust trees. Pass through a second tree line at a fork joining three fields at 0.9 mile, going straight into a section of woods that is older still. Elms and poplars create a canopy above walnuts and serviceberry—a tree known alternately on the eastern seaboard as shadbush, for the reliability of its flowers to bloom when the shad run, and Juneberry.

At 1.5 miles reach the remains of a metal barn and assorted outbuildlings. Soon a deep stream gorge opens below on the right. In autumn the woods below host great flocks of migratory birds who stop over and make a racket to rival a hotel full of seniors on a bus tour. Descend steeply to stream level and cross the creek. A pond on the left is an inviting rest stop. If you approach it silently, you will be treated to glimpses of wood ducks. Look for the distinctive, colorful helmet of the male.

Enter another field and walk with the tree line and Morgan Run on the left. You will circle this field and enter the woods uphill, to the right of where you entered it. If you need to cut the hike short, omit this field. At 2.0 miles there are nice views of the ridge above Morgan Run just as you enter the woods. Turn left at the T and follow a faint path with the stream on your right for a few hundred yards before crossing a seasonal run. Then recross the stream running the gorge. At the other side of the creek, turn right and follow a wide path as it ascends above the gorge. At the top of the grade, emerge from the woods at the farm buildings you passed earlier. Turn left and ascend, retracing your earlier steps.

At the top of a long climb, at 3.0 miles, reach a junction you passed earlier. Take the soft left here (not the extreme left), and walk a wide path between tall shrubs and dense thicket. The path wraps around this old field. As you go, you might scare up a grouse or two or, in spring, happen upon a fawn hiding deep in the dark thicket. After a long, gradual climb, step left through an opening in the trees, at 3.6 miles, and continue walking uphill until you reach the picnic clearing at the hike's beginning. Turn left to return to the trailhead.

Miles and Directions

0.0 Start from trailhead kiosk.

0.5 Pass through first line of trees and enter wildlands.

0.9 Reach forks of three fields; go straight.

1.5 Arrive at farm buildings.

2.0 Enjoy views of ridge, then turn left at T.

2.2 Cross a smaller stream.

2.5 Pass farm buildings for a second time.

3.0 Take soft left at junction.

3.6 Step left through opening in the trees; continue uphill.

4.1 Arrive back at trailhead.

Options: Because much of the trail network follows tree lines around old fields, you can pick your own combination of paths.

Soldier's Delight Natural Environment Area

The 2,000-acre serpentine grasslands that make up Soldier's Delight Natural Environment Area are the largest prairie ecosystem in the eastern United States. The soil, composed of green magnesium silicate, is so dry it supports only the hardiest of grasses and shrubs. A much larger area of northern Maryland once was covered in this unusual grass-and-pine vegetation. At first glance, the rock-strewn soil and short grasses might seem an unglamorous scrub forest, but a hike through the grasslands reveals a diverse ecosystem of hundreds of plant species. However, it is not the twisting grasses that give the landscape its name. The dull green, mottled mineral that forms the underlying bedrock is serpentine. Because both hikes start from the same trailhead, information common to both hikes is provided once below, followed by information specific to each hike.

25 Soldier's Delight East Loop, Soldier's Delight Natural Environment Area

A short hike through pine forest and grasslands.

Location: Soldier's Delight Natural Environment Area is located in Baltimore County, 10 miles northwest of the Baltimore Beltway.
Type of hike: 3.0-mile loop.
Difficulty: Easy.
Season: January through April; October through November.
Fees and permits: No fees or permits required.
Maps: USGS Reisterstown, Maryland.
Special considerations: On a hot, cloudless summer day, the area heats to ten to fifteen degrees warmer than the hardwood forests only several miles away. Although the hikes pass into and out of pine groves, offering relief from the sun, it is a lot easier to enjoy the ecology of the area in autumn, winter, or spring. There are two hikes described below, one to the east of Deer Park Road in the flatland and one white-blazed loop to the west that descends into the stream bottom.
Camping: No camping is available.
For more information: Soldier's Delight Natural Environment Area.
Trailhead facilities: None. On weekdays and Saturday morning, the visitor center, 0.25 mile past the trailhead on Deer Park Road, is open.

Finding the trailhead: From the Baltimore Beltway (Interstate 695), drive north on Interstate 795 to exit 7, Franklin Boulevard. Go west on Franklin Boulevard for 2 miles, then turn left onto Berrymans Lane. In 0.5 mile turn left onto Deer Park Road. Trailhead parking is on the right in 2 miles.

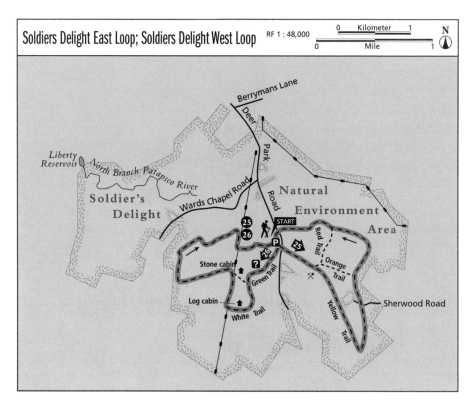

Soldiers Delight East Loop; Soldiers Delight West Loop   RF 1 : 48,000

The Hike

Cross Deer Park Road and look for colored blazes to the right leading down a wide path. Follow the path into the woods, and come to the site of a former chromium mine. The surrounding area was the first chromium mine in the world; the openings at this site are the last known shafts. Continue on the path with the mine on the right.

At 0.5 mile turn right, following the yellow blazes at a junction where the orange blazes continue straight and the red blazes break right.

The trail makes a long, very gradual descent into and out of the woods and then breaks sharply left at about 1.3 miles. Cross Sherwood Road and reenter the woods. The orange-blazed trail joins from the left at 1.7 miles. A trail marker at 2.0 miles shows the way west; do not continue straight.

Follow a slow-moving stream on the right, then cross a small branch on a foot-bridge. Leave the stream and continue an easy ascent. Emerge into a clearing and, at 2.2 miles, join the red-blazed trail, which cuts sharply right into a grove of oaks and pines. Cross a small stream and emerge into open, sandy grassland. At the end of the field, the trail follows a narrow "green tunnel," with underbrush and saplings growing close to the trail.

At 2.8 miles emerge from the woods onto Deer Park Road. Turn left and follow the road 350 yards back to the trailhead.

Miles and Directions

0.0 Start at trailhead, crossing Deer Park Road.

0.3 Reach mine site.

0.5 At junction, turn right onto yellow trail.

1.7 Orange trail joins from the left.

2.0 Turn west at trail marker; do *not* continue straight.

2.2 Reach junction with red trail.

2.8 Emerge from woods onto Deer Park Road.

3.0 Arrive back at trailhead.

Options: For a 2.0-mile hike just to get the flavor of grasslands, go straight on the orange trail at 0.5 mile and follow the description above from 1.7 miles.

26 Soldier's Delight West Loop, Soldier's Delight Natural Environment Area

A walk through wild grasses and over rugged, rocky terrain.

See map on page 109

Location: Soldier's Delight Natural Environment Area is located in Baltimore County, 10 miles northwest of the Baltimore Beltway.

Type of hike: 3.0-mile loop.

Difficulty: Moderate.

Season: January through April; October through November.

Fees and permits: No fees or permits required.

Maps: USGS Reisterstown, Maryland.

Special considerations: On a hot, cloudless summer day, the area heats to ten to fifteen degrees warmer than the hardwood forests only several miles away. Although the hikes pass into and out of pine groves, offering relief from the sun, it is a lot easier to enjoy the ecology of the area in autumn, winter, or spring. There are two hikes described below, one to the east of Deer Park Road in the flatland and one white-blazed loop to the west that descends into the stream bottom.

Camping: No camping is available.

For more information: Soldier's Delight Natural Environment Area.

Trailhead facilities: None. On weekdays and Saturday morning, the visitor center, 0.25 mile past the trailhead on Deer Park Road, is open.

Finding the trailhead: From the Baltimore Beltway (Interstate 695), drive north on Interstate 795 to exit 7, Franklin Boulevard. Go west on Franklin Boulevard for 2 miles, then turn left onto Berrymans Lane. In 0.5 mile turn left onto Deer Park Road. Trailhead parking is on the right in 2 miles.

The Hike

This is an odd little hike that leaves you wondering which ecosystem you are in. There are oak-beech hardwoods, open prairie grasses, pine groves, and an almost lunar, rocky knoll at the westernmost part of the loop. The trip is somewhat marred by several hundred yards of following a utility right-of-way, but the landscape is so varied that your mind will not focus on the cable lines for long.

From the trailhead, follow the green trail south along Deer Park Road; duck into a stand of trees, enjoying the shade while you can. Emerge at a dead end in a clearing, and go right following the green blazes into an open meadow. From here there is an expansive southwest view of the North Branch Patapsco River and the Liberty Reservoir watershed.

Pass right of the visitor center, staying on a dirt road, and come to a stone cabin. Go left before the cabin. Descend on an old cart path, with oak and remnant American chestnut scattered among loblolly and red pines. At 0.5 mile the green trail forks west (right) and the white trail continues straight into the woods. Remember this spot. The cabin route ahead may be difficult to find in the vegetation. If you cannot find the way, retrace your steps to this fork and follow the green-blazed trail to the green junction at 1.3 miles. If you are burning to see an old log cabin, you can find it more easily by reversing the route from that spot.

The trail levels off; at the end of the field from which the green trail diverged, the woods on both sides form a dense thicket. A white blaze on a tree points left. Fifty yards past this blaze is an opening to the right that cuts through the woods and leads to an old log cabin at 0.8 mile. Continuing, come to a clearing at 1.0 mile, where the immense power lines cut a swath through the landscape, offering a bit of irony in the fact that the land here is managed as a natural environment area. To its credit, the power company is participating in a management plan to restore the prairie grasses.

Turn right and ascend steeply under open skies. At the top of the hill, at 1.3 miles, the green trail enters from the right and continues along beneath the power lines. Turn left here, following the white blazes in their descent into the woods. Stay on the trail, which may be difficult to follow at times, until you reach a fork with two trails. Here, take the hard right. You may not see blazes for a time.

At 1.8 miles descend into a dense, cool canopy of hardwood. Cross a stream without a bridge and climb a small knoll, emerging from the woods. Were it not for the trees bordering the open area, you would swear you were on another planet. Baseball-size rocks form the terrain, and the open rocky ground takes on ethereal shade in the late-day sun. This is the landscape that lends the name serpentine to the grasslands. Hug the treeline to the right, ascending. In an open meadow, watch for the trail crossing to the north of the clearing.

Continue to climb the next 0.5 mile in the open rocks. At the top of the hill, a line of oaks offers a brief respite from the sun before you emerge once again into the power line right-of-way. Turn right and descend to a stream in the hollow, the same stream you crossed at 1.8 miles. At 2.7 miles turn left before crossing; hike upstream into the woods, following the green blazes.

Cross the spring twice while continuing to ascend, steeply at times. Emerge from the woods for a steep final ascent to the trailhead.

Miles and Directions

0.0 Start at trailhead, following green trail south along Deer Park Road.

0.5 At fork, continue straight, now on white trail.

0.8 Opening to right leads to log cabin.

1.0 Come to clearing at power lines.

1.3 Reach junction with green trail; turn left, following white blazes.

1.8 Cross stream (no bridge); climb small knoll and emerge from woods.

2.0 Reach junction with trail crossing to north of clearing.

2.3 Turn right onto right-of-way.

2.7 Turn left before stream.

3.0 Arrive back at trailhead.

27 Little Bennett Loop, Little Bennett Regional Park

An easy loop through several forest types that includes a pleasant stroll along Stoney Brook and Sopers Branch.

Location: The hike is in Little Bennett Regional Park, part of the Montgomery County, Maryland, system, located just east of Maryland Highway 355, about 25 miles northwest of Washington, D.C.

Type of hike: 4.1-mile loop.

Difficulty: Easy.

Season: Year-round.

Fees and permits: No fees or permits required.

Maps: USGS Urbana, Maryland.

Special considerations: To manage automobile traffic within the park, park officials sometimes limit automobile access to the nature center parking area. In this case you can park at the Clarksburg Road trailhead at the junction of Hyattstown Mill and Clarksburg Roads and start this loop at Mound Builder Trail. To reach the trailhead, reverse your driving route back to Clarksburg Road and go left. In about a mile, at the left intersection with Hyattstown Mill Road, there is trailhead parking on the right. To reach Mound Builder Trail, walk 0.25 mile west on Hyattstown Mill Road and go left at the first trail leaving the road. In 200 yards cross Little Bennett Creek on a footbridge, and continue straight for about 50 yards to Mound Builder Trail. Turn right and follow the directions of the hike as described below; when you reach the nature center, follow the directions from the beginning back to this spot.

Camping: Camping is available; a permit and a fee are required. Call (301) 972-9222.

For more information: Little Bennett Regional Park.

Trailhead facilities: Water and vending machines at nature center; restrooms during business hours.

Finding the trailhead: From the Capital Beltway, drive north on Interstate 270. Exit at Maryland Highway 121 North toward Clarksburg. Go left onto Maryland Highway 355, Frederick Road. Proceed to the park entrance on the right.

The Hike

This splendid little hike offers Washington, D.C., and Montgomery County urbanites an almost instant retreat from the city. Although the woods here have a wild feel about them, the park area actually encompasses the former settlement of Kingsley.

As early as the eighteenth century, the Little Bennett Valley was the scene of farms and small-scale industries capitalizing on the region's abundant resources of timber, water, and vast acreage for farming. Several gristmills and sawmills, a sumac mill, and a whiskey manufacturer were established at various times along the creek. The steep and rocky slopes did not encourage farming, but farmers gave it their best, raising tobacco first and then grain crops well into the twentieth century. A small community flourished, which was called Kingsley—named for a prominent Montgomery County family whose surname, King, now identifies several subdivisions in the region.

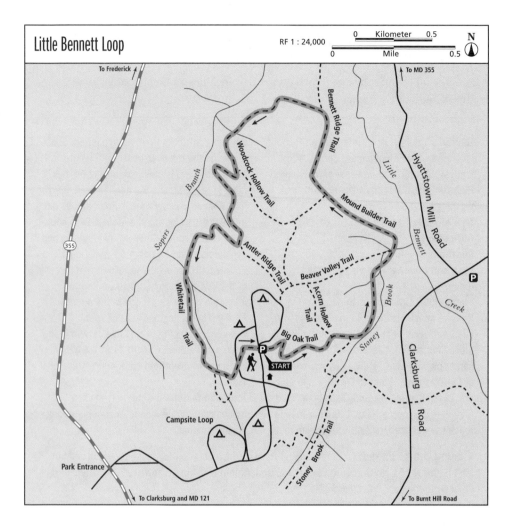

Little Bennett Loop

RF 1 : 24,000

0   Kilometer   0.5

0   Mile   0.5

N

To Frederick

To MD 355

Bennett Ridge Trail

Little

Hyattstown Mill Road

Woodcock Hollow Trail

Branch

Mound Builder Trail

Bennett

Sopers

355

Antler Ridge Trail

Beaver Valley Trail

Brook

Creek

P

Whitetail

Acorn Hollow Trail

Stoney

Clarksburg

Trail

Big Oak Trail

START

P

Road

Campsite Loop

Stoney Brook Trail

Park Entrance

To Clarksburg and MD 121

To Burnt Hill Road

Start the hike on Big Oak Trail, which begins behind the nature center. In addition to the oaks along the path, there are silver maples and a pine grove. Turn right onto Acorn Hollow Trail, and descend easily into the small valley created by Stoney Brook. Reach the brook and turn left onto Stoney Brook Trail at 0.5 mile.

Walk through the wonderfully quiet hollow, interrupted only by a short rise over a small knob and a crossing of a spring babbling under cover of red cedar. At the junction with Beaver Valley Trail are the remnants of Wilson's Sawmill, one of the many sawmills that utilized Little Bennett Creek, which is about a hundred yards east of the trail.

Reach Mound Builder Trail at 1.0 mile, but before turning left continue straight for another 50 yards to enjoy a rest stop at Little Bennett Creek. From the bridge over the creek, it is a short hike to Hyattstown Mill Road and on to the Clarksburg Road Trailhead (see Special considerations). Back at Mound Builder

Trail, ascend through red cedar and pine. Watch for the mounds near the trail and in the woods. These are huge anthills—by themselves a worthy attraction on this hike.

Turn right onto Bennett Ridge Trail, a wide former farm road, at 1.5 miles; walk along an open field crest until you reach Woodcock Hollow Trail at 2.0 miles. Turn right. Descend into the woods through a glade dotted with sycamore and red pine; then enter a cool woods amid much older, larger sycamore and oaks. For the next 1.5 miles walk just above Sopers Branch. Watch for the descent onto Whitetail Trail, at 2.7 miles. It is a little tricky; just stay right and descend.

Cross a small stream in an open glade, and pass Antler Ridge Trail at 3.1 miles. In this vicinity you will see old farm implements and machinery still standing where they were left when the farms were sold to the county. Cross a small stream and ascend beside it. The horizontal gashes you see in the oaks, resembling huge human lips, are created by ant-loving birds. They chop the outer bark to allow the sap to run—which attracts ants and other insects—and then swoop in for their feasts.

Reach the nature trail at 3.7 miles, staying left at the fork. Cross the stream and ascend to the nature center on a wide, accessible pathway.

Miles and Directions

0.0 Start at Big Oak trailhead, behind nature center.

0.5 Turn left at junction with Stoney Brook Trail.

1.0 Come to junction with Mound Builder Trail; start of trail to Hyattstown Mill Road.

1.5 Turn right onto Bennett Ridge Trail.

2.0 Turn right onto Woodcock Hollow Trail.

2.7 At Whitetail Trail junction, descend to the right.

3.1 Pass Antler Ridge Trail.

3.7 Reach nature trail; stay left at fork and cross stream.

4.1 Arrive back at trailhead.

Options: There are several options for short loops in the north section of the park; site maps are available at the contact station.

28 Schaeffer Farm Trail, Seneca Creek State Park

An easy loop that meanders in and out of new and mature woods and cornfields along several creeks in the Seneca Creek drainage. A good chance of seeing deer and other wildlife.

Location: The hike is in Seneca Creek State Park in the Schaeffer Farm Trails System, just off Maryland Highway 117, 20 miles northwest of Washington, D.C.
Type of hike: 3.5-mile loop.
Difficulty: Easy.
Season: September through May.
Fees and permits: No fees or permits required.
Maps: USGS Seneca, Maryland.
Special considerations: The trails in the system were built largely by members of area mountain bicycling and equestrian organizations and are maintained cooperatively. Trail use guidelines call for cyclists to yield to hikers, but it is often easier for a hiker to step aside to allow an oncoming cyclist to pass. Be courteous. Summer months are the most popular for trail cyclists here. Trail closures are routine from mid-December to mid-March.
Camping: No camping is available.
For more information: Seneca Creek State Park.
Trailhead facilities: None.

Finding the trailhead: From the Capital Beltway, drive north on Interstate 270 to the Maryland Highway 118 exit. Go 3 miles west and turn right onto Maryland Highway 117; then almost immediately turn left onto Schaeffer Road. In 2.5 miles, just as the road takes a hard right, turn left into the trail system parking area. The trailhead is at the back of the parking area.

The Hike

Start at the far end of the parking area, continuing past a trailhead sign for the white- and yellow-blazed trails. Turn left to walk the loop counterclockwise. Enter an open field, and follow white blazes into the woods. The terrain is easy, and the trail's path is serpentine, more for esthetics than necessity. Enter a farm field and walk its perimeter. At 0.4 mile, reenter the woods along a seasonal run and begin a stretch of passing into and out of the woods.

Enter mature woods at 0.5 mile and cross two small bridges; cross the same run (without bridges) twice more beginning at 0.7 mile. Climb a small knoll and enter another field, turning right, with the woods on your right. Circle halfway around the field, and cut through a stand of maple into yet another field. Walk along Black Rock Road for 200 yards, and enter the woods beside a giant red oak surrounded by a grove of white pine and cedar, crossing an old farm road. Still in the pine, pass close to a farmhouse, 100 yards to the right, and then break from the road and ascend toward the open field. This is a perfect location for spotting deer. If you sit still for ten minutes, you will almost certainly be rewarded with a sighting.

The trail bends right, and the hillside drops dramatically to the left. You can hear Seneca Creek 300 yards south and 70 feet below. The trail hugs the slope, following

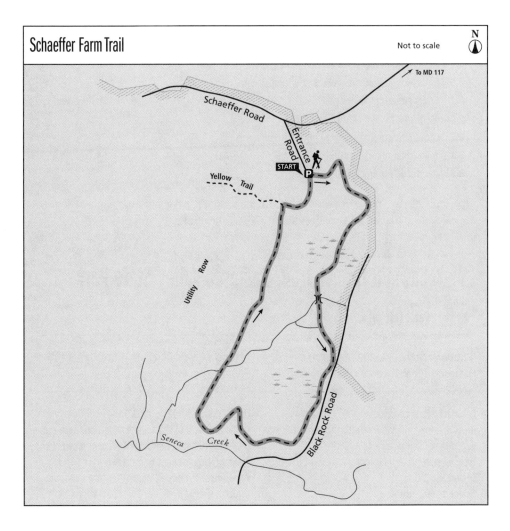

a tunnel of mountain laurel. At 1.3 miles the trail moves up the ledge of a narrow hollow containing a stand of huge, mature oaks. At the top of the hollow, the trail enters the corner of a field, then ducks back into the woods at 1.7 miles. Remnant fence posts from the farm still stand.

At 2.0 miles, merge with a utility right-of-way as the trail descends, following the ground above a buried telephone line. The orange posts infringe somewhat on the scenery, but the clearing brings out berries and other edge-loving plants that attract wildlife. At the bottom of the hill, cross two small streams just above their confluence, and reenter the woods at 2.2 miles. Cross the streams again and climb steeply, with the stream on the right. For the next 0.5 mile the trail follows mostly level ground punctuated by gentle descents and rises over small knobs.

The yellow trail enters from the left at 3.1 miles, sharing the route with the white blazes back to the trailhead on a gentle woodland trail.

Miles and Directions

0.0 Start at trailhead at far end of parking area.

0.5 Enter woods and cross two small footbridges.

0.7 Cross streams (no bridges).

2.0 Merge with utility right-of-way.

2.2 Cross streams (no bridges) and reenter woods.

3.1 Yellow trail enters from the left.

3.5 Arrive back at trailhead.

Options: There are several color-blazed trails in the park system. Contact Seneca Creek State Park for information about these other trails.

29 Sawmill Branch Trail, Patapsco Valley State Park, Hilton Area

A surprisingly rugged and remote descent into a wooded stream valley to the Patapsco River.

Location: Patapsco Valley State Park Hilton Area is a few miles outside the Baltimore Beltway near U.S. Highway 40.

Type of hike: 3.2-mile loop.

Difficulty: Moderate.

Season: Year-round.

Fees and permits: $2.00 per person over age fifteen on weekends, April through October.

Maps: USGS Ellicott City, Maryland.

Special considerations: Throughout the hike, remnant junctions from older versions of these routes sometimes cause moments of misdirection, especially at the bottom of Sawmill Branch. Stay with the fresh blazes. On the return, a dozen downed trees over 0.5 mile cut down on traffic and add to the feeling of remoteness, but they require some hurdling. If you are hiking with children, be prepared to go slowly.

Camping: Developed campsites are available through the park office. For reservations call Maryland's statewide reservations line for state parks and forests: (888) 432-2267.

For more information: Patapsco Valley State Park.

Trailhead facilities: There is a spigot at the comfort station, 50 yards before the parking area, as well as restrooms and a playground for children.

Finding the trailhead: From the Baltimore Beltway (Interstate 695), take the US 40/West Frederick Road exit. Drive 2 miles and then turn left onto South Rolling Road. At the first intersection bear left onto Hilton Avenue. Patapsco Valley State Park Hilton Area entrance is 0.8 mile ahead on the right. Once inside the park, take the first right turn and proceed to Shelter 245. The trailhead is 100 yards down the access road to the camping area, leaving from behind the shelter.

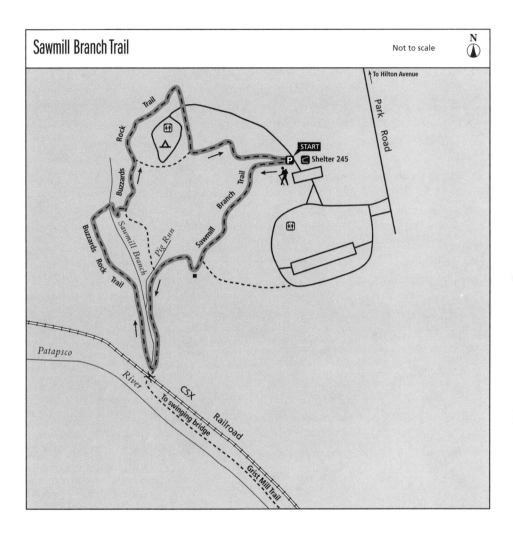

Sawmill Branch Trail — Not to scale — N

The Hike

From the trailhead, follow the road behind the picnic pavilion 100 yards to where the red-blazed trail breaks left and descends 150 yards to a junction with the yellow and red blazes leading right. After you pass this junction and cross under power lines in an open meadow, the real hiking begins when you reenter the woods.

The trail passes under a canopy of huge, mature red oaks, some of which are nearly 3 feet in diameter. Dogwoods cling to the rocky soil, and everywhere on the open knobs there is moss and lichen. Pass through and near picnic sites; just as the park drive becomes visible, break hard right, following the sign for Sawmill Branch Trail and continue the casual descent toward the river.

At a T intersection, at 0.4 mile, take a moment to follow a path leading left 50 yards to a ledge overlooking the shallow gorge cut by the Patapsco River—a particularly fine view in winter when the trees are leafless. Return to the T, and follow the trail's switchback into a darker, deep stream hollow, where the trail runs head on into Pig Run, a spring hatched 0.25 mile uphill that at this point tumbles beneath a vegetative cover most of the way. The trail breaks sharply left. Here the understory drapes over the path a mere 10 to 15 feet overhead, and several downed trees left to their natural decay require minor scrambling to navigate.

Pig Run disappears just as the sound of Sawmill Branch takes over above the occasional knock-knock-knock of a pileated woodpecker or the sounds of smaller birds hobnobbing in the undergrowth. The trail meets Sawmill Branch just below its confluence with Pig Run and follows it ever downward. Beware of a false crossing of Sawmill Branch about 100 yards farther down. Sawmill Branch Trail did once cross here and make a steep ascent of the south bank, but the trail now crosses at the railroad bridge 150 yards farther.

The railroad bridge, at 0.9 mile, is a marvel of stone construction, creating a tunnel through which Sawmill Branch passes and Grist Mill Trail begins its southeast route along the Patapsco. Take a few minutes here to explore the Patapsco, perhaps finding a sunny spot for a picnic or a splash around on the shore. Back through the railroad tunnel, Sawmill Branch Trail crosses the creek over stones. From this point on called Buzzards Rock Trail, it climbs upstream on the opposite side.

The trail has a much-less-traveled feel on this side, and for the next mile you will hike above and next to Sawmill Branch. A series of cascades beginning at about 1.3 miles offers pools for wading and oversize granite rocks for napping, especially where the sun breaks through. The trail above the cascades may be difficult to follow because of overgrowth and downed trees. Your options are to follow a faint high-water trail for 175 yards, slabbing over a knob to rejoin the trail, or to stay with the water and make your way past the bad section—which is only about 200 feet if you follow the water.

Cross the creek, stepping over rocks onto the yellow trail at 1.8 miles, and head east back toward the park. On the way, there are more outstanding red oaks and white ash, as well as a few more false trails left from recent trail relocations. Just above the switchback after crossing Sawmill Branch, stay right with the yellow blaze at the T. Turn left at the next junction, where a trail leads right. Stay left at the red-blazed campground trail, at 2.2 miles, and loop around the campground in the woods. Cross a campground access road at 2.5 miles; stay left at a junction at 2.8 miles marking the other end of the red-blazed campground trail.

At 3.1 miles turn left at the fork with Sawmill Branch Trail and ascend out of the forest. The trail comes to the access road behind Shelter 245 and returns to the trailhead at 3.2 miles.

Miles and Directions

0.0 Start at trailhead behind Shelter 245.

0.1 Bear right at junction with yellow/red trail.

0.4	At T intersection, follow path 50 yards to view. Return to T and continue on trail.
0.9	Reach railroad bridge and Patapsco River.
1.3	Reach series of cascades.
1.8	Cross creek onto yellow trail; head east back toward park.
2.2	Cross campground access road. Stay left on yellow/red trail.
3.2	Arrive back at trailhead.

Options: The park map outlines a few shorter options.

30 McKeldin Area Loop, Patapsco Valley State Park

Starting from the swift rapids of the South Branch, to the confluence of the North and South Branches and beyond, this hike follows the mood of the Patapsco River—sometimes lively, sometimes lazy. About two-thirds of the hike comes into very close contact with the river. The return is a woodland walk through a narrow hollow favored by white-tailed deer.

Location: This trail is located in the McKeldin Area of Patapsco Valley State Park on the Baltimore–Howard County line, about 15 miles west of Baltimore.
Type of hike: 3.5-mile loop.
Difficulty: Easy.
Season: Year-round.
Fees and permits: No fees or permits required.
Maps: USGS Ellicott City; Maryland.
Special considerations: The lush Maryland vegetation can overtake a trail in a summer. If a trail segment seems overgrown, it may be in need of a volunteer. The park is used extensively by equestrians and bicyclists. On weekdays it is possible to find solitude in the park, but the bottomlands have undergone significant damage in recent years.
Camping: Camping is available for youth groups only.
For more information: Patapsco Valley State Park.
Trailhead facilities: Restrooms.

Finding the trailhead: From the Baltimore Beltway (Interstate 695), drive west on Interstate 70 for 11 miles to Marriotsville Road, exit 83. Go north 2 miles to the park entrance on the right. Circle the open field, and then continue right until the park road ends at the trailhead parking. Continue the final 150 yards to the river on foot, following the blacktop.

The Hike

Thanks to the topography of the area, it is possible to find solitude even when large groups are enjoying picnics in the park pavilions. The rolling landscape and cliffs provide a buffer that allows for quiet enjoyment of the stream valley.

Take some time at the outset to enjoy the cascades on the South Branch, and then walk southeast with the river on your right. A quarter of a mile downstream, the trail breaks north; a narrow path leads to a rocky point that juts into the river,

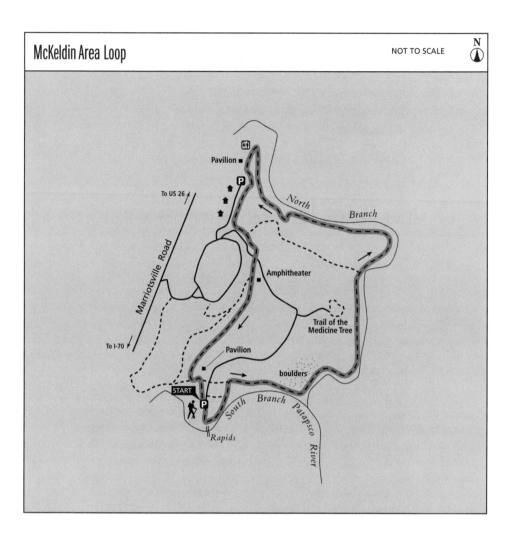

creating a narrow rapids. Emerge from the woods, and cross over huge boulders that seem to slide into the stream. At 0.4 mile reach the confluence of the South and North Branches of the Patapsco River. Continue straight, now upstream, along the North Branch.

Follow the trail through a wide bottomland, which creates a broad bend. Then, as the river course comes from due north, walk beneath a steep and rocky hillside rising about a hundred feet left. For nearly the next mile, the trail follows the North Branch closely, usually through maple and scattered oak and hickory. There are some very old, immense oaks along the bottomland here, spared from farming because of the rough terrain directly uphill. Perhaps the most interesting features along this lazy stretch of water are the occasional boulder fields, especially a sprawling one at 1.3 miles. Where the huge rocks protrude from the creek bottom, they form shady pools favored by the trout stocked here each spring.

At 1.5 miles go left at the cutoff trail and climb, first through a long switchback and then rather steeply for a hundred yards or so. A second switchback takes the trail north again. Follow the ledge above the North Branch, moving upstream; then descend into a narrow hollow to cross a small stream, taking care not to cause further erosion. Ascend again, slowly from the hollow and then steeply for a final sprint to reach the park access road near a comfort station and picnic pavilions, at 1.7 miles.

Follow the park road 0.1 mile to a fork; go left, then left again through a parking area. Turn left onto the park road, and follow it 100 yards; cross the road and enter the woods marked by a trail sign at 2.0 miles. At the amphitheater just inside the woods, take the left trail at the fork. From here the trail follows a narrow, shallow stream valley, which drops to your right. The valley is home to scores of deer, giving you ample opportunities to watch the youngest testing their gallops.

After crossing a small stream, stay right at the fork and continue along the stream valley. At 2.7 miles, just above the South Branch, go left and follow the trail 0.4 mile to the park road, emerging at the rest area. Turn right and walk 0.4 mile along the road to return to the trailhead.

Miles and Directions

0.0 Start at trailhead walking down to river.

0.4 Reach confluence of North and South Branches; continue straight.

1.3 Reach boulder field.

1.5 Go left at trail junction.

1.7 Reach park access road; and picnic pavilion.

2.0 Cross road.

2.7 Reach trail to trailhead; turn left onto trail.

3.5 Arrive back at trailhead.

Options: Several variations on this hike are made possible by trails weaving through the park, at various stages of maintenance. The Trail of the Medicine Tree is a nice 0.5-mile interpretive nature trail.

31 Wincopin–Quarry Run Loop, Savage Park

A short ramble along the Middle Patuxent River to its confluence with the Little Patuxent River, then upstream, with a return via an abandoned quarry road. Most of the hike follows the streams closely.

Location: This trail is located in Howard County, Maryland, about 20 miles north of Washington, D.C.

Type of hike: 2.4-mile loop.

Difficulty: Easy.

Season: Year-round.

Fees and permits: No fees or permits required.

Maps: USGS Savage, Maryland.

Special considerations: The first 0.5 mile of the hike is within loud earshot of I-95, which intrudes upon the remote feeling of the river bottomland. Still, considering its proximity to the few million residents of the Baltimore–Washington Corridor, it provides a quick escape into the woods. Nearby Savage Mill is a great spot for an after-hike lunch.

Camping: No camping is available.

For more information: Howard County Recreation and Parks.

Trailhead facilities: Kiosk with map of area.

Finding the trailhead: From the Capital Beltway, drive north on Interstate 95 (from the Baltimore Beltway, drive south on I-95). Exit onto Maryland Highway 32 South. In 2.5 miles turn south onto U.S. Highway 1. In 0.25 mile turn right onto Howard Street, then left onto Baltimore Street. Take the third right onto Savage Road. In 1 mile go left onto Vollmerhausen Road. The trailhead is 0.25 mile on the left, just over the bridge.

The Hike

Within minutes of setting off, you will be transported from one of the most densely populated suburbs in America to a lovely woodland along two former mill streams. Sandwiched between I–95 and US 1, Savage Park is the population epicenter of the Baltimore–Washingon Corridor; however, you would never know it on this hike (except for the intrusion of highway noise in the first 0.5 mile).

From the Vollmerhausen Road trailhead, follow the red blazes along a paved trail that turns to a dirt footpath in 100 yards. Enter the woods, and follow the trail past one left junction with the green-blazed Quarry Run Trail; at 0.4 mile go left at the second junction with Quarry Run Trail.

At 0.5 mile an overlook offers a vista over the Middle Patuxent bottomland. This is an especially nice view in winter, when the trees are leafless. Descend into a hollow along a ledge, with sycamore and hickory above, and walk over a footbridge, coming to the river's edge. Turn left, walk downstream, and enter an area of old-growth shagbark hickory and chestnut oak, at 0.8 mile. Watch for copperheads in the shallow water along the riverbank.

At 1.3 miles come to an old bridge abutment that offers an open view of the river and, in winter, of the confluence. Go left onto an old dirt road, still following

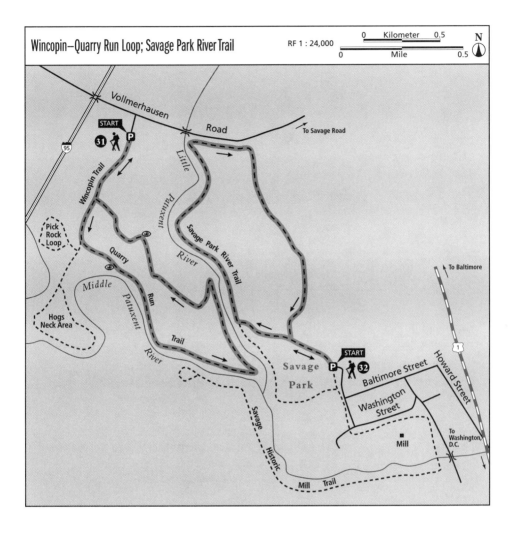

Wincopin–Quarry Run Loop; Savage Park River Trail   RF 1 : 24,000

START

Vollmerhausen Road

To Savage Road

95

31

Wincopin Trail

Little Patuxent River

Savage Park River Trail

Pick Rock Loop

Quarry Run

Middle Patuxent River

Hogs Neck Area

Trail

To Baltimore

1

Savage Park

START

32

Baltimore Street

Howard Street

Savage Historic

Washington Street

Mill

To Washington, D.C.

Mill Trail

Quarry Run Trail, and walk along the Little Patuxent, which is about 50 yards to the right and will emerge in about a hundred yards. Following the dirt road under a canopy, at 1.7 miles come to the ruins of a concrete dam abutment; a bench here offers a nice view of the river and a shady rest stop.

At 1.9 miles the dirt road continues left and the green trail switches back abruptly left and climbs. Do not continue straight on the dirt road. A sign 200 yards farther warns hikers: NO TRESPASSING. VIOLATORS WILL BE SHOT; SURVIVORS WILL BE PROSECUTED.

Ascend steeply for 150 yards; as the trail finds level ground, come to a wooden overlook to the right. Just beyond, the green trail ends at a T intersection with the red-blazed Wincopin Trail, at 2.1 miles. Turn right to return to the trailhead.

Miles and Directions

0.0   Start at trailhead, just over bridge.

0.4   Reach second junction with Quarry Run Trail; turn left.

0.5   Arrive at overlook.

0.8   Enter old-growth forest.

1.3   At bridge abutment, turn left onto dirt road.

1.7   Reach dam ruins.

1.9   Follow green trail or left ascent.

2.1   Turn right at T intersection with Wincopin Trail junction.

2.4   Arrive back at trailhead.

32 Savage Park River Trail

A quiet stream valley walk along the Little Patuxent River, with an upland return on a rail-trail.

See map on page 125
Location: This trail is located in Howard County, Maryland, about 20 miles north of Washington, D.C.
Type of hike: 2.5-mile loop.
Difficulty: Easy.
Season: Year-round.
Fees and permits: No fees or permits required.

Maps: USGS Savage, Maryland.
Special considerations: The rail-trail that provides the return loop is part of a planned path to Elkhorn Lake.
Camping: No camping is available.
For more information: Howard County Recreation and Parks.
Trailhead facilities: None.

Finding the trailhead: From the Capital Beltway, drive north on Interstate 95 (from the Baltimore Beltway, drive south on I-95). Exit onto Maryland Highway 32 South. In 2.5 miles turn south onto U.S. Highway 1. In 0.25 mile go right onto Howard Street and then left onto Baltimore Street. Take the fifth right into Savage Park. Follow the access road to the northwest corner of the ball fields. The road ends at a parking area. The hike begins at the paved pathway into the woods.

The Hike

Anyone living within quick access of I–95 in the Baltimore–Washington Corridor can be out the door and on the trail in less than thirty minutes to enjoy a quiet stroll along the Little Patuxent River. There is not a lot to describe in this hike because it is, after all, a short jaunt through a suburban wood. Still, it is a splendid walk for a late afternoon when you have the desire for a woodland hike but not the time to get away.

Equestrian trails are an integral part of Maryland's recreation scene. PHOTO COURTESY OF MARYLAND DNR

The hike begins behind the ball fields, following an asphalt path to a campfire ring used by youth groups. At the ring, at 0.2 mile, a dirt footpath provides access west to the river trail. Descend through the trees and hike upstream.

From here it is an unremarkable but lovely hike along the narrow, shallow Little Patuxent. At about 1.0 mile the trail breaks from the river, climbs a little, then descends again to the stream just before reaching Vollmerhausen Road, at 1.3 miles. Turn right and walk along a sidewalk, watching for a wide rail-trail leading right just before the parking lot of Patuxent Valley Middle School, at 1.7 miles. Follow the paved trail for about 0.5 mile.

At 2.3 miles rejoin the asphalt path just below the fire ring; turn left and ascend to return to the trailhead.

Miles and Directions

- **0.0** Start at trailhead behind ball fields.
- **0.2** Reach access trail to river trail.
- **1.3** Reach Vollmerhausen Road; turn right.
- **1.7** Rail-trail leads right just before school.
- **2.3** Rejoin asphalt access trail.
- **2.5** Arrive back at trailhead.

Options: For a short 1.5-mile walk along the Middle Patuxent River on a wide path, park at Savage Mill, a renovated collection of shops and galleries. Walk down Foundry Street 200 yards to a footbridge. Follow the trail along the river, and retrace your steps to return. Be sure to stop at the French bakery!

33 Cash Lake Loop, Patuxent Research Refuge

A walk through pine forests and near marshy lakes in an area that is arguably the wildest place within 75 miles of Washington, D.C.

Location: Patuxent Research Refuge is located in Prince Georges County, about 10 miles north of Washington, D.C.

Type of hike: 4.7-mile double loop.

Difficulty: Easy.

Elevation gain: Minimal.

Season: September through May.

Fees and permits: No fees or permits required.

Maps: USGS Laurel, Maryland.

Special considerations: Because the area is managed for wildlife research, Zero Impact Hiking is especially important. No picnicking is allowed along the trail. Bring some water, but leave the food at home. Spring rains and heavy rains sometimes make the south section of

Cash Lake impassable. When this is the case, after visiting the fishing pier, retrace your steps to continue your hike via the northern section. Also, the south side of Cash Lake Trail is closed mid-October to mid-June to provide undisturbed lakeshore for wintering and nesting waterfowl.

Camping: No camping is available.

For more information: Patuxent Research Refuge, National Wildlife Visitor Center.

Trailhead facilities: The visitor center has wonderful exhibits on wildlife habitat and many other topics important to world ecology. There are restrooms, water fountains, and a gift shop featuring natural history books.

Finding the trailhead: From Washington, D.C., travel north 3.5 miles on Maryland Highway 295, the Baltimore–Washington Parkway (from Baltimore, travel south). Exit onto Powder Mill Road East. In 2 miles turn right into the National Wildlife Visitor Center. The hike begins from the parking area in front of the center. The trailhead is adjacent to the exit road, just where the road leaves the parking area.

The Hike

Follow the wide path through pine and hardwoods dominated by beech and red oak. The odd-looking cuts in the forest you pass are remnants of research on the regeneration of forest species. Cross the exit road and reenter the woods. At 0.9 mile cross the old telegraph road and reach the junction with Laurel Trail.

Just beyond, go left on the Valley Trail, traveling east. Mature oaks and beech tower above, and a woodland valley opens below. From here it is hard to believe the Baltimore–Washington Parkway is less than 2 miles away. At 1.5 miles turn left onto Cash Lake Trail, crossing two wooden bridges and then a fishing pier right off the

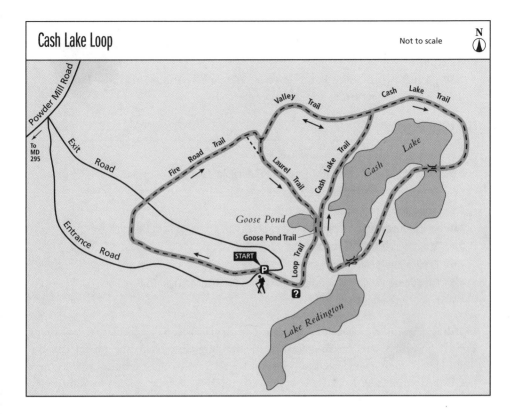

Not to scale

N

Powder Mill Road

To MD 295

Exit Road

Fire Road Trail

Entrance Road

Valley Trail

Laurel Trail

Cash Lake Trail

Cash Lake Trail

Goose Pond

Goose Pond Trail

Loop Trail

START

P

Cash Lake

Lake Redington

trail. This is a great spot to watch the amazing variety of waterfowl and the activities of beavers building their lodges. To make the most of your viewing, consider stopping at the visitor center to purchase a booklet to help identify the birds.

Mid-June to mid-October, you can round the lake to the south side, crossing a bridge over an arm of the lake. When the trail is closed, retreat and pick up the hike at the Fire Road Trail (or skip this section). Cross another bridge, now just below the visitor center, and turn right onto the paved Loop Trail at 2.5 miles.

Enter the woods on Goose Pond Trail, traveling through a forested wetland and reaching Goose Pond at 3.0 miles. Plan to spend some time here. There are waterfowl coming and going and interesting demonstrations of wildlife management practices.

From the north end of Goose Pond, turn right onto Cash Lake Trail's north section, which offers outstanding views of the lake en route to a junction with Valley Trail at 3.4 miles, at the spot where you entered the lake area earlier. Turn left to retrace your steps on Valley Trail.

Turn left onto Laurel Trail at 4.0 miles. In late spring this short trail is alive with the sounds of songbirds and the bloom of the countless mountain laurels along the trail. The trail is also known to local birders as Robbins Trail; it is dedicated to Chandler S. Robbins, a researcher whose more than fifty years of work greatly expanded the knowledge of migratory birds and the effects of habitat fragmentation on their populations.

At 4.4 miles pass Goose Pond on your right, and continue on Goose Pond Trail to Loop Trail for a return to the visitor center.

Miles and Directions

0.0 Start at trailhead adjacent to the exit road.

0.9 Cross old telegraph road to junction with Laurel Trail and then Valley Trail.

1.5 Reach Cash Lake Trail junction; turn left.

2.5 Turn right onto paved Loop Trail.

3.0 Reach Goose Pond. From north end of pond, turn right onto Cash Lake Trail.

3.4 At junction with Valley Trail turn left.

4.0 Turn left onto Laurel Trail.

4.4 Pass Goose Pond on your right. Follow Goose Pond Trail to Loop Trail.

4.7 Arrive back at trailhead.

Options: This hike is described using a loop that utilizes Valley Trail, first traveling easterly and then, after circling Cash Lake, traveling westerly to the top of Laurel Trail. This is done to include the beautiful Laurel Trail in the circuit, as well as the north section of Cash Lake Trail. A nice 3.3-mile hike can be created by returning directly to the visitor center after visiting Goose Pond.

34 Cedarville State Forest Loop

An easy walk through deep, shady forest along the banks of meandering creeks.

Location: Prince Georges County, Maryland, about 20 miles southeast of Washington, D.C.
Type of hike: 5.1-mile loop.
Difficulty: Easy.
Season: Year-round.
Fees and permits: No fees or permits required.
Maps: USGS Bristol, Maryland.

Special considerations: During hunting season, check with forest managers to see which trails are open and safe.
Camping: Youth group camping is permitted with advance registration.
For more information: Cedarville State Forest.
Trailhead facilities: Chemical toilet.

Finding the trailhead: From Interstate 495, travel 11.5 miles south on Maryland Highway 5 to Cedarville Road. Turn left, go 2.1 miles, and turn right into Cedarville State Forest on Bee Oak Road. Follow Bee Oak Road 1.7 miles to Forest Road. Turn right onto Forest Road, and go 0.1 mile to the trailhead parking on the right.

The Hike

On a hot summer day, there is a drowsy, languid feel to the creeks that run through Cedarville State Forest. They are known to rise up and wash out bridges, and if their steeply cut banks are any measure, they have done so often. But there is little babble to these sandy-bottomed brooks. Walking by them through stands of hardwood and meadows of lush ferns, you are more likely to hear a breeze in the trees than a wild torrent. It is a good setting for a tranquil afternoon stroll.

From the trailhead parking area, enter the woods and turn left onto the blue-blazed trail, which you will follow for the entire loop counterclockwise. Descend to placid Wolf Den Branch, staying left where the orange-blazed trail goes right, and follow the trail through the woods along the creek. The trail soon joins a white-blazed trail, becoming wide and gravelly, and then crosses Wolf Den Branch at 0.3 mile.

After crossing the stream, follow the creekbank through oak and hickory groves with understories both dense and spacious. The fern-covered meadows are especially pleasing and can give the woods the lush feel of a Pacific Northwest rain forest. They may also have provided cover for moonshiners who once used the area's creeks and streams for their subtle art.

Passing a big, fat-stumped oak at 1.0 mile, climb slightly—a rare and enjoyable occurrence in this region. At 1.2 miles bend left, splitting off from the white-blazed trail, which continues straight ahead.

Leaving the moist woods by the creek, proceed through stands of pine on a drier, sandier trail. At 1.7 miles go across Cross Road and follow the blue blazes through an area used for target shooting. The trail bends gradually left, traveling through

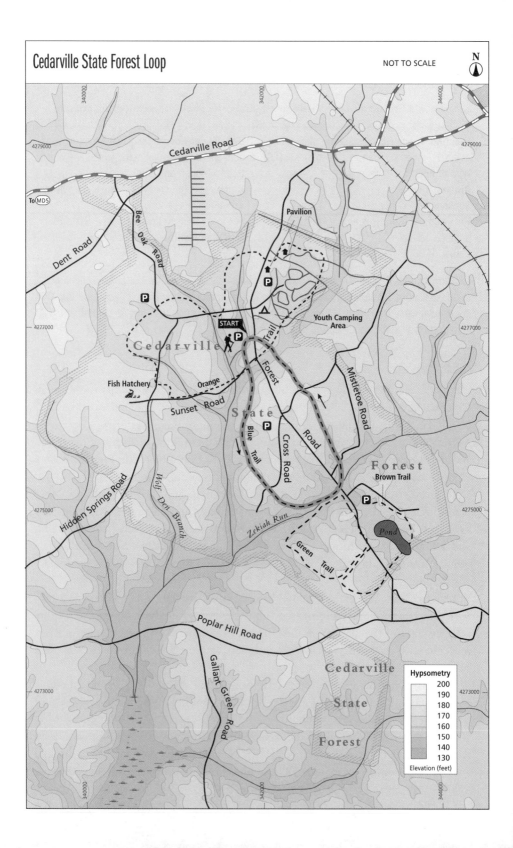

young oak and pine, and meets Zekiah Run, another languid watercourse. Turn left and cross Forest Road at 2.9 miles.

Continue through the woods, crossing Mistletoe Road at 3.3 miles and Cross Road at 4.1 miles. After Cross Road, enter a beautiful stand of mature oak and poplar. Travel through the venerable trees slowly to enjoy their stature; then turn right, following blue blazes, and continue to Wolf Den Branch at 4.6 miles. Cross the bridge over the creek. Reach Forest Road at 4.9 miles. Follow the road briefly; then cross the road and reenter the woods, following orange and blue blazes back to the trailhead.

Miles and Directions

0.0 Start at trailhead parking area.
0.3 Cross Wolf Den Branch.
1.7 Go across Cross Road.
2.9 Turn left at Zekiah Run and cross Forest Road.
3.3 Cross Mistletoe Road.
4.1 Cross Cross Road.
4.6 Cross bridge over Wolf Den Branch.
4.9 Reach Forest Road; follow briefly, then cross to reenter woods.
5.1 Arrive back at trailhead.

Options: There are 14 miles of trails at Cedarville State Forest. For a long hike, you can include most of them in a bigger loop.

35 Parkers Creek Loop, American Chestnut Land Trust

This hike offers a combination of upland forest, transitional hillsides of holly trees and pines, wetland woods, and the broad marsh along Parkers Creek. There are first-rate interpretive signs along the Double Oak Farm Trail section.

Location: Parkers Creek Loop is in the northern tracts of lands owned or managed by the American Chestnut Land Trust (ACLT) in Calvert County, Maryland, about 40 miles southeast of Washington, D.C.
Type of hike: 3.0-mile loop.
Difficulty: Moderate.
Elevation gain: 200 feet.
Season: Spring and autumn.

Fees and permits: No fees or permits required.
Maps: USGS Prince Frederick, Maryland.
Special considerations: Check for hunting schedule in season, especially on trails traversing private land (see www.aclt.org).
Camping: No camping is available.
For more information: American Chestnut Land Trust.
Trailhead facilities: Privy, kiosk.

Finding the trailhead: From Baltimore drive south on Interstate 97 to U.S. Highway 301; then go south 19 miles to Maryland Highway 4. Turn left, and drive 23 miles to Prince Frederick. Turn left on Dares Beach Road and go 2 miles. Turn right on Double Oak Road and go 1 mile. Turn left onto a lane across from an open field and proceed past the house to trailhead parking.

From Washington, D.C., exit onto MD 4 from the Capital Beltway (Interstate 495). Go 32 miles to Prince Frederick, then follow the directions above.

The Hike

It is hard to prefer one time of year over another to visit the Parkers Creek Loop, but it is also hard to imagine a better place to spend a late autumn morning. The understory has opened for winter, revealing views of Parkers Creek marsh while you are still deep in the woods. The last of the migratory birds darken the sky above the marsh like a pointillist moving picture, the final colors of the canopy perform hang-gliding routines from the ledges. With the pace of growth in Calvert County, it is hard to say what the landscape out on MD 4 will look like in 2020. Fortunately, along this stretch of Parkers Creek watershed, nature will have the say in what types of changes transpire.

From the kiosk, walk away from the entrance road with the woods on the right; poke through a small woods line back into the field, then follow the Turkey Trail into the woods on the right. The hardwood trees around you include southern red oak, black cherry, and northern red oak. All around is evidence of a hurricane that tore through in 2003. Songbirds have made great use of all the downed trees; in season you will see Carolina chickadees and hooded warblers darting in and out of the long branches smashed into the ground. If you don't see them, you will surely hear them. All this tree fall has created quite a haven for red-bellied woodpeckers, too.

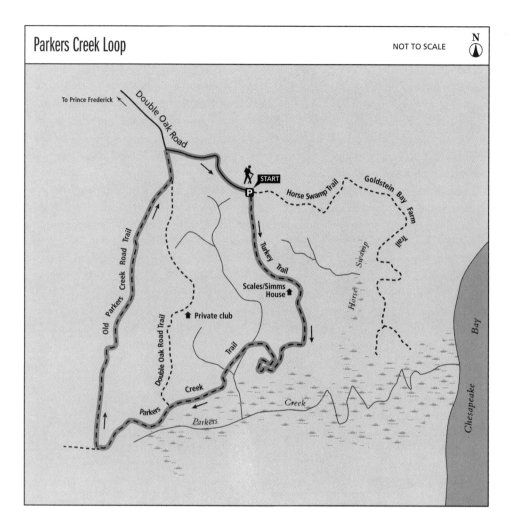

NOT TO SCALE

N

To Prince Frederick

Double Oak Road

START

P

Horse Swamp Trail

Goldstein Bay Farm Trail

Old Parkers Creek Road Trail

Double Oak Road Trail

Turkey Trail

Scales/Simms House

Private club

Horse Swamp

Trail

Creek

Parkers

Parkers

Creek

Chesapeake Bay

Chesapeake

Keep an eye open to the right at about 0.5 mile to see the remains of the Scales/Simms House, named for two African-American families who lived and farmed here in the nineteenth century. Just beyond the house, to the left, are long views of the Chesapeake Bay in the distance.

Reach the junction with Parkers Creek Trail at 0.6 mile. The Turkey Trail descends about 0.25 mile downhill to the marsh. After turning right onto Parkers Creek Trail, follow the path through mature poplar and oaks over a wide flat plain. Then you walk a roller coaster of ups and downs circling a deep hollow. Just before dropping into Parkers Creek, reach a vista overlooking the creek at 1.0 mile. Descend steeply into the hollow and walk through wetlands woods, keeping an eye out for the yellow blazes (or ribbons to guide you through the blowdowns). After crossing a small footbridge, turn left and follow the creek downstream.

This bottomland is a real treat. It seems that all the habitat and land types of the region converge down in this hollow and on the steep hills that surround it. At the end of the hollow, reach the tall marsh grasses of Parkers Creek's 0.5-mile-wide drainage. It is a classic Chesapeake view, and yet when you look behind you, you cannot help but be reminded of forest above the fall line. The trail follows the marsh, just inside or just outside the tree line for 0.5 mile, wending in and out of hollows and passing the junction with Double Oak Road Trail at 1.3 miles. This trail passes through a private hunt club, but the owners generously allow hikers passage—stay on the trail if you take that route.

Parkers Creek Trail continues straight ahead, crossing another stream on a bridge, then arriving at the junction with Old Parkers Creek Road Trail at 1.6 miles. Before turning right to head up the wide path, follow the detour left about 50 yards to the old bridge crossing over the creek. It is remarkable to see how different the creek valley appears here—only a narrow passage at the foot of two hills, rather than the broad marsh 0.5 mile back. Begin the long ascent up Old Parkers Creek Road Trail, a wide old dirt road that once carried traffic over the creek.

Settle in for a long gradual climb from the stream. As you climb, the many changes of forest type you encountered in the descent replay themselves in reverse. As the trail levels out at the top, there are a dozen or more vernal pools, created by tires spinning in mud but now appreciated by salamanders and frogs in one of nature's ironies. They lay their eggs in these pools, secure in knowing no fish are present to gobble them up and that insect larvae will provide food for the infants.

Reach Double Oak Road at 2.7 miles. Turn right and walk the paved road 150 yards to the main entrance to Double Oak Farm. Follow the gravel road 0.25 mile back to the trailhead.

Miles and Directions

0.0 Start at trailhead near kiosk.

0.6 Reach junction with Parkers Creek Trail; turn right.

1.0 Reach Parkers Creek overlook.

1.3 Pass junction with Double Oak Road Trail; continue straight on Parkers Creek Trail.

1.6 Reach junction with Old Parkers Creek Road Trail.

2.7 Reach Double Oak Road; turn right.

3.0 Arrive back at trailhead.

Options: For an out-and-back hike to spectacular views of the bay and Parkers Creek, take the Horse Swamp and Goldstein Bay Farm Trails.

36 American Chestnut Land Trust Loop

This is a rare place of mixed hardwoods, bottomland swamp, and creeks making their way to the Chesapeake Bay. The land is privately owned and permanently protected by the American Chestnut Land Trust. There is indeed a mature chestnut tree on the grounds.

Location: The trails are within the American Chestnut Land Trust's southern tract, located in Calvert County, Maryland, about 40 miles southeast of Washington, D.C.
Type of hike: 3.5-mile loop.
Difficulty: Easy.
Season: September through May.
Fees and permits: No fees or permits required.
Maps: USGS Prince Frederick, Maryland.
Special considerations: The landscape and hiking trails here are a real marvel of private initiative on the part of the American Chestnut Land Trust. Hikers are urged to support this nonprofit organization by sending a donation to the address shown in Appendix A.
Camping: Camping is available under pre-arranged circumstances, such as work exchanges. Contact the office for details.
For more information: American Chestnut Land Trust.
Trailhead facilities: There is a privy about 0.25 mile into the hike. The American Chestnut Land Trust (ACLT) offices are across the street from the trailhead.

Finding the trailhead: From Baltimore drive south on Interstate 97 to U.S. Highway 301, then go south 19 miles to Maryland Highway 4. Turn left and drive 23 miles to Prince Frederick. From Washington, D.C., exit onto MD 4 from the Capital Beltway (Interstate 495); go 32 miles to Prince Frederick. From the intersection with Maryland Highway 231 in Prince Frederick, go 4 miles south on MD 4 (also Maryland Highway 2 here). Turn left onto Parkers Creek Road, cross Maryland Highway 765, and turn right onto Scientists' Cliffs Road. In about a mile, the main entrance parking is on the left.

The Hike

The American Chestnut Land Trust is a moving story of community-inspired conservation. Working in partnership with the State of Maryland and The Nature Conservancy, ACLT owns or manages some 3,000 acres of public and private land in Calvert County, Maryland. In addition to preserving the ecologically important lands of the Parkers Creek watershed, the group has had a major impact in preserving cultural resources, such as old farmsteads that tell the history of Chesapeake Bay settlement. This hike and Parkers Creek Loop explore upland forests, old fields, and marshlands as the trail weaves among the remains of early homesteads.

Follow Gravatt Lane, a wide dirt farm road, 400 yards to its junction with the yellow-blazed Swamp Trail. Turn right, and follow the trail as it winds between mature hardwoods. Walk along an old farm road beneath mature hardwoods. Most of the area was cleared for agriculture, so these big trees are just entering second-growth maturity. At 0.5 mile a path leads left to a lone, mature American chestnut. Once the tree that defined eastern North America, it was said a squirrel could hop

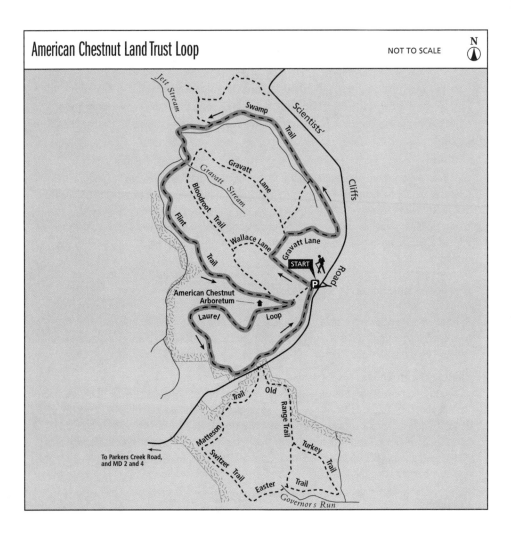

from chestnut to chestnut from Maine to Georgia without touching the ground. Chestnut forests spared from farming or settlement were destroyed by a blight introduced from Asia in the early 1900s.

A 900-foot boardwalk, starting at about 0.7 mile, navigates you over swamp and stream crossings. Cross Gravatt Stream at 1.1 miles. Gravatt Lane climbs from here 1.0 mile back to the trailhead. Continue on Flint Trail, following the red blazes, to the American Chestnut Arboretum, a research area planted with hybrid American chestnuts, at 2.0 miles. Turn right onto Laurel Loop. In spring the woods here are alive with mountain laurel; you would guess you were 70 miles west in the Maryland foothills. Turn left onto Scientists' Cliffs Road at 2.4 miles, and follow the road for 100 yards before getting back on the trail. Part of this trail crosses through, and at times borders, private property. Please respect this property to retain the privilege of the trail experience.

Miles and Directions

0.0 Start at trailhead on Gravatt Lane.

0.5 Reach side path to mature American chestnut.

0.7 Begin 900-foot boardwalk.

1.1 Cross Gravatt Stream.

2.0 Arrive at American Chestnut Arboretum; turn right onto Laurel Loop.

2.4 Turn left onto Scientists' Cliffs Road; follow 100 yards and return to trail.

3.5 Arrive back at trailhead.

Options: There is a 1.5-mile hike along the east loop on the other side of Scientists' Cliffs Road. Parking for the loop is 0.25 mile back on Scientists' Cliffs Road. The trails, blazed in green, are well marked.

37 Calvert Cliffs State Park

A hike through forest and bog down to the Chesapeake Bay where fossils are abundant below the sandstone cliffs.

Location: Calvert Cliffs State Park is on Chesapeake Bay at the southern end of Calvert County, Maryland, about 7 miles north of Solomon's Island.

Type of hike: 3.6-mile out-and-back.

Difficulty: Moderate.

Season: Spring through autumn.

Fees and permits: No fees or permits required.

Maps: USGS Cove Point, Maryland.

Special considerations: About half the park is open to hunting in various seasons, including spring turkey season. Check at the kiosk for schedule. There is no hunting along the red trail to the beach.

Camping: Group camping is available by registration.

For more information: Calvert Cliffs State Park.

Trailhead facilities: Restrooms, vending machines.

Finding the trailhead: From Baltimore or Washington, go south on U.S. Highway 301 to Maryland Highway 4 South. Go 22 miles to Prince Frederick, then 14 more miles to Maryland Highway 765. Turn left and follow signs to the park.

The Hike

Calvert Cliffs State Park is unique among hiking opportunities in the region for its up-close views of the Calvert Cliffs from below, fossil hunting opportunities, and hiker-only access to the Chesapeake shoreline along a mile of sandy beach. The cliffs and the shores below contain more than 600 species of fossils from the Miocene epoch, more than ten million years ago. The cliffs were formed when southern Maryland was under a shallow sea. Adding to the pleasure: Foraging for fossils on

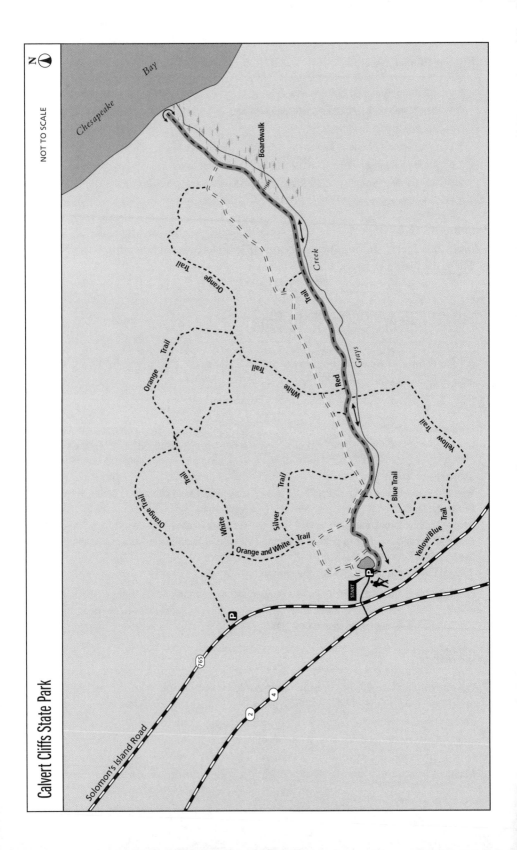

Calvert Cliffs State Park

N

NOT TO SCALE

Chesapeake Bay

Boardwalk

Trail

Orange Trail

Grays Creek

Orange Trail

White Trail

Red Trail

Orange Trail

White Trail

Yellow Trail

White Trail

Silver Trail

Blue Trail

Orange and White Trail

Yellow/Blue Trail

START

P

P

Solomon's Island Road

765

2

4

the sandy beach is permitted—but no digging. Kids love it. Pair the trip to Calvert Cliffs with a visit to St. Michael's or Battle Creek Cypress Swamp, and you have a great day of wandering.

Calvert Cliffs is designated as a state wildland. So while the Red Trail to the fossil beach is the most popular path, it is on the park's other trails that you will find solitude. Still, on a mile of beach below the cliffs, you are sure to hear more birds than people.

From the trailhead kiosk, follow the path over the wooden bridge by a small pond and enter the woods to the left. Hike along the unpaved service road. Although cliffs and fossils get top billing, the woods here are pleasing. There is surprising diversity in the variety of trees in this transition zone from upland forest to swampy land below. As you descend toward the bay, you can watch the character of the woods and topography change.

Leave the dirt road about 0.25 mile in, turning right onto a narrow footpath and dropping down the bank beside Grays Creek. The service road continues left to the beach; to make a loop of this hike, you can walk back via the road. Pass the yellow-blazed Grays Nature Trail at 0.3 mile, and enjoy the pines and black oaks along the stream.

The Blue Trail, 0.6 mile, and the White Trail, 0.7 mile, lead left toward circuit options in the park. No trails lead up to the top of the cliffs. Public access to the cliffs was halted in 2001 because the cliffs are eroding—they are literally falling into the bay over time.

The marsh overlook, at 1.3 miles, is a scenic place for a rest stop. A boardwalk leads 80 yards into a shallow pond formed by Grays Creek as it bottoms out in a broad, flat shelf just above the bay. All around the pond you see evidence of beaver, the originators of the pond long ago—it is now managed with the use of culverts as a kind of perpetual beaver pond. While it is tempting to take a snack out to the overlook, this should be resisted. There is no way to retrieve the inevitable accidental litter that will fall over the boards and become a blight in the still water.

Pass the service road leading back to the trailhead at 1.6 miles. This road makes for a slightly longer return and makes a nice quiet loop out of this hike. It also connects with other trails in the park. Reach the beach 300 yards farther. If possible, time your hike for low tide so that you can see what the sea has stirred up.

Miles and Directions

0.0 Start at the trailhead kiosk.

0.3 Pass Grays Creek cutoff.

1.3 Reach marsh overlook.

1.6 Pass service road leading back to trailhead.

1.8 Arrive at beach. This is your turnaround point.

3.6 Arrive back at trailhead.

Options: Create a loop by returning on the dirt service road; explore other trails in the park.

38 Greenwell State Park

Take a swim in the river after a walk along the western shore of Maryland's Patuxent River. The trail travels through fields, meadows and woods, and offers dramatic views of the river, with visits to two historic barns.

Location: Greenwell State Park is located in St. Mary's County, Maryland.
Type of hike: 3.5-mile double loop.
Difficulty: Easy.
Season: Year-round.
Fees and permits: $5.00 parking fee.
Maps: USGS Bristol; Upper Marlboro, Maryland.

Special considerations: Some trails are closed to hikers during hunting season; check with the park office.
Camping: No camping is available.
For more information: Greenwell State Park.
Trailhead facilities: Water, portable privy.

Finding the trailhead: From the Baltimore Beltway, travel south on Interstate 97/Maryland Highway 3 to U.S. Highway 301. Go south on US 301 to the junction with Maryland Highway 5. (From the Capital Beltway, travel south on MD 5.) Take MD 5 south to Maryland Highway 235, toward Hollywood. Turn left onto Maryland Highway 245 East (Sotterley Gate Road) and travel 2.5 miles. Make a right onto Steerhorn Neck Road. The park entrance is the second drive on the left.

The Hike

The Patuxent River is the star of this hike. Here the river is wide and the views it offers are downright dramatic. The hike visits three coves, one with a sandy beach. Greenwell's trails take you through a variety of settings typical of traditional rural St. Mary's County. In a nod to local recreational preferences, the land is managed primarily for game wildlife and hunting. Open fields separated by hedgerows and stream valley woodlands predominate. These open fields offer hikers a welcome change of view, a chance to see many birds you miss on a forest hike. The delightful surprises include two historic barns left alone far from anywhere for hikers to discover.

Because the trail system is designed in part to provide separation for hunters, there are a lot of trails and junctions. It can be confusing—but with such openness it is hard to get lost. To help you stay on track, the description that follows is more detailed than is typical for a hike of this length.

From the kiosk, walk down the paved access trail between the manor house and the ranger station. From the outset you are greeted with great river views. At the fishing pier turn right and follow the beach toward a cove with a sandy beach. Circle the cove. On the far side of the cove, turn right between the trees and climb

NOT TO SCALE

N

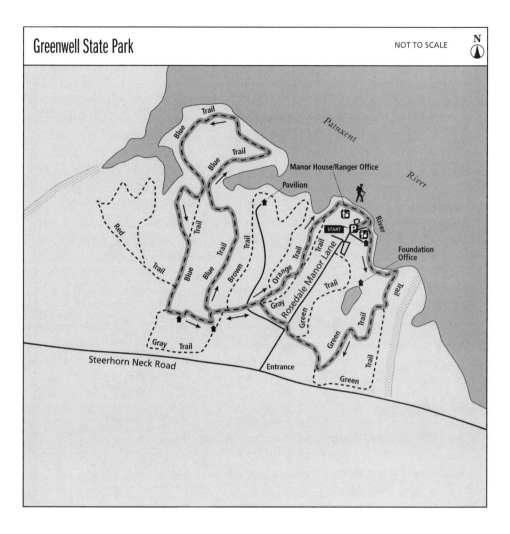

a short hill. Turn right at the top and follow the woods, with the field on your left.

At 0.3 mile at the junction with the green trail, turn right, keeping the field on your left. Follow the path in and out of the woods to a clearing and a junction with the gray trail. Turn right, then in 100 yards emerge into a farm field. Turn left onto the gray trail (the trailhead is to the right on the green trail).

Cross the park road at 0.6 mile, then turn right and immediately left, following the gray trail along the gravel road. At a kiosk for the orange trail at the end of the road, turn left to stay on the gray (and blue) trail. Circle the field (with the field on the right) to a junction with three trails at the next wood line, at 1.1 miles. Go straight into the woods for 50 yards and emerge into a field on the blue trail. Turn right and walk the woods line, keeping the field on your left to the end. Bear left at the angle at the end of the field, then turn right through the gap in the trees to a clearing at the junction of three fields at 1.3 miles. Turn right onto the blue loop.

From here you will make a long circle of this field, visiting the river for a long stretch, returning to the same stop at the junction of three fields at 2.2 miles. Turn right, then right again at the post, circling this field with the tree line on the right. At the junction with the red trail, at 2.6 miles, go straight on the gray/red trail (blue trail goes left). Follow the path 175 yards and go left at the T to visit a beautiful old barn. What's really unusual, and most welcome, is that the barn has been left alone for visitors to enjoy. There are two picnic tables in the barn and some interpretive displays.

Leaving the barn, walk down the tree line, with the field on the right, then poke through a hedgerow to a second, smaller barn. Just beyond, turn left on the gray trail and descend to the same junction you passed at 1.1 miles. Go through the trees and turn right, circling the same field you circled earlier, now with the field on the left. Reach the kiosk for the orange trail at 3.0 miles. A hundred feet past the kiosk, the orange trail turns left into the woods, following the pawpaw trees along a narrow spring, then emerging into a field. Turn left and follow the field, ducking in and out of the woods a couple of times, making sure to stay in the woods when the field leads uphill to the barn.

Reach a cove and small sandy beach on the Patuxent at 3.3 miles. Turn right to circle the cove—at high tide you might have to scamper on the high rocks for a very short distance. When you reach the river, turn right and enjoy the stroll back to the fishing pier and the start of the hike.

Miles and Directions

0.0   Start at trailhead at kiosk.

0.3   Reach junction with green trail; turn right.

0.6   Cross park road; turn right and immediately left.

1.1   At junction of three trails, go straight into woods.

1.3   At junction of three fields, turn right onto blue loop.

2.6   Reach junction with red trail; go straight on gray/red trail.

3.0   Reach kiosk for orange trail; follow this trail, going left 100 yards past kiosk.

3.3   Reach cove on the Patuxent.

3.5   Arrive back at trailhead.

Options: The park trail system offers a number of shorter options; check at park headquarters.

Land between the Bays

Delaware's parks contain miles of quiet, hidden trails. PHOTO COURTESY OF MARYLAND DNR.

39 Judge Morris Estate, White Clay Creek State Park

A quiet walk in the woods over varied terrain above Pike Creek, just minutes from Newark, Delaware.

Location: The Judge Morris Estate area of White Clay Creek State Park is on Polly Drummond Road just north of Kirkwood Highway (Delaware Highway 2), 3 miles northeast of Newark, Delaware.
Type of hike: 3.0-mile loop.
Difficulty: Easy to moderate.
Season: Year-round.

Fees and permits: Parking fee is $2.50 for in-state and $5.00 for out-of-state vehicles.
Maps: USGS Newark East, Delaware.
Special considerations: None.
Camping: No camping is available.
For more information: White Clay Creek State Park.
Trailhead facilities: Kiosk map and composting privy.

Finding the trailhead: From Newark, travel east on Kirkwood Highway (Delaware Highway 2) approximately 3 miles to Polly Drummond Road. Turn left and travel 1 mile to the park entrance on the right (about 0.25 mile past the Judge Morris House entrance).

The Hike

It would be easy to say there is little notable about this nice ramble on the Chestnut Hill Trail through woodlands east of Newark, but that would miss the mark. The quiet and solitude offered by this trail is remarkable because the park's southern edge is adjacent to busy Kirkwood Highway. The Judge Morris Estate forms the southeastern corner of the nationally renowned conservation effort in the White Clay Creek watershed. Since the 1970s, as the population epicenter of New Castle County has shifted from Wilmington to Newark, the collaboration among Delaware, Pennsylvania, and local agencies and nonprofits has created a kind of "Central Park." The White Clay is designated part of the nation's Wild and Scenic River system. Hikers interested in a real leg stretcher can depart from the Judge Morris trailhead and walk the Tri Valley Trail into Chester County, Pennsylvania, through woods, meadows, and farm fields—crossing only five roads en route.

This little ramble on the Judge Morris Estate begins at the trailhead kiosk. Follow the gravel path past the junction with the Middle Run (Tri Valley) Trail to the post marking the beginning of the Chestnut Hill Trail loop. Go straight, entering the woods under 70-foot chestnut oaks and beech and poplar trees, sidling around a small hill. Turn right at the junction with the cutoff trail, at 0.3 mile; cross the creek on a footbridge, then ascend steeply beneath towering trees.

As you continue through dense woods, there might be a faint sound of traffic, but even at rush hour bird song is more likely to get your attention, especially in

Old farms and young forests form the foundation of Delaware's parks. PHOTO COURTESY OF MARYLAND DNR ▶

Judge Morris Estate

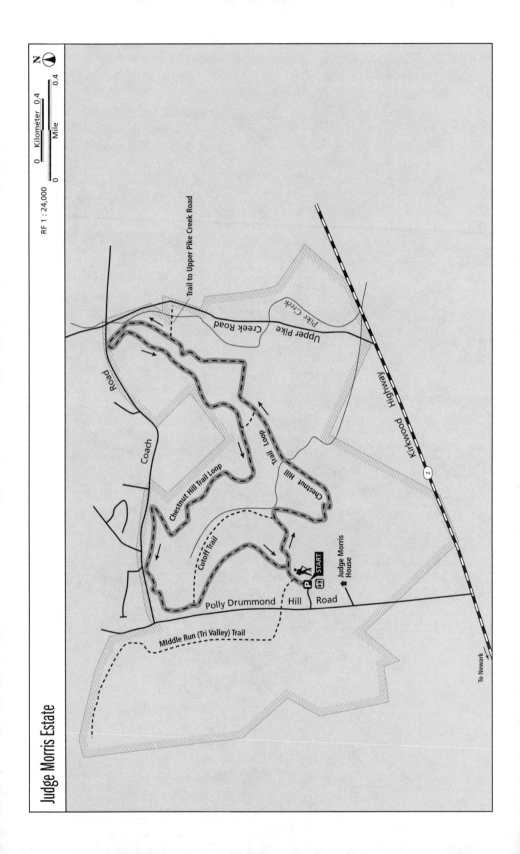

RF 1 : 24,000

Kilometer 0 0.4
Mile 0 0.4

N

Coach Road

Trail to Upper Pike Creek Road

Upper Pike Creek Road

Pike Creek

Chestnut Hill Trail Loop

Chestnut Hill Trail Loop

Cutoff Trail

Polly Drummond Hill Road

Middle Run (Tri Valley) Trail

Judge Morris House

START

P

Kirkwood Highway

2

To Newark

spring when wood thrushes and chickadees are in full voice. At 0.6 mile pass a short-cut trail on the left. You can use it to cut a mile or so from the trip, but it trims some of the nicest parts of the hike.

The terrain is flat and the hiking easy as you pass through a small clearing and through younger woods. The open meadow serves up wildflowers in spring and blackberries in summer. Pass an access trail to Upper Pike Creek Road on the right, at 0.8 mile, then cross a footbridge over a small run. The understory is open, with scattered witch hazel and serviceberry. There are lush ferns along the streambank, hanging on despite pretty serious degradation of the streambank caused by visitors failing to follow wet-weather rules (for hikers this means staying on the trail and walking through puddles; for bicyclists it means taking the day off and awaiting drier weather).

Soon the forest character changes yet again. Now there are hollies on the hillside leading to Pike Creek's wide bottomland as you slab around the hill above the creek and the adjacent road. You descend for a closer look at the creek just as the trail makes 180-degree turn left near the junctions of Upper Pike Creek and Coach Roads, just outside the park's northeast boundary, at 1.4 miles. While there is no parking or trailhead at Coach Road, an informal path makes it possible to make an emergency exit there.

Leaving the road behind, ascend Chestnut Hill again. You'll only gain 50 feet or so in altitude, but a breeze will greet you atop the hill. The woods here are more tangled with vines and opportunistic plants such as mile-a-minute and multiflora rose, indicating a younger part of this forest in succession from farm fields. The trail passes between two massive poplars, a site itself worth the hike, into a pine grove followed by a stand of beech. At 1.9 miles, at the top of a steep and lovely hollow, there is a bench—perfectly placed by volunteers. Just beyond, at 2.0 miles, is the other end of the shortcut trail you passed earlier.

A half mile downtrail a small clearing offers up succulent blackberries in season. Just beyond, the woods change character yet again, passing on a boardwalk through a boggy area of ferns and skunk cabbage. You will pass two more seasonal runs—primarily drainages from Polly Drummond Hill Road. At 2.6 miles reach the second junction with the cutoff trail. If you want to stay in the shade of the woods, turn left and proceed to the end of the cutoff trail; then turn right to return to the trailhead. To wander through the farm field on your return, stay straight (right) at the junction and enter the field. The path through the field might be tough to discern, but it is obvious which way you should go. If you have never walked through a field of hip-high soy beans, this is your chance.

Miles and Directions

0.0 Start at trailhead kiosk.

0.3 Reach first junction with cutoff trail; turn right.

0.8 Pass access trail to Upper Pike Creek Road.

1.4 Turn left near junction of Coach and Upper Pike Creek Roads.

2.0 Reach other end of cutoff passed earlier.

2.6 Reach second junction with cutoff trail.

3.0 Arrive back at trailhead.

Options: You can shorten your hike by taking the shortcut.

40 Lenape Loop South, Middle Run Natural Area

A short, easy loop in a peaceful, wooded stream valley, not far from Newark, Delaware.

Location: Middle Run Natural Area is 2.5 miles north of Main Street, Newark, in northwestern New Castle County, Delaware.
Type of hike: 3.6-mile loop.
Difficulty: Moderate.
Season: Year-round.
Fees and permits: No fees or permits required.
Maps: USGS Newark West, Delaware.

Special considerations: You might find yourself crossing Middle Run at a bridgeless crossing. The creek is only 20 feet wide and several inches deep.
Camping: No camping is available.
For more information: New Castle County Department of Parks and Recreation.
Trailhead facilities: Information kiosk and map.

Finding the trailhead: From Newark travel north on Paper Mill Road 1.6 miles to Possum Park Road (Delaware Highway 72). Turn right, then immediately left onto Possum Hollow Road (Road 299). Proceed 0.4 mile to Middle Run Natural Area on the left. Follow the gravel entrance road around a big bend 0.4 mile to the parking area.

The Hike

You can get totally lost in Middle Run Natural Area. In an area as densely populated as middle New Castle County, this is a real blessing. You can also get lost on the many informal side trails created by mountain bikers; inconsistent trail signage is another challenge. These inconveniences are more than offset by the scenic, wild surroundings. The terrain is varied, the woods are deep, and the trail system devised to make maximum use of the acreage. The paths visit tall poplar stands and pass through quarter-mile-wide fields. There is a quiet segment where the trail hugs the high side of a steep, narrow gorge. Other than one bridgeless stream crossing and a few steep hills, the Lenape South route is a casual leg-stretcher.

Middle Run Natural Area lies in the eastern reaches of the rambling White Clay Creek Preserve, a network of parks and open space that stretches from busy Kirkwood Highway, near Newark, Delaware, into Chester County, Pennsylvania.

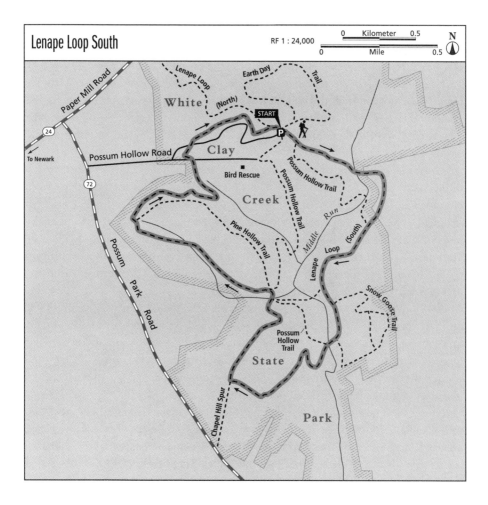

From the kiosk at the trailhead, follow a gravel walking path toward the woods about 50 feet; turn right just before entering the woods. A faint dirt path in the grass, called the Lenape Cutoff Trail, skirts the field and descends gradually for a short hundred yards, then ducks left into the tree line. Descend through "old fields," a recovering forestland sprouting up in the overgrown field, to the junction with the Lenape Trail. Go straight—left leads to the north Lenape Loop and the Earth Day Trail.

If the bridge is out over Middle Run and the water is too high to rock-hop, you will have to go shoeless for the crossing (or keep a cheap pair of beach shoes in your day pack). In a small clearing a hundred yards farther, turn right and cross a small stream on a footbridge. At another junction just beyond, turn right and walk along Middle Run with the stream on the right. Tall beeches and chestnut oak accompany the abundant tulip poplar as you climb above the stream. At 0.6

mile pass the junction with Possum Hollow Trail on the right (if you are seeking solitude away from bikes, the Possum Hollow Trail is a hiker-only trail). The remains of a mill race are visible below the trail, near the creek.

Continue straight at a couple of junctions, marked and unmarked. With the number of informal trails ducking into the woods, this is an easy spot to get turned around. At 1.1 miles descend stone steps in the hillside to reach Middle Run. The scene here is a real delight any time of year. The pools in the creek are inviting and worthy of a rest stop.

Cross the stream on foot stones created for the task—themselves almost worthy of the visit. They are cylindrical footings of concrete and river rock that have been fashioned to look like logs. Standing upright in the stream, they form a series of stepping-stones. After crossing the stream, in a span of 30 yards, go straight at the junction with Possum Hollow Trail on the right, ignoring the washed-out Lenape Trail on the left, then turn left on the interim Lenape on the left just as you begin a steep ascent. The Lenape Trail now follows Middle Run downstream from the opposite side of the creek.

At about 1.7 miles reach the junction with Chapel Hill Trail; stay right to stay on the Lenape Trail and begin ascending a long hill. At the top, turn left and continue through the woods to a clearing where you will see deer and, if you're lucky, foxes. Bear right and walk along the faint path with the woods on your left, then reenter the woods. Here the woods take on a different character; there are more pines, some holly, and a small hemlock grove.

Come to another junction with Pine Hollow Trail at 2.2 miles. The next 200 yards can be confusing. The trail signs may not match the maps posted at the kiosk. Turn left, descend, and cross the creek, still on the Lenape Trail. Climb the hill and, just as it levels out, go left as the Possum Hollow Trail breaks right. In 100 feet, at 2.3 miles, stay left (straight) at the junction with Double Horseshoe Trail, which leads right through a clearing. A lovely gorge opens up to the left. You lose trail signs and blazes for the next mile or more.

This is perhaps the most scenic part of the hike—walking above the gorge, with tall tulip poplars and chestnut oaks creating a dense canopy. The path makes a long descent to a footbridge, then climbs back up on lazy switchbacks to emerge into a broad field at 2.5 miles. When you emerge from the woods, follow a faint path in the grass toward, then through, a clump of trees; continue toward the woods on the opposite side of the field.

From here it's another descent into a stream-valley gorge via switchbacks. After crossing a footbridge, the trail sidles the hill and ascends to Possum Hollow Road at 3.1 miles. Go left and walk 50 feet, then turn right into the trees. In about 75 feet you emerge onto the access road. If you've had enough of the woods, turn right and follow the gravel 0.5 mile back to your car. To continue on Possum Hollow Trail, turn left onto the access road and go 20 yards, then turn right to walk along the field with the trees right.

Turn right, into the trees, to follow the Lenape Trail. By this point you've noticed that no matter where you are, signs for the Lenape and Possum Hollow Trails seem to pop up almost randomly. This is because the two trails are braided and because there are north and south loops to the Lenape Trail. There are also a few Lenape Cutoff Trails that link sections of the Lenape.

Cross a small footbridge at 3.5 miles, then ascend 175 yards to reach the clearing at the trailhead and the end of the hike.

Miles and Directions

0.0 Start at trailhead kiosk.

0.6 Pass junction with Possum Hollow Trail.

1.1 Cross Middle Run on foot stones.

1.7 Reach junction with Chapel Hill Trail; stay right.

2.2 Come to junction with Pine Hollow Trail.

2.3 Reach Double Horseshoe Trail—stay left.

3.1 Ascend to Possum Hollow Road; go left.

3.5 Cross footbridge.

3.6 Arrive back at trailhead.

Options: From the trailhead, follow the Earth Day Trail for a 1.5-mile loop.

41 White Clay Creek Preserve Loop, White Clay Creek State Park

A hike through the floodplain woodlands along White Clay Creek.

Location: White Clay Creek State Park is in northwestern New Castle County, Delaware, about 4 miles from Newark.
Type of hike: 2.1-mile loop.
Difficulty: Easy.
Season: Year-round.
Fees and permits: Entrance fee is $2.50 for Delaware residents, $5.00 for nonresidents.
Maps: USGS Newark West; Newark East, Delaware.

Special considerations: Pets are permitted in some areas of the park, but they must be leashed. Check the signs at the trailhead or inquire at the contact station. Some trails are closed during the hunting season.
Camping: No camping is available.
For more information: White Clay Creek State Park.
Trailhead facilities: Restrooms, nature center.

Finding the trailhead: From Newark travel north on New London Road (Delaware Highway 896) 2.9 miles to Hopkins Road. Turn right onto Hopkins Road and proceed 1 mile to the preserve entrance on the left. Follow the dirt road 0.3 mile to the nature center parking area on the left.

The Hike

White Clay Creek Preserve Loop is the only trail in the several sections of the park that actually runs along White Clay Creek, following its banks to the Pennsylvania line, where the preserve extends across the border. The area is popular with birders, botanists, and other naturalists who like "going afield." A public journal at the nature center notes sightings of the many local birds, including red-bellied, downy, and pileated woodpeckers, osprey, kingfishers, wild turkeys, cedar waxwings, and blackburnian warblers. There are also wild geraniums, wood violets, trillium, and trout lily in abundance, as well as mammals large and small. Reports say there is even a mountain lion roaming this neck of the woods!

From the parking lot, cross the dirt entrance road and enter the woods on the marked hiking trail. The path travels along the banks of the creek in the shade of maples, oaks, poplars, and sycamores, making even a midsummer walk a refreshing experience. The water is slow moving, splashing easily along, and birdsong rings from the branches of the big, old trees.

Pass a field edge full of darting butterflies in summer, and continue along the stream's still, sunlit pools and running torrents to Chambers Rock Road at 0.6 mile. As you approach the road in the heat of summer, the smell of hot tar mixes with the sweet and snaky smell of the creek. The trail splits as it comes to the road. Go left, cross the road, and then turn right onto a grassy path, following blue blazes. Continue across the parking lot and onto a mown path that bends left along the edge of

Creative planning has helped create suburban wildlands along White Clay Creek in Delaware and Maryland. PHOTO COURTESY OF MARYLAND DNR

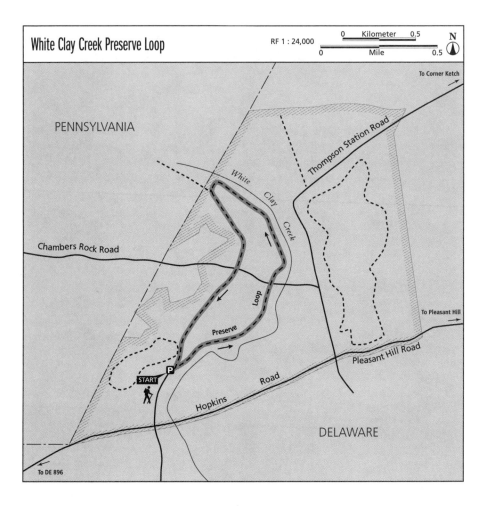

RF 1 : 24,000

0   Kilometer   0.5

0   Mile   0.5

N

To Corner Ketch

PENNSYLVANIA

Thompson Station Road

White

Clay Creek

Chambers Rock Road

To Pleasant Hill

Loop

Preserve

START

P

Road

Hopkins

Pleasant Hill Road

DELAWARE

To DE 896

a field, under the bowing branches of sycamores and a chorus of birdsong.

Follow a woodland edge, with the field and a border of young trees on the left. To the right are bigger, more mature trees and the now-slow, still creek. Leaving the field, the path plunges into deep forest and continues along the stream. Follow the trail as it bends left where rapids shoot over the rocks beneath the stone ruins of an old bridge, and continue to the Pennsylvania state line at 1.2 miles.

At the Pennsylvania state line, the blue blazes can appear to point straight ahead. Turn left here, and proceed on a wide path marked by a white arrow on a brown post. You are now traveling on the western slope of the creek valley.

At 1.6 miles leave the woods, cross Chambers Rock Road again, and continue on a wide path, with a wooded thicket on the right and open fields on the left. As you walk along in open country, watch for red-winged blackbirds perched in the tall grasses or for the blossoms of Queen Anne's lace and goldenrod.

The trail bends left into the woods at the edge of the field, passes through a gate, and continues back to the trailhead on a dirt road that winds downhill, passing near private property. Please stay on the trail.

Miles and Directions

0.0 Start at trailhead at dirt entrance road.

0.6 Reach Chambers Rock Road. Go left before crossing.

1.2 Reach Pennsylvania state line.

1.6 Cross Chambers Rock Road.

2.1 Arrive back at trailhead.

Options: You can continue into the Pennsylvania section of the preserve on a 3.0-mile trail that follows the east branch of White Clay Creek to London Tract Road.

42 Whitetail Trail, White Clay Creek State Park

A hike on the rolling hills of Delaware's piedmont through meadows, old fields, and impressive woodlands.

Location: The Walter S. Carpenter Recreation Area of White Clay Creek State Park is in northwestern New Castle County, Delaware, 2.6 miles north of Newark.

Type of hike: 3.0-mile loop.

Difficulty: Easy.

Season: April through November.

Fees and permits: Entrance fee is $2.50 for Delaware residents, $5.00 for nonresidents.

Maps: USGS Newark West; Newark East, Delaware.

Special considerations: Observe signs regarding pets; they are permitted in some areas of the park but must be kept on a leash.

Camping: No camping is available.

For more information: White Clay Creek State Park.

Trailhead facilities: Restrooms, water, picnic area, telephone.

Finding the trailhead: From Newark travel north on New London Road (Delaware Highway 896) 2.6 miles to the entrance of White Clay Creek State Park's Walter S. Carpenter Recreation Area on the right. Turn right into the park, and proceed 0.2 mile through the fee booth to the picnic area parking.

The Hike

One of several sections of White Clay Creek State Park, the Walter S. Carpenter Recreation Area lies to the west of White Clay Creek's floodplain, its gently rolling hills rising up from the valley. Like the other small parcels of the preserve,

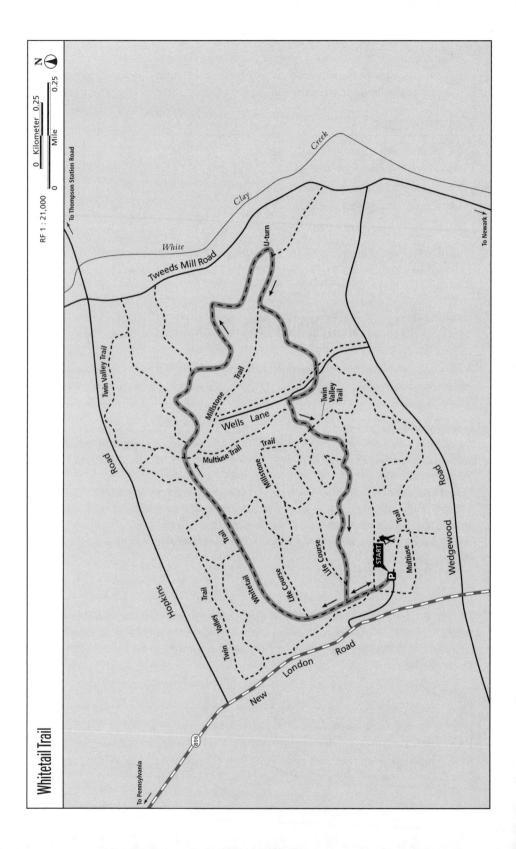

Whitetail Trail

RF 1 : 21,000

0 Kilometer 0.25

0 Mile 0.25

N

To Thompson Station Road

White

Clay

Creek

Tweeds Mill Road

U-turn

Twin Valley Trail

Millstone Trail

Wells Lane

Multiuse Trail

Twin Valley Trail

Millstone Trail

Hopkins Road

Twin Valley Trail

Whitetail Trail

Life Course

Life Course

Life Course

Multiuse Trail

START

P

Wedgewood Road

New London Road

886

To Pennsylvania

To Newark

the landscape is a mixture of old fields, thickets of honeysuckle and blackberries, saplings, and stream-laced woodlands with wonderful groves of beech and tulip trees. When you are finished hiking in the woods here, the preserve's shady picnic area and disc golf course make this area a great place for an all-day family outing.

From the trailhead just north of the parking area, follow Whitetail Trail, which is marked with a white arrow in a blue blaze. It is a wide grassy path passing hedgerows and open meadows. The trail bends right at a red marker. Travel up the hill past the junction with the Life Course fitness trail, and continue along the hilltop overlooking the fields and forests rolling down to White Clay Creek.

Passing through a thicket on the hilltop, you may see a blue blaze on the left. Do not go left. Continue to follow the white arrow in the blue blaze straight across the hilltop. Just ahead is a bench beneath an apple tree with more nice views of the creek valley.

At 0.7 mile the red-blazed Millstone Trail breaks off to the right. Proceed through a picnic area into the woods, following the blue markers. The trail bends right, descends a hill, and then bends left. This begins a wonderful stretch through an impressive grove of tulip trees. As you follow the trail down to a stream crossing and on to the 1.0-mile marker, stop and survey the stately tulip poplars, so called for the bright, yellow-orange flowers that bloom on their high branches each spring. The tallest hardwood in North America, tulip trees grow up to 200 feet tall in the southern Appalachians. This stand does not reach that height, but it is glorious nonetheless.

The trail bends right at the mile marker and rises slightly, climbing through a young forest, and then descends, widening and winding to a U-turn at 1.5 miles. Follow the sharp bend to the right; proceed 200 yards and turn left where the red- and yellow-blazed trails join the path. From here the trail travels through mature forest again. Walking the rolling ridge above a streambed, peer into the dense canopy below and through the boughs of immense old trees.

Passing through a sycamore stand, reach Wells Lane at 2.0 miles. Turn right; proceed on the road past a house on the left, and then turn left onto a gravel path to the edge of a field. Pass the multiuse trail on the right, and continue around the bend to the left.

At a trail junction at 2.2 miles, with Millstone Trail on the right and Twin Valley Trail on the left, follow the blue-blazed path straight ahead. Climb through the woods to another field and turn right, following the path along the bottom edge of the field, where groundhogs lumber into the tall grass as you pass. Enter the woods, following the trail as it bends to the right, and proceed on the wide, grassy path back to the picnic area and the trailhead.

Miles and Directions

0.0 Start at trailhead just north of parking area.

0.7 Reach junction with Millstone Trail; follow blue markers through picnic area and into woods.

1.5 Follow U-turn sharply to the right.

2.0 Reach Wells Lane; turn right onto road.

2.2 Reach junction with Millstone and Twin Valley Trails; follow blue-blazed trail straight ahead.

3.0 Arrive back at trailhead.

Options: Several footpaths wind through the park, from a 5.0-mile multiuse trail to a 1.5-mile fitness trail. Create long or short circuits from the 12 miles of trails.

43 Carousel Park

The 217-acre park's main attraction is its equestrian center and pond. A nice place to introduce children to the outdoors or to get outside with visitors who are not outdoor types.

Location: Carousel Park is on Limestone Road about halfway between Milltown and Paper Mill Roads.

Type of hike: 2.6-mile loop.

Difficulty: Easy.

Season: Year-round.

Fees and permits: No fees or permits required.

Maps: USGS Newark East, Delaware.

Special considerations: None.

Camping: No camping is available.

For more information: New Castle County Department of Parks and Recreation.

Finding the trailhead: Carousel Park is on Limestone Road about halfway between Milltown and Paper Mill Roads. From Newark, travel north on Paper Mill Road to its end at Limestone Road. Turn right and go about 0.5 mile to the park entrance on the right.

The Hike

Kids love horses, and in this corner of New Castle County there are not many public places to watch them trotting, walking the trails, or grazing on the meadow. Carousel Park does its level best to please a range of interests, from picnicking to trail riding and hiking to special events. This is not the place for hikers seeking solitude in the deep woods; it's just a nice county park combining open, grassy fields with narrow, wooded groves. Somehow, along busy Limestone Road, Carousel evokes pastoral calm.

Because there are many open fields, it is difficult to get lost at Carousel. You can park at any one of the three trailheads and wander. The hike described here is meant to show you a variety of what the park has to offer.

Start the hike at the equestrian center, a fancifully designed compound reminiscent of a frontier town. Passing through the piazza, turn right at the paddock and

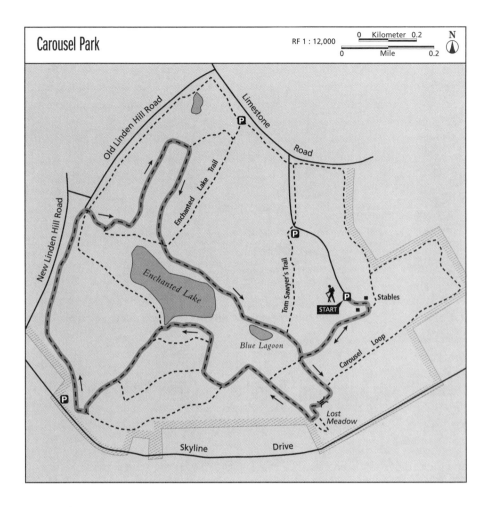

RF 1 : 12,000

0   Kilometer   0.2

0   Mile   0.2

N

Old Linden Hill Road

Limestone

Road

Enchanted Lake Trail

New Linden Hill Road

Enchanted Lake

Tom Sawyer's Trail

Stables

START

Blue Lagoon

Carousel Loop

Lost
Meadow

Skyline   Drive

follow the fence a hundred yards before it ducks into the trees and descends on a paved service road. At the bottom, a sign points right toward the pond. Go left and follow the trail a hundred yards or so to a junction with the Carousel Loop. Turn right, cross a footbridge, and climb the stairs to emerge into an open field known as Lost Meadow. Turn right.

Keeping the tree line on the right, you will pass the path leading back to the trail-head on the right, then circle the field and ascend the hill. At 0.5 mile turn right to pass through the tree line. Take the first right into the woods and descend toward Enchanted Lake. At the bottom of the hill, at 0.7 mile, turn left and walk along the lake's south shore, pausing as long as you please. At the end of the woods, just as the shore trail enters a clearing, turn left and climb the hill on Camelot's March just inside the woods line. After leaving the woods continue uphill, with the tree line on your right.

Reach the Skyline Drive parking area at 1.1 miles; turn right to pass behind a few houses, then poke through the next tree line. Descend into and out of the woods and reach the western edge of the Enchanted Lake Trail. This is slightly confusing as you will turn right, then turn left to get on the northern part of the loop. In less than a hundred yards, turn left onto Robin Hood's Trail and walk with the cultivated field on your left. The trail eventually turns sharply right into the thicket and ends at a T. Turn left and follow the path to its end; turn left, again joining the Enchanted Lake Trail.

Follow the lake past its spillway into Blue Lagoon and the woods, meeting Tom Sawyer's Trail at 2.1 miles. Turn left to return to the equestrian center.

Miles and Directions

0.0 Start at equestrian center.

0.7 At bottom of hill, turn left and walk along Enchanted Lake's south shore.

1.1 Reach Skyline Drive trailhead; turn right.

2.1 Reach junction with Tom Sawyer's Trail; turn left.

2.6 Arrive back at equestrian center.

Options: Park at the Skyline Drive trailhead and hike the perimeter of the park on the Carousel Loop.

44 Creek Road Trail, Brandywine Creek State Park

Alternating long views and close contact with Brandywine Creek along Creek Road Trail, which here aligns with the Northern Delaware Greenway, the hike includes an interlude above the scenic Rocky Run gorge. A 1.5-mile option creates a circuit through and above the gorge.

Location: Brandywine Creek State Park's Thompsons Bridge Area is in northern New Castle County, Delaware, 4 miles north of Wilmington.
Type of hike: 2.8-mile lollipop.
Difficulty: Moderate.
Season: Year-round; autumn is best for seeing migrating hawks.
Fees and permits: Entrance fee during summer and weekends in spring and fall: $2.50 for Delaware residents, $5.00 for nonresidents.

Maps: USGS Wilmington North, Delaware.
Special considerations: Pets are permitted but must be kept on a leash.
Camping: A youth camping area is available for official groups only.
For more information: Brandywine Creek State Park.
Trailhead facilities: Composting toilet, interpretive kiosk.

Finding the trailhead: From Delaware Highway 52 in Wilmington, travel 2.4 miles north on Delaware Highway 100 to the intersection with Delaware Highway 92 and Adams Dam Road. Turn right; go 0.6 mile and cross the Brandywine River. Take an immediate left into a town house neighborhood. Trailhead parking for several cars is at the end of the street.

Tall tulip poplars shade the old carriage road along Brandywine Creek. PHOTO COURTESY OF
DELAWARE DIVISION OF PARKS AND RECREATION/DNREC

The Hike

The Thompsons Bridge Area of Brandywine Creek State Park lies on the east side
of Brandywine Creek. The wide, even trail surface along the river allows for easy
going and side-by-side walking, as the path leads through a dense poplar forest above
the floodplain. There are wonderful views of the river from above. Downtrail the
path moves close to the river and passes through picnic grounds.

This hike is most rewarding when a loop around Rocky Run is included. However, check with officials before adding in this loop unless you are comfortable poking around in the woods for a very short stretch looking for blazes (see Options). This
hike is described leaving out the Rocky Run loop but gives directions to explore it.

To put the hike into a historical context, visit the interpretive display just below
the parking area before you hike. From the trailhead parking area, walk straight
down the hill toward the river (or follow the lane on which you entered to the
sidewalk and enter the trail from the road). Near the kiosk you will find the rest-
room as well.

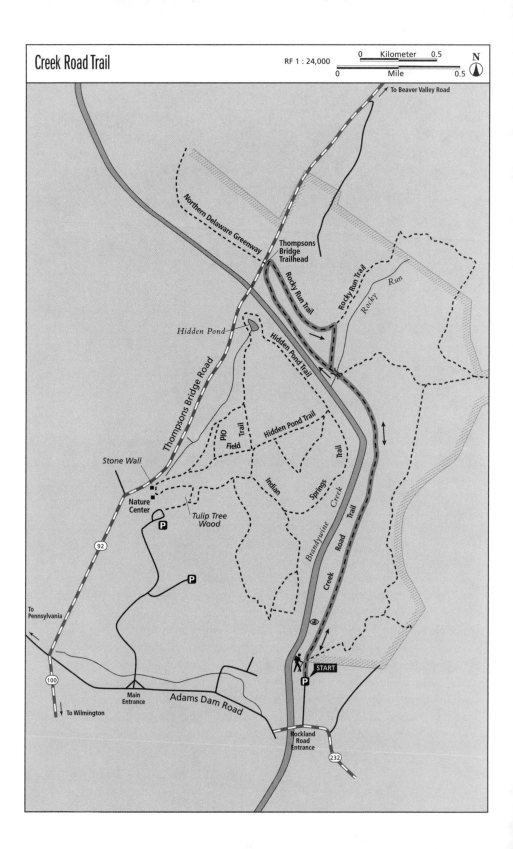

Creek Road Trail

RF 1 : 24,000

Kilometer 0.5
Mile 0.5

N

To Beaver Valley Road

Northern Delaware Greenway

Thompsons
Bridge
Trailhead

Rocky Run Trail

Rocky Run Trail

Rocky Run

Hidden Pond

Hidden Pond Trail

Thompsons Bridge Road

PIO
Field
Trail

Hidden Pond Trail

Stone Wall

Nature
Center

Tulip Tree
Wood

Indian

Springs

Trail

Brandywine Creek

Creek Road Trail

92

To
Pennsylvania

100

Main
Entrance

Adams Dam Road

To Wilmington

START

Rockland
Road
Entrance

232

From the kiosk follow the trail upstream. The paved trail quickly gives way to a crushed-stone path. As the trail climbs, the views of Brandywine Creek become more expansive. At 0.1 mile pass a trail junction on the right, then come to Brandywine Creek Overlook on the left at 0.2 mile. Although you've just started hiking, this is a fine place to watch the slow-moving river roll by and to read the interpretive displays.

The trail enters a woods of tall poplars and oaks, where a steep slope climbs to the right. An old stone wall is one of few reminders that the land around the trail was once grazing land for a du Pont family dairy farm. At any time of year, the view of the trail ahead, stretching out for half a mile or so, is as fine a woodland scene as can be seen outside New England.

The trail imperceptibly descends to creek level. At 0.9 mile cross Rocky Run on a beautiful wooden bridge with stone wall approaches. Take a moment and watch the run tumble into the Brandywine. Across the river from here are the Hidden Pond and Indian Springs Trails—opportunities to visit some of the oldest forest in the Diamond State.

The stream valley is much wider and the canopy open as you approach Thompsons Bridge. Picnic greens and barbecue grills dot the riverside, inviting a lunch stop. It's also a fine spot for angling after smallmouth bass and bluegill (license required).

The Thompsons Bridge trailhead is at 1.3 miles. There are restrooms, parking, and an easy put-in location for paddlers. The Northern Delaware Greenway continues north under the bridge.

From the parking area, continue to the DE 92 entrance, then turn right without crossing the road. Within about 25 yards a faint path enters the woods to the right. Follow the path and ascend steeply for about 125 yards. For a short stretch, the path here is somewhat more rugged than what you've been following. But it soon levels off atop a knoll overlooking the Brandywine. In winter there are long views through the trees.

Just as the trail begins an ascent, watch for dark-green blazes leading left—a false trail continues straight ahead. Descend 150 yards to an open meadow and the junction with Rocky Run Trail at 1.8 miles. Rocky Run cuts a lovely, narrow gorge through upland forest. It's really worth a diversion. To explore, turn left here and follow the blue blazes (sometimes green blazes) above and along the creek as far as you like. When you reach the creek crossing, return to this spot to continue. (See Options to continue on the Rocky Run loop.)

Turning right onto Rocky Run Trail, follow the wide, even path above the creek. There are a couple of paths leading down to the creek. If you descend to play in the creek, stay on the established trails to get there—the steep hillside is susceptible to erosion.

Return to the Creek Road Trail and the Rocky Run bridge at 1.9 miles; turn left. Follow the wide trail back to the trailhead.

Miles and Directions

0.0 Start at the trailhead kiosk.

0.2 Reach Brandywine Creek Overlook.

0.9 Cross Rocky Run on wooden bridge.

1.3 Reach Thompsons Bridge trailhead.

1.8 Reach junction with Rocky Run Trail; turn right onto Rocky Run Trail.

1.9 Return to Rocky Run bridge; turn left.

2.8 Arrive back at trailhead.

Options: For a scenic circuit around Rocky Run, turn left when arriving at Rocky Run Trail, 1.8 miles. This is one of the most scenic hikes in Northern Delaware—opened too late to be included in its entirety in this edition. The loop follows Rocky Run through a narrow gorge, then loops above the gorge under a canopy of tall oaks and tulip poplars. Rocky Run Trail is well marked and easy to follow. The trail returns to the stone bridge over Rocky Run on the Creek Road Trail, adding about 1.5 miles to the hike. From the bridge turn left to return to the trailhead. You can finish the hike without retracing your way on the Creek Road Trail. About a quarter mile past the cut-off trail to the Westcliff Road trailhead, look for an unmarked and unmaintained, but well-traveled trail turning left.

45 Swamp Forest Trail, Lums Pond State Park

A long but easy hike through the woods around Delaware's largest freshwater pond.

Location: Lums Pond State Park is in central New Castle County, Delaware, just north of the Chesapeake & Delaware Canal.

Type of hike: 7.5-mile loop.

Difficulty: Easy.

Season: Year-round.

Fees and permits: Park entrance fee is $2.50 for Delaware residents, $5.00 for nonresidents.

Maps: USGS St. Georges; Delaware Trails Guidebook; state park map.

Special considerations: Hunting is permitted in the park; check with the park office for season information.

Camping: A sixty-eight-site camping area is open March through November. For reservations call (877) 987-2757.

For more information: Lums Pond State Park.

Trailhead facilities: Restrooms, water, picnic area.

Finding the trailhead: From Interstate 95 near Newark, follow Delaware Highway 896 south 5.6 miles. Turn left onto Howell School Road, following Lums Pond State Park signs. Turn right into the park at 0.4 mile. Continue past the park office and fee booth to the Whale Wallow Nature Center on the left.

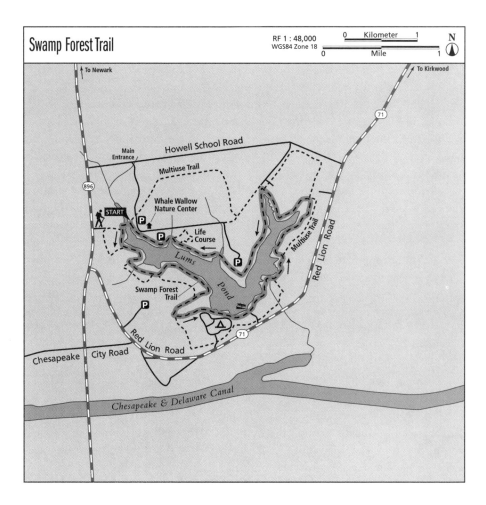

RF 1 : 48,000
WGS84 Zone 18

0 Kilometer 1

0 Mile 1

N

To Newark

To Kirkwood

71

Main
Entrance

Howell School Road

Multiuse Trail

896

Whale Wallow
Nature Center

START

Life
Course

Lums

Multiuse Trail

Red Lion Road

Swamp Forest
Trail

Pond

71

Red Lion Road

Chesapeake City Road

Chesapeake & Delaware Canal

The Hike

Delaware's largest freshwater pond, Lums Pond, was created in the early 1800s when St. Georges Creek was impounded to supply water for the locks of the new Chesapeake & Delaware Canal. Today the pond covers 200 acres and is surrounded by oak forests, wetlands, and beaches. Swamp Forest Trail circles the entire pond, following the shoreline and occasionally drifting from the water's edge into the forest and along the edges of a wooded swamp.

From the parking area, cross the park entrance road and proceed to the far right corner of the grassy picnic area to pick up the trail. Cut through a hedgerow of trees on the right, and then turn left onto the Swamp Forest Trail. Cross the spillway and then turn left onto the footpath, which is well marked for its entire length.

Follow the pond edge through a forest of red maples, poplars, and sweet gums. The presence of these trees, which tend to be adaptable colonizers of cleared land, shows that the shores of the pond were logged into the beginning of the twentieth century, probably supplying the mill powered by the dammed St. Georges Creek. There are also big, old oaks in the pondside forest, and many of the fast-growing poplars have also reached impressive proportions.

Within the first 0.5 mile, the trail also crosses wetland areas on a series of board-walks, where you may see herons or ducks in the tall reeds. At 0.4 mile the trail bends right, leaving the pond edge and briefly sharing a multiuse trail before turning left and continuing through the woods. At 0.6 mile follow the trail left, where it briefly shares the multiuse path again and then returns to the edge of the pond.

Continue on the edge of the pond, with views across the green rippling water to the woods on the opposite side. It is a nice stretch of easy, pleasant walking. The path travels in the shade of oaks and poplars while the sun glitters on the water. Ducks are often visible on the pond. Another vocal resident, the kingfisher, which favors wooded areas along waterways, may be seen diving for a fresh catch. Anglers here have a lot of luck reeling in bluegill, largemouth bass, catfish, crappie, and pickerel.

At 1.5 miles, after passing many gnawed stumps and fallen trees—the work of several active beaver colonies in the park—the trail breaks from the pond again, tracing a triangle around the edge of a wooded swamp and returning to the shoreline. Here there are more nice open views across the pond, and on the trailside in early summer there is an abundance of bright orange day lilies.

Cross the boat ramp access road at 2.7 miles and continue through the woods. For the next 3.0 miles, the trail follows the pond's doglegged shoreline. The views from the water's edge continue to be nice, and the trail begins to have a wilder feel as you pass the youth camping areas on the right and, at 4.0 miles, begin tracing a fishtail around the northeast edge of the pond. Perhaps it is the distance from the park's swimming and picnic areas that makes this stretch seem more remote than it actually is—whatever the cause, it is quiet here and feels far from the surrounding civilization.

Midway through the fishtail, from 4.6 to 5.6 miles, the well-marked trail makes several short breaks from the pond and travels along the edge of fields and thickets. At 5.6 miles the footpath traces the wooded edge of a park recreation area, popular with disc golf players. At the south edge of this area, turn right into the clearing; then, in 25 yards, turn left, following the edge of the playing fields and passing the swimming area on the left, at 6.0 miles. If you are walking on a summer day, this is a great place for a rest and a swim (the swimming area is open only when guards are on duty, during summer daylight hours).

Cut through the beach picnic area on the wide gravel path and cross a footbridge at 6.5 miles. The pond is picturesque here, especially to the right, where it has the look of a mountain lake. The trail bends left, then follows the shoreline and continues through the boat rental pavilion. After passing the Life Course fitness trail on the right, at 7.0 miles, cross another footbridge, bend left at the parking area, and continue through the woods along the shore back to the trailhead.

Miles and Directions

0.0 Start at trailhead at far right corner of picnic area.

0.6 Follow trail left.

1.5 Reach wetlands; follow trail along edge.

2.7 Cross boat ramp access road; continue through woods.

4.0 Begin tracing fishtail around edge of pond.

6.0 Reach swimming area.

6.5 Cross footbridge; trail bears left.

7.0 Pass fitness trail on your right; then cross another footbridge.

7.5 Arrive back at trailhead.

Options: Make a day of your visit to Lums Pond—there are picnic areas, playing fields, a swimming beach, boat rentals, and a nature center.

46 Blackbird State Forest Loop, Tybout Tract

An easy walk through natural and managed coastal-plain woodlands in Blackbird State Forest, famous for its Delmarva bays—the small upland ponds of mysterious origin that dot the forest's ten tracts.

Location: Blackbird State Forest's Tybout Tract is in southwestern New Castle County, Delaware, about 15 miles north of Dover.
Type of hike: 2.7-mile loop.
Difficulty: Easy.
Season: February through October.
Fees and permits: No fees or permits required.
Maps: USGS Clayton, Delaware.

Special considerations: Delaware state forests are open to hunting during fall and winter. Hiking during the state's deer hunting season is not recommended.
Camping: Camping is available; a permit is required.
For more information: Blackbird State Forest.
Trailhead facilities: Picnic area.

Finding the trailhead: From U.S. Highway 13, 5 miles north of Smyrna, travel southwest on Blackbird Forest Road (Delaware Highway 471) 2.2 miles to the picnic area parking on the right. The trail begins across Blackbird Forest Road.

The Hike

Like many of Delaware's other managed woodlands, much of Blackbird State Forest has been a "forest" for less than fifty years. The trails on the Tybout Tract, for instance, pass through areas that were tilled fields until 1941, when the state acquired the land and began cultivating stands of loblolly and white pine. Along with the managed

Blackbird State Forest Loop

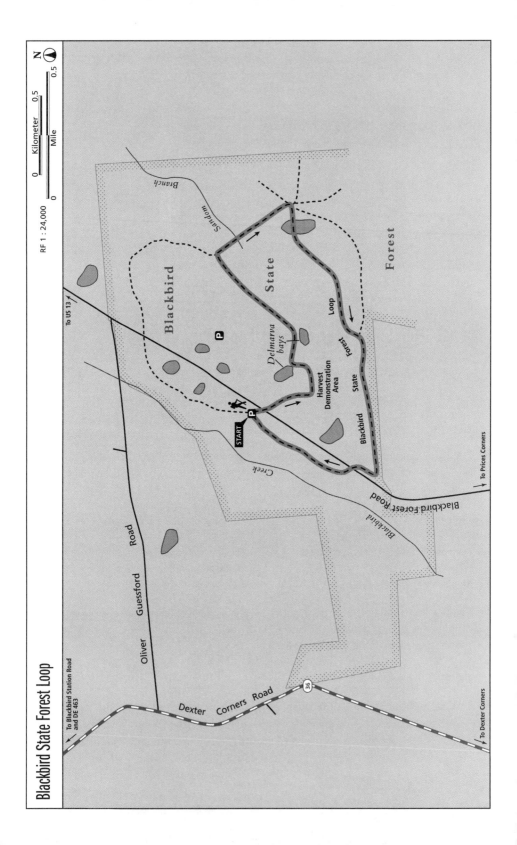

RF 1 : 24,000

N

0   Kilometer   0.5

0   0.5
Mile

To US 13

Blackbird

State

Forest

Sandom

Branch

Delmarva
bays

Harvest
Demonstration
Area

Forest

Loop

State

Blackbird

P

P

START

Creek

Oliver   Guessford   Road

To Blackbird Station Road
and DE 463

Dexter   Corners   Road

36

To Dexter Corners

Blackbird Forest Road

To Prices Corners

parcels, acres of natural hardwood forests border the Blackbird trails. These are lovely tracts of red oak and maple, sweet gum and poplar, with the lush understory of flowering trees and shrubs common in wild coastal-plain woodlands.

The trail begins across Blackbird Forest Road from the picnic area, heading into the woods perpendicular to the road. Follow the path through young sweet gums and poplars, the colonizers of fields and clearings, to the junction at the Harvest Demonstration Area at 0.2 mile. Here you'll see two parcels that were cut and replanted—one in pine and spruce in 1951, the other in hardwoods in 1994—to demonstrate forest recovery. Turn left, and proceed through the young stands to the Delmarva bay on the right at 0.3 mile.

Small upland ponds that harbor a variety of rare plants, Delmarva bays are also known as Carolina bays, loblollies, and whale wallows. The latter refers to just one of the many origin stories of these unique depressions: Legends say "wallowing" beached whales made the ponds. Others suggest that meteorites created them. Whatever their origins, the bays are considered a natural treasure and are protected by the Delaware Natural Areas Preservation System.

At the junction just past the bays, turn right and proceed on a sandy dirt road with pines on the left and hardwoods on the right. Trails will intersect, first from the right and then from the left, before you enter a nice stand of mixed hardwoods. At 0.8 mile, at the red marker, turn right onto the trail to Sandom Branch, a wetland stream forded by two short bridges. Continue on the hiking path into the fragrant, wild woods among scrambling squirrels and lively songbirds.

At 1.2 miles come to an unusual woodland intersection, a kind of star with trails radiating in six directions. Simply turn right, following the red-blazed metal post, and continue through the forest. At 1.4 miles pass a path entering from the right. At 1.5 miles proceed through the junction, bearing slightly right. Here, still in the wild forest, dogwoods and pink azaleas blossom abundantly in spring.

The trail bends right at a junction at 1.8 miles and proceeds 100 yards through a yellow gate to an access road. Turn right onto the crushed-rock road, and continue through shady groves of mixed hardwoods. Listen here for songbirds, woodpeckers hammering away at old snags, and deer bounding among the trees.

At 2.4 miles the trail intersects Blackbird Forest Road. Turn right, cross the road, and turn left into a triangular picnic area. Cross the picnic area, and pick up the trail on the right just before the yellow gate. The blue-blazed path crosses a marsh area and then meanders through the woods to the trailhead.

Miles and Directions

0.0 Start at trailhead, across Blackbird Forest Road from picnic area.

0.2 Reach Harvest Demonstration Area; turn left.

0.3 Arrive at Delmarva bays (or "whale wallows"). Turn right at junction just past the bays.

0.8 Junction with trail to Sandom Branch; turn right onto this trail.

1.2 Reach "star junction"; turn right, following red-blazed post.

1.8 Trail bends right at junction. Proceed 100 yards through yellow gate to access road.

2.4 Trail intersects Blackbird Forest Road; turn right and cross the road.

2.7 Arrive back at trailhead.

Options: There are 80 miles of trails and access roads in Blackbird State Forest. Pick up maps from the Tybout Tract office, just 0.2 mile from the trailhead, and design your own shuttle and circuit hikes.

47 Bombay Hook National Wildlife Refuge Loop

A circuit hike on the dirt roads of a Delaware Bay wildlife refuge. This is an especially rewarding hike for those interested in watching migrating shorebirds and waterfowl, nesting bald eagles, and resident woodland mammals, such as deer, fox, woodchucks, and raccoons.

Location: Bombay Hook National Wildlife Refuge is in eastern Kent County, Delaware, about 15 miles northeast of Dover.

Type of hike: 8.3-mile double loop.

Difficulty: Easy.

Season: September through May.

Fees and permits: No fees or permits required.

Maps: USGS Bombay Hook, Delaware; Refuge Auto Tour Map.

Special considerations: The wildlife is abundant on the refuge year-round. In summer bring insect repellent. Pets must be kept on a leash.

Camping: No camping is available.

For more information: Refuge Manager, Bombay Hook National Wildlife Refuge.

Trailhead facilities: Restrooms, water, nature center, gift shop.

Finding the trailhead: From U.S. Highway 13 halfway between Smyrna and Dover, travel 3.8 miles east on Delaware Highway 42 to Delaware Highway 9. Turn left onto DE 9; proceed north 1.5 miles, and turn right onto Whitehall Neck Road. Go 2.3 miles to Bombay Hook National Wildlife Area; continue through the entrance 0.2 mile to parking at the visitor center on the left.

The Hike

Bombay Hook National Wildlife Refuge, on the shores of the Delaware Bay, is one of the best birding sites in the region, rivaling New Jersey's Cape May and Brigantine National Wildlife Refuge. Its extensive salt marsh—at 13,000 acres one of the largest undisturbed tracts on the East Coast—along with its 3,000 acres of freshwater pools, wooded marshes, upland forests, and cultivated fields, provides diverse habitat for more than 260 species of nesting and migrating birds. And the birds are not alone; 34 species of mammals and a wide variety of reptiles, amphibians, and fish

The cool seasons are a magical time to hike oceanside trails. PHOTO COURTESY OF DELAWARE DIVISION OF PARKS AND RECREATION/DNREC

also make the refuge their home. The dikes, dirt roads, and short walking trails that circle and cross the refuge pass through all the area's landscapes and provide great opportunities for watching wildlife.

Please note before embarking on a trip to Bombay Hook that you may share some of your walk with cars. The dirt roads you will travel are designed for slow-moving automobiles, most driven by avid birders cruising and stopping, cruising and stopping, with binoculars in hand. But serious birding does not really draw a crowd. Hiking here, especially on weekdays, is a lot like walking on an old country road. If that sounds appealing, you should enjoy a day of exploring Bombay Hook.

Pick up the trail—here a gravel road—in front of the visitor center, and turn left into the refuge. At 0.2 mile turn right and begin a partial loop around Raymond Pool, one of the refuge's freshwater impoundments. Before drawing close to the edge of the pool, at 1.1 miles, you will pass through marshland grasses, meadows, open fields, and stands of sweet gum and red maple, a sampling of refuge habitats clearly favorable to the local birds: Their songs and wild flights here seem to be expressions of pure delight.

Proceed around the edge of Raymond Pool, with marshland stretching far into the distance on the right. On the flats near Raymond Pool, look for long-legged

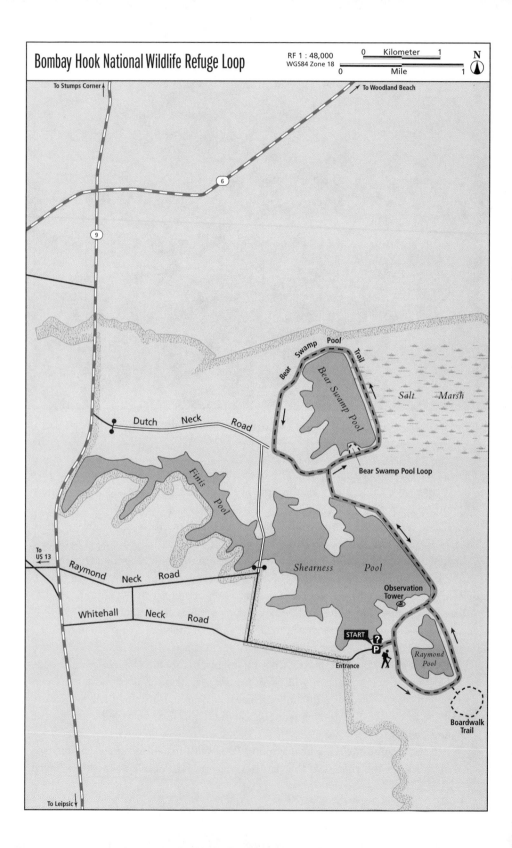

Bombay Hook National Wildlife Refuge Loop

RF 1 : 48,000
WGS84 Zone 18

Kilometer
Mile

N

To Stumps Corner

To Woodland Beach

6

9

To US 13

Dutch   Neck   Road

Finis Pool

Raymond   Neck   Road

Whitehall   Neck   Road

Bear   Swamp   Pool   Trail

Bear Swamp Pool

Salt   Marsh

Bear Swamp Pool Loop

Shearness   Pool

Observation Tower

START

Entrance

Raymond Pool

Boardwalk Trail

To Leipsic

waders, such as black-necked stilts, ibis, and great blue heron. At 1.7 miles go right, following signs to Shearness Pool, and continue along the edge of the vast salt marsh. This stretch is prime birding territory. During fall Shearness Pool is alive with some thirty species of ducks passing through the refuge. In spring look for migrating shorebirds—black-bellied plover, red knot, and ruddy turnstone—resting and feeding on the mudflats of the marsh. And soaring over the whole scene are the bald eagles that nest in the edge of the woods behind Shearness Pool.

At 3.0 miles the trail bends to the left away from the salt marsh, traveling through forest as it passes Parson Point Trail, a 0.5-mile spur into the woodland to the edge of Shearness Pool. If you are up to adding a mile to your hike, Parson Point Trail is a nice walk through the woods, where you may see eagles' nests, black-crowned night herons, wild turkeys, and spring wildflowers such as the jack-in-the-pulpit.

After Parson Point the road travels briefly through woods and grassland and then splits at 3.3 miles. Go right and begin a loop around Bear Swamp Pool. At 3.6 miles another short spur, the 0.3-mile Bear Swamp Pool Loop, takes you to an observation tower on the edge of the pool. It is worth the detour. From the tower, which feels like a tree house set in the branches of the surrounding oaks and maples, there are great views across the mudflats of Bear Swamp and the salt marsh to the east. In the flats, look for the meandering, crisscrossing tracks of many creatures, from herons and egrets to the peculiar trails of tail-dragging turtles.

Back on the road, continue around Bear Swamp Pool with marsh on either side. At 4.7 miles the road bends away from the marsh and travels through the woods. Look for deer on the flats to the left or for one of the refuge's resident foxes retreating lazily from a sunny spot in the road into the surrounding forest.

Continue through woods and cultivated fields. At 5.8 miles, at Dutch Neck Road (the road to Allee House), turn left and follow the road to the junction, at 6.1 miles, to complete the loop around Bear Swamp Pool. From the junction retrace the road past Parson Point and Shearness Pool to the loop around Raymond Pool, at 7.7 miles. Go straight at the junction with the Raymond Pool loop. Pass the Shearness Observation Tower on the right and then turn right, at 8.1 miles, to return to the trailhead at the visitor center.

Miles and Directions

0.0 Start at trailhead in front of visitor center.

0.2 Turn right and begin loop around Raymond Pool.

1.1 Draw close to edge of pool.

1.7 Go right, following signs to Shearness Pool.

3.0 Pass Parson Point Trail junction.

3.3 Come to split in road; go right and begin loop around Bear Swamp Pool.

3.6 Reach junction with Bear Swamp Pool Loop. Follow spur to observation tower if you wish before returning to road.

4.7 Road bends away from marsh to travel through woods.

5.8 Reach Dutch Neck Road (to Allee House); turn left and follow road.

6.1 Reach junction, completing Bear Swamp Pool loop.

7.7 Go straight at junction with Raymond Pool loop.

8.1 Reach spur to visitor center; turn right.

8.3 Arrive back at trailhead.

Options: There are short but interesting detours on Parson Point, Bear Swamp Pool, and Boardwalk Trails. You also can create an 11.6-mile round-trip by including other roads and trails; see the auto tour map at the visitor center for additional routes.

48 Norman G. Wilder Wildlife Area Loop

A long, easy walk on dirt fire roads through mature forests and upland swamps in an area managed for wildlife.

Location: The Norman G. Wilder Wildlife Area is in Kent County, Delaware, about 10 miles southwest of Dover.

Type of hike: 8.2-mile loop.

Difficulty: Easy.

Season: February through August.

Fees and permits: No fees or permits required.

Maps: USGS Marydel; Wyoming, Delaware.

Special considerations: Use insect repellent during summer.

Camping: No camping is available.

For more information: Delaware Division of Fish and Wildlife.

Trailhead facilities: None.

Finding the trailhead: From Dover travel 8.5 miles south on U.S. Highway 13 to Delaware Highway 32. Turn right onto DE 32, and proceed 0.7 mile to the intersection of Delaware Highways 108 and 240. Go straight on DE 108 (here called Evans Road) 1.1 miles to the stop sign. Turn right, continuing on DE 108 (now called Firetower Road), and go 0.5 mile to the Norman G. Wilder Wildlife Area headquarters on the right.

The Hike

Named for a notable Delaware conservationist and wildlife biologist, Norman G. Wilder Wildlife Area is a preserve managed primarily for hunting. The trails are well-maintained fire roads, closed to vehicles, that pass through fields, forests, and swamps protected to provide habitat for game. During the hunting seasons, September through January, a trip here would be ill advised. But the rest of the year, the lengthy trail and the flat, wooded terrain make this a good hike for those who like to walk far and fast.

The trail begins on the dirt road to the left of the office, with the fire tower visible above the trees to the left. Walk between a thicket on the left and a wooded

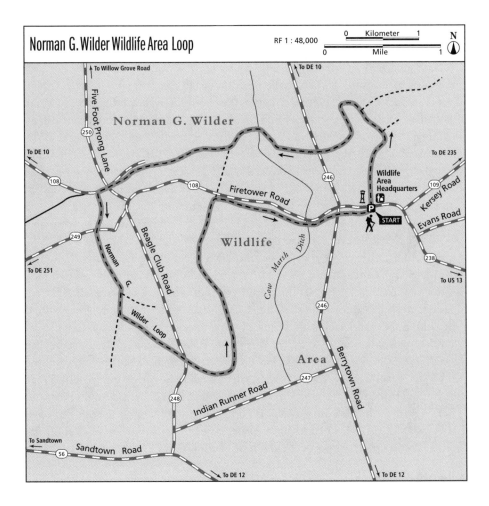

RF 1 : 48,000

0   Kilometer   1

0   Mile   1

N

To Willow Grove Road

To DE 10

Five Foot Prong Lane

Norman G. Wilder

250

To DE 10

To DE 235

108

108

246

Wildlife
Area
Headquarters

109

Kersey Road

Firetower Road

START

Evans Road

249

Norman

G.

Wildlife

Cow Marsh Ditch

246

238

To DE 251

To US 13

Wilder

Beagle Club Road

Loop

246

Area

Berrytown Road

248

247

Indian Runner Road

To Sandtown

56

Sandtown Road

To DE 12

To DE 12

hedgerow on the right where young red maples, sweet gums, and willows shade the path. Pass fields and meadows on the left, and then enter the woods. The trail here is wide, soft, and shady; the forest is young but lush, with holly and bayberry tangling beneath a canopy of loblolly pine, sweet gum, and tulip poplar.

Stay to the left as the trail passes two spurs and a wildlife clearing on the right. Continue through the woods as the fire road makes a horseshoe bend and crosses Road 246 at 1.5 miles. Barricades block automobile access to the fire road on both sides—duck under the gates or step around them.

Past the road, the trail is sandy and the trees beside the lane provide little shade. A hat, sunglasses, and some extra water will help get you through this sunny stretch. And it is worth it. Soon the trail passes through an impressive stand of mature oaks, some as tall as 100 feet. Also look for honeysuckle and wild azalea.

At 1.8 miles, after passing a clearing on the right, cross Cow Marsh Ditch, which is aptly named. It is a drainage channel that looks every bit like a ditch. The water is a dark, muddy shade of brown that appears rather toxic but is actually colored by the organic content of the soil.

Leaving Cow Marsh Ditch behind, continue on the sunny trail past a side trail on the left, at 2.1 miles, and on to the junction of DE 250 and DE 108 at 3.3 miles. Cross Road 250, which enters the intersection from the right, and then cross Road 108. Turn right and follow Road 108 for about 150 yards on a rutted horse trail, then turn left into the woods on a narrow, shady footpath.

Go straight into the woods, passing a fire road on the right. The trail winds through a holly grove and crosses Road 249 at 3.7 miles. Again a sandy fire road, the trail continues through the woods. At 4.3 miles a spur shoots off the trail to the left. Soon after, follow the narrow hiking trail that cuts off the road to the left. Be careful here—the trail is not marked, and it is easy to miss. If you come to an area of wide-open croplands, you have gone too far.

Once on the shady foot trail, pass through a young pine forest and then cross Road 248 at 5.1 miles. Passing a field on the left, the fire road then makes a long bend to the left and continues through the woods. This is a nice stretch. The trail does not cross a road for nearly 2.0 miles, and it passes through shady groves of old oaks with honeysuckle and wild azalea winding through the understory.

At 7.0 miles the fire road meets Road 108. Turn right and continue along the roadside. The shoulder is not wide, but the band of grass between the road and the woods gives you enough room to walk safely. If you are with a group, walk single file. Although roadside walking can be annoying, here it is actually quite pleasant. There is little traffic, and the roadway is bordered by the forest on the left and open fields on the right, where birds are plentiful. Ahead, the fire tower appears on the horizon, where the road passes the trailhead.

Miles and Directions

- **0.0** Start at trailhead on dirt road to the left of office.
- **0.5** Cross Road 246 (Berrytown Road).
- **1.8** Cross Cow Marsh Ditch.
- **3.3** Cross Road 250 and then Road 108 (Five Foot Prong Lane and Firetower Road).
- **3.7** Cross Road 249 (C&R Center Road).
- **5.1** Cross Road 248 (Beagle Club Road).
- **7.0** Fire road meets Road 108 (Firetower Road); turn right.
- **8.2** Arrive back at trailhead.

Options: There are 16.0 miles of fire road trails in the wildlife area. It would be hard to create a longer loop, but you could add some spurs to your walk or plan a shuttle hike.

49 Killens Pond Loop, Killens Pond State Park

A walk around an eighteenth-century millpond through diverse wetland and upland forests.

Location: Killens Pond State Park is in Kent County, Delaware, 13 miles south of Dover.
Type of hike: 3.2-mile loop.
Difficulty: Easy.
Season: Year-round.
Fees and permits: Fee charged May through October; $3.00 for state residents, $6.00 for nonresidents.

Maps: USGS Harrington, Delaware.
Special considerations: Bring insect repellent in summer.
Camping: Primitive and improved sites are available in addition to cabins.
For more information: Killens Pond State Park.
Trailhead facilities: Restrooms, water, picnic areas, telephone.

Finding the trailhead: From U.S. Highway 113, travel west on Delaware Highway 12 through Frederica and continue 5 miles to Chimney Hill Road. Turn left onto Chimney Hill Road and go 1.2 miles to Killens Pond Road. Turn right and in 0.1 mile turn left into the park. Continue 0.7 mile on the park entrance road to the parking lot.

The Hike

Set in the farm country of central Delaware, Killens Pond State Park straddles the boundary between southern and northern forests. Here you will see the loblolly pine and American holly forests typical of the wet, sandy plain to the south as well as stands of mature hardwoods common in the rolling hills to the north. In places on the Killens Pond Loop, the trail itself seems to be the boundary between the two habitats, with the tall pines and dense undergrowth of coastal lowlands on one side and groves of giant poplars and oaks on the other—both, in rather different ways, quite beautiful. Add several nice views of the pond, and you have all the ingredients for an interesting, scenic, and refreshing walk.

The well-marked loop begins at the wooden sign marking Pondside Nature Trail. The pine duff path enters the woods and, at 0.1 mile, meets the trail's return loop. Go right, and continue along with the pond to the left. For the next 0.5 mile the trail passes through the pine and hardwood forests mingling at the edges of the path. Here flowering dogwoods and several species of oaks mingle between the sweetbay, ferns, and climbing vines of the marsh and the upland stands of poplar. There may not be a better place to experience the diversity of Delaware's woodlands.

At 0.5 mile, at a fork in the trail, you may go left 50 yards for a view of the sixty-six-acre pond. It is worth the detour. In spring the pinxter flower, sometimes called pink azalea, blooms abundantly here. From the edge of the pond, you can gaze over the still water, listen to birdsong, and watch for ducks and cormorants. Back at the

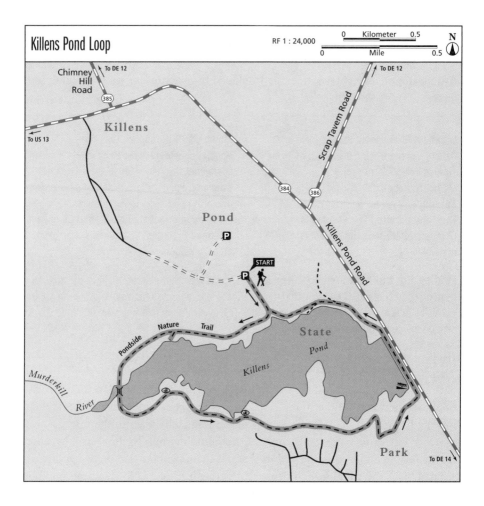

RF 1 : 24,000

0   Kilometer   0.5
0   Mile   0.5

N

Chimney Hill Road

To DE 12

To DE 12

385

To US 13

Killens

Scrap Tavern Road

384   386

Pond

P

Killens Pond Road

START

P

Nature   Trail

Pondside

State

Pond

Killens

Murderkill

River

Park

To DE 14

fork, bear to the left and continue through a lovely grove of tall, stately poplars. The trunk of one giant, just to the left of the trail, takes two people to reach around!

At 0.8 mile the trail bends left around the edge of the pond and then intersects a sandy road. Turn left and, at 0.9 mile, cross a bridge over the narrow Murderkill River. Before it was made a millpond in the late 1700s, the Killens Pond area was the floodplain of the Murderkill and the site of several Native American settlements and hunting camps. The river's peculiar name, legend has it, commemorates the massacre of a group of Dutch traders by the local tribe. And the name is not redundant; the Dutch *kil* is a stream, creek, or channel. From the bridge the view of the pond and the surrounding marsh forest is quite nice.

Turn left after the bridge. The trail bends along the pond through holly and up a rise to a bench and a view at 1.1 miles. From a little clearing surrounded by oak and poplar, dogwood and pink azalea, the view and the setting here invite a rest.

Bear left at the fork, following trail markers down the rise and close to the pond. Watch the snags for sunning turtles and perching ducks, and note the dead bald cypress, well drilled by woodpeckers. Continue in the lowlands over boardwalks and then up a slight rise at 1.5 miles to another nice view of the pond.

At 1.7 miles the trail enters Killens Pond Campground, with cabins on the right. Continue straight, across an unpaved access road, and head back into the woods on a slope above the marsh. The trail runs through the woodlands behind the campground and, at 2.1 miles, turns right. To the left is a short spur to the pond.

Proceed, winding through hardwoods, to the boat launch at Road 384 at 2.5 miles. Turn left and walk the shoulder over the spillway at the edge of the pond, then turn left through the opening in the post-and-rail fence at 2.6 miles. Follow the pond edge on the left, past a canoe rental area, and enter the woods on a wide, sandy trail in the shade of loblolly pines. To the right, a short nature trail loops through a stand recovering from a severe winter storm in 1994. From the path you can see the many trees and limbs downed by five bitter days of ice and wind.

Continue to the fork, at 2.8 miles, and bear to the left, following the PONDSIDE NATURE TRAIL sign. After 50 yards, another spur breaks left from the trail to the edge of the pond. Proceed to the right through mixed pines and hardwoods to the entrance spur, at 3.1 miles. Turn right, and return to trailhead.

Miles and Directions

0.0 Start at trailhead marked by wooden sign.

0.1 Pondside Nature Trail junction; go right.

0.5 Reach fork; go left on spur for a view of the pond. Back at fork, bear left.

0.9 Cross bridge over Murderkill River; turn left after bridge.

1.1 Reach bench with a view, then bear left at fork.

1.7 Enter Killens Pond Campground; continue straight.

2.1 Trail turns right.

2.5 Reach boat launch at Road 384; turn left.

2.8 Bear left at fork, following Pondside Nature Trail.

3.1 Entrance spur junction; turn right.

3.2 Arrive back at trailhead.

Options: Bring a fishing rod, or rent a canoe and try the Murderkill River Canoe Trail.

50 Prime Hook National Wildlife Refuge Loop

A short walk through coastal forest and wetlands on the western shore of Delaware Bay. A great hike for birders.

Location: Prime Hook National Wildlife Refuge is in Sussex County, Delaware, 22 miles southeast of Dover and 13 miles northwest of Rehoboth Beach.
Type of hike: 1.6-mile lollipop.
Difficulty: Easy.
Season: October through April.
Fees and permits: No fees or permits required.
Maps: USGS Lewes; Milton, Delaware.

Special considerations: Mosquitoes in late spring and summer make the Refuge Loop a true October-to-April trail. In any season, bring binoculars for birding.
Camping: No camping is available.
For more information: Refuge Manager, Prime Hook National Wildlife Refuge.
Trailhead facilities: Visitor center, restrooms, picnic tables.

Finding the trailhead: From Delaware Seashore resorts, travel north on Delaware Highway 1, 1.5 miles north of the Broadkill River, to Delaware Highway 16. Go right on DE 16 and, after 1.2 miles, turn left onto Road 236 (Turkle Pond Road) into Prime Hook National Wildlife Refuge. Trailhead parking is 1.5 miles ahead at the visitor center.

The Hike

Prime Hook National Wildlife Refuge—8,817 acres of fresh and tidal marsh, upland forest, and croplands on the shores of the Delaware Bay—is home to a wonderful array of birds, mammals, and reptiles and is an important stopover for migrating waterfowl. On an easy 1.5-mile stroll on the Refuge Loop, you can see fine examples of each of the coastal habitats as well as of the area's abundant wildlife.

The Refuge Loop begins on Boardwalk Trail, across the parking lot from the visitor center. For the first 0.25 mile, the trail is like a garden path: a wide, grass walkway bordered on both sides by multiflora roses teeming with songbirds, rabbits, and groundhogs.

A short detour to the left, at 0.1 mile, leads to the site of the Jonathan J. Morris Homestead, thought to have been established around 1750. Fruit trees, the bright white stones of the family cemetery, and grassy cropland are all that remain, but in this peaceful setting it is easy to imagine life on the Morris farm.

Continue on the trail under sweet gum trees to the marsh boardwalk at 0.2 mile, and proceed into wetlands about 50 yards. Where the boardwalk turns right, pause to observe the teeming life of a marsh community. Close to the boardwalk you may see turtles and green frogs sunning or ducks and muskrats swimming by in the shallow water. In the marsh grass, red-winged blackbirds roost and hunting hawks glide just above. Across the vast wetlands there are forested islands bright with color in spring and fall.

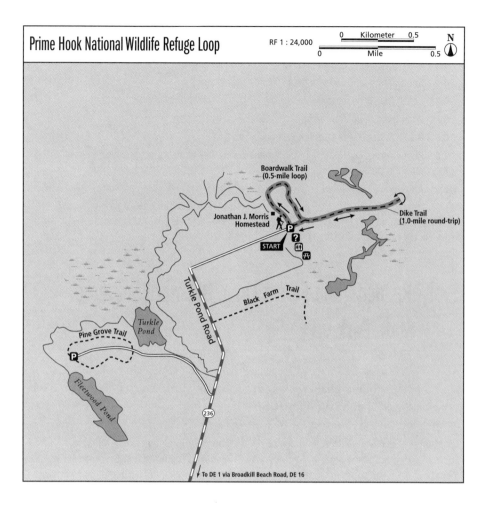

Prime Hook National Wildlife Refuge Loop

RF 1 : 24,000

Kilometer

Mile

N

Boardwalk Trail
(0.5-mile loop)

Jonathan J. Morris
Homestead

Dike Trail
(1.0-mile round-trip)

START

Turkle Pond Road

Black Farm Trail

Pine Grove Trail

Turkle
Pond

Fleetwood Pond

236

To DE 1 via Broadkill Beach Road, DE 16

Proceed on the boardwalk another 50 yards, turn right; wind through a forest of young maples and sweet gums, groves of holly, and an occasional stately pine. The woods here rustle with warblers and thrashers hopping in the brush, blue jays flitting in the branches, and woodpeckers hammering away at rotten trunks.

At the forest edge, the trail enters a field. Turn left on the sandy path, and proceed to the Dike Trail junction, at 0.5 mile. Dike Trail runs a straight 0.5 mile along the edge of another great expanse of marsh. With the woods to the left and the marsh to the right, the birding is excellent. While walking the path, you may see such residents as great blue herons, egrets, hawks, and vultures, as well as ducks and shorebirds. In fall, the legions of migrating geese are an annual Atlantic-shore spectacle.

At 1.0 mile the trail dead-ends in the marsh. Turn around here and return to the trailhead, perhaps focusing your attention on the woodland birds and wildlife, now on your right.

Miles and Directions

0.0 Start at trailhead across parking lot from visitor center.

0.1 Short detour leads to Jonathan J. Morris Homestead.

0.2 Reach marsh boardwalk.

0.3 Wind through upland forest.

0.5 Reach junction with Dike Trail; turn left onto trail.

1.0 Reach end of Dike Trail, your turnaround point. Stay straight past boardwalk turnoff to return to trailhead.

1.6 Arrive back at trailhead.

Options: Pine Grove Trail, a 0.8-mile loop, and Black Farm Trail, a 1.2-mile walk, are two more easy hikes in the Prime Hook wildlands.

51 Redden State Forest Loop, Delaware Seashore State Park

An easy walk through a tract of Delaware's largest state forest in the heart of loblolly pine country. A good hike for exploring the natural and cultural history of a relatively new wild and managed forest.

Location: Redden State Forest is in central Sussex County, 3.5 miles north of Georgetown and about 35 miles south of Dover.
Type of hike: 5.0-mile loop.
Difficulty: Easy.
Season: Year-round.
Fees and permits: No fees or permits required.

Maps: USGS Georgetown, Delaware.
Special considerations: State forest lands are open to hunting during the fall and winter seasons. The trail is unmarked but easy to follow.
Camping: Primitive camping is available with a permit. No fee is required.
For more information: Redden State Forest.
Trailhead facilities: None.

Finding the trailhead: Travel 3.5 miles north from Georgetown on U.S. Highway 113 to East Redden Road. Traveling east on East Redden Road, go 0.4 mile and turn right at the entrance to the Headquarters Tract of Redden State Forest. Proceed 0.2 mile to parking at the office.

The Hike

Early in the 1900s, Redden State Forest was not a forest at all. Until the 1930s, the 1,767 acres of woodlands here were primarily open fields and meadows separated by hedgerows—a quail-hunting retreat for the executives of the Pennsylvania Railroad Company. All the forest growth, both natural and managed, has occurred since then. A walk through the forest's natural groves of mixed hardwoods and its planted

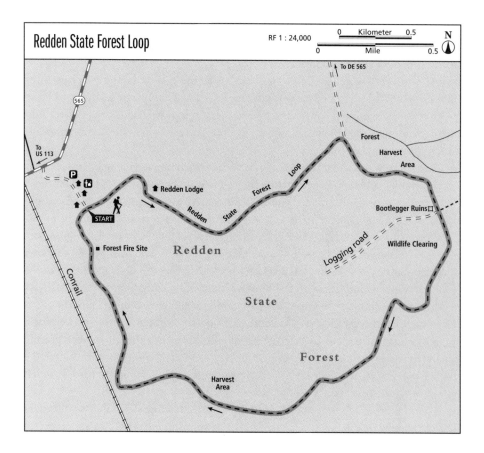

Redden State Forest Loop

RF 1 : 24,000

0   Kilometer   0.5

0   Mile   0.5

N

To DE 565

565

To
US 113

Forest
Harvest
Area

Forest Loop

Redden Lodge

Redden State

START

Bootlegger Ruins

Forest Fire Site

Redden

Logging road

Wildlife Clearing

Conrail

State

Forest

Harvest
Area

and harvested stands of loblolly pine reveals the young woodland's many layers of human and natural history.

From the parking lot, walk past the state forest office and turn left onto an unpaved access road, following the sign for Redden Lodge. An educational trail, perpendicular to the road, also begins here. This 0.1-mile path is a good introduction to the area's ecology.

Proceed on the wide, unimproved road through a natural stand of loblolly pine and mixed hardwoods. This is an area of the forest left to develop in its natural state. The canopy of pines, maples, and oaks and the understory of holly and maple and sweet gum saplings are typical of a young forest on the coastal plain.

At 0.4 mile the trail loops around Redden Lodge, built in the early 1900s to house the Pennsylvania Railroad's hunting retreats. The lodge was placed on the National Register of Historic Places in 1980. Renovated in 1995, it is wheelchair-accessible and available for meetings, celebrations, and educational programs.

Continue on the wide, sandy trail through pine forest. Although there are some Virginia and yellow pines, the predominant tree throughout the forest is the loblolly pine, a southern species that occurs from east Texas to central Delaware. The tree—

used for lumber, plywood, and paper—is the most valuable timber species in Delaware. It is also wonderfully fragrant, musical in the wind, and a provider of a shady home for many woodland creatures.

As you will see at 1.5 miles, clear-cutting is the typical method of harvesting loblolly pines. This type of harvest yields a high financial return and, according to forestry officials, mimics natural fire by exposing loblolly seedlings to the direct sunlight they require to mature. However, the method also alters the forest landscape and remains controversial.

Turn right where the trail meets the clear-cut, and continue on. The harvest area will be on your left and the uncut forest on the right. As unsettling as the harvest may be, it does provide an edge habitat for birds and animals. As you walk along between woodlands and clearing, you may see hawks and songbirds or a fox retreating into the forest.

The trail soon bends to the right, turning into a refreshing woodland. In season, dogwoods blossom here beneath the tall pines. At 2.0 miles the path passes the mossy foundations of two small houses, believed to be the homes of bootleggers early in the century. Whether they supplied the hunting lodge with spirits is purely speculative.

Just past the bootlegger ruins, an old logging road intersects the trail on the right. Continue straight ahead to the "wildlife plot," on the right at 2.3 miles. The plot is a narrow strip of pasture between the trail and the woods that provides a grazing area for wildlife. At the end of the pasture, stay to the left and turn right where the trail changes from slightly primitive to the harder surface of the access road. Turn left at a short stone post with a yellow blaze.

Continue through pine forest to another harvest area at 3.5 miles. At 4.0 miles the trail bends to the right near the state forest border and, at 4.7 miles, enters an area burned by a fire in April 1995. The fire was caused by a spark from a train on the nearby railroad and burned 209 acres of forest. You will see the charred bark of burned trees and a new generation of loblolly pines taking root in the clearing. The trail turns right at the edge of the clearing and returns to the office and parking area.

Miles and Directions

0.0 Start at trailhead, past state forest office.

0.4 Trail loops around Redden Lodge.

1.5 Reach state forest harvest area. Turn right where trail meets the clear-cut.

2.0 Pass bootlegger ruins; continue straight at junction with logging road.

2.3 Reach wildlife plot; at end of pasture stay left, then turn right where trail changes to access road.

3.5 Reach another state forest harvest area.

4.0 Trail bends right near state forest border.

4.7 Trail enters forest fire site and turns right at edge of clearing.

5.0 Arrive back at trailhead.

Options: Walk the 1.0-mile educational trail to start or finish the state forest loop.

52 Gordons Pond, Cape Henlopen State Park

This walk weaves around a mile-long tidal pond and ends at the ocean, offering arm's-length views of more than a dozen species of shorebirds.

Location: Cape Henlopen is in Sussex County, Delaware, along the Atlantic coast, stretching from Rehoboth Beach to Lewes. The Gordon Pond loop is 1 mile north of Rehoboth.
Type of hike: 4.0-mile loop.
Difficulty: Easy.
Season: Fall through spring (see Special considerations).
Fees and permits: Entrance fees are collected daily during summer and on weekends and holidays in spring and fall; $4.00 per car for state residents, $8.00 for nonresidents. No fee for bicycle or pedestrian entry.

Maps: USGS Cape Henlopen, Delaware.
Special considerations: Some areas of the preserve are subject to closure during nesting season. Check the trailhead kiosk. For much of the hike, there is no shade—a hat is advisable.
Camping: Camping is permitted in the park's north end; fee required.
For more information: Cape Henlopen State Park.
Trailhead facilities: Restrooms, concession.

Finding the trailhead: In Rehoboth Beach, from the intersection of Rehoboth Avenue and First Street, go north on Rehoboth (if you're facing the beach, go left). Go 5 blocks to Lake Avenue; turn right. Turn left onto Surf Avenue and follow to Henlopen Avenue/Ocean Drive. Turn right and follow Ocean Drive to the park entrance. The trailhead is in the left parking lot. Look for the kiosk.

The Hike

Crouching near the great tidal pool known as Gordons Pond, you watch from behind the rushes as a great blue heron prepares to strike a fish at its feet. When it does, the commotion sets a dozen plovers into flight. As you follow them, you notice a small plane in the distance. It will be flying beyond the sand dunes, out over the ocean. This is your only clue that you're just a couple of beach miles from busy Rehoboth Beach. Otherwise, it's you and the shorebirds—and the foxes that hope to feast on them.

For the first 0.7 mile this easy stroll follows a crushed limestone path, open to bicycles, along the southern shore of Gordons Pond to an observation deck. From there a footpath meanders close to the shore amid the reeds and berry bushes for more than a mile, dropping you high on a sand dune overlooking the ocean from 0.5 mile. The return is a walk along the ocean to the trailhead.

Begin at the trailhead kiosk. Your first ten steps from the parking area are like stepping behind a curtain into the wild. Look for marsh wrens darting among the cattails and bulrushes. Little more than a quarter mile in, a bench welcomes you to

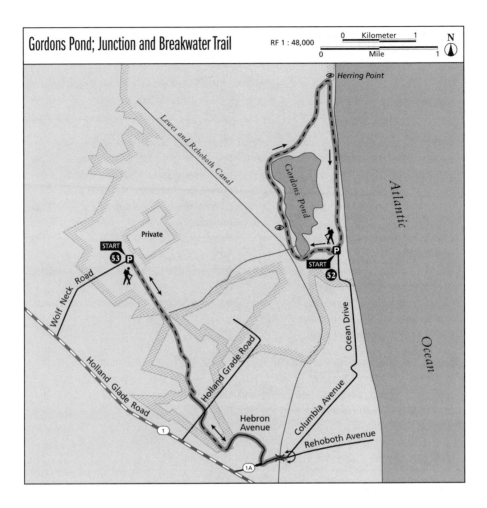

dawdle in the hope of seeing a willet in flight, flashing its distinctive black-and-white wing pattern.

Circling the pond's lower reaches, at about 0.5 mile there is a long view of a World War II watchtower a mile away. Except to Delawareans accustomed to the sight of them along the seashore, the towers seem a bit out of place in their surroundings. They were built to triangulate targets at sea, working in tandem with guns placed down the coast or on the water. An interpretive display tells the story.

Reach the observation deck at 0.7 mile. In winter you might be treated to the sight of showy snow geese. In summer great egrets, with their white plumage and black legs, ply the shallow waters. A splendid spot any time of year, the deck is downright dramatic during migration.

Leaving the deck, the trail narrows to a footpath and things get even quieter. Walking close to the pond, listening to the reeds rustle, lulled by the breezes, you might be startled by a sudden splash nearby as a bird dives for its supper. Along the way, where you least expect, some wise birder has placed a rustic bench several feet from the pond and a world away from everything else. It's a fine place to sit and listen.

At about 1.8 miles the trail enters a pine grove, which offers up the first shade of the hike. Just beyond, the trail climbs a low sand dune and emerges onto the open, dune-covered beach. Grasses, scrub pines, and berry bushes dot the dunes. The ocean is 0.25 mile over the sand. It's tempting to explore, but it's best to stay on the trail— and, by all means, off the grasses.

Follow the path left leading toward the overlook and building at Herring Point, just visible to the north. At 2.2 miles reach the beach at Herring Point. After a visit to the observation deck, walk south along the beach. You might share the beach with a few trucks, as there is vehicle access for fishing.

At 3.5 miles reach Cape Henlopen State Park's south beach. If you haven't stopped along the way for a swim yet, now is the chance. From the beach it is 175 yards up the path to the trailhead.

Miles and Directions

0.0 Start at trailhead kiosk.

0.7 Reach observation deck.

1.8 Trail enters pine grove.

1.9 Emerge onto dune-covered beach with ocean vistas.

2.2 Reach Herring Point scenic overlook; walk south along the beach.

3.5 Reach state park's south beach.

3.7 Meet access path to trailhead.

4.0 Arrive back at trailhead.

Options: Hike to the overlook (0.7 mile) or the dunes (1.9 miles), and return by the same route.

53 Junction and Breakwater Trail, Cape Henlopen State Park

This hike passes through scenic Holland Glade, highlighted by a scenic overlook on a wooden bridge with views of marshland and the ocean in the distance. It follows a wide graded trail through coastal forest and farm fields.

See map on page 188
Location: The Wolf Neck–Holland Glade section of Cape Henlopen State Park is a greenway connecting Rehoboth Beach and Lewes, Delaware.
Type of hike: 6.4-mile out-and-back.
Difficulty: Easy.
Season: Year-round.
Fees and permits: Deposit $3.00 per car state park entrance fee in box.
Maps: USGS Cape Henlopen, Delaware.
Special considerations: At the date of this

publication, the Junction and Breakwater Trail was still in development. Plans show the trail eventually connecting with Lewes, making possible a long loop hike with a return using the Gordons Pond Trail. Check the Delaware State Parks Web site for updates.
Camping: No camping is available.
For more information: Cape Henlopen State Park.
Trailhead facilities: Information kiosk and park area map.

Finding the trailhead: You can begin this hike at The Grove Park at Shaw Circle in Rehoboth Beach, or you can start at the Wolf Neck Road trailhead. To reach Wolf Neck Road from Rehoboth Beach, travel northwest on Delaware Route 1 about 2 miles. Turn right onto Wolf Neck Road just beyond Midway and just before the junction with Delaware Highway 24. Follow Wolf Neck Road about a mile to the trailhead parking on right.

The Hike

For many visitors to Delaware beaches, the stretch of Route 1 from Lewes to Rehoboth Beach gives the impression that Sussex County's natural values have been completely overrun by commerce. Little do they know that the western reaches of Cape Henlopen State Park extend practically to the back lot of the stores along the strip. Hiding from the sounds of travelers and shoppers are glades, marshes, and pine forests leading all the way to the ocean. You can dodge the heat of the day along a trail that ducks in and out of pine-holly groves and hedgerows. You can skirt a cornfield and watch a hawk hunt among the rows. Best of all is the rest stop at the wooden bridge over Holland Glade.

From the trailhead kiosk, walk down the gravel path through the field, then through the tree canopy to reach the Junction and Breakwater Trail. Turn right and walk among loblolly pines, chestnut oaks, and hollies on a wide, crushed-stone path. The trail is plenty wide for two people to walk side by side while passing twosomes coming from the opposite direction. In the coastal woods astride the trail, birds dart

A hiker pauses to enjoy the marsh and waterfowl at Holland Glade. PHOTO COURTESY OF
DELAWARE DIVISION OF PARKS AND RECREATION/DNREC

in and out of the berry bushes. Occasionally you are surprised by the unlikely sight
of shorebirds poking around in the woods.

At 0.9 mile the trail emerges into sudden open sky as you cross Holland Glade
on a magnificent wooden bridge that doubles as a wayside rest stop. The view of
shore grasses waving in the breeze stretches to the horizon. If the morning mist has
burned off, you can see the ocean just above the horizon. Leaving the bridge, the
trail enters woods just as suddenly as it had emerged. There is the smell of pine and
crape myrtle and the red of sumac berries in season. Over the next mile a theme
emerges: into the woods for a spell, then into daylight as the trail skirts cropland.
When the field is planted in corn, the sense of solitude is heightened. Other than
the birds and the breeze, the only sound in summer is the occasional small plane—
usually pulling an advertisement over land on its return trip.

At 1.8 miles turn right toward "the outlets" at the trail marker, and follow the
trail through the field toward the road. Don't bear right at the Y toward Route 1
(DE 1). Cross Holland Glade Road at 2.0 miles, and follow the trail as it wends

through the woods. The path skirts The Tides Condominiums—you're leaving the glades and marshes behind, but the walk is altogether pleasant.

Reach a paved trail abutting cinder-block buildings at 2.5 miles, and follow it to Hebron Avenue at 2.6 miles. Turn left; follow Hebron Avenue to the north end of the road and turn right onto the sidewalk at 2.8 miles. At the end of this road (3.0 miles) turn right and make an immediate left at the fork onto Rehoboth Avenue.

At 3.1 miles reach the drawbridge over the canal. The Grove Park is on the left, about 100 yards beyond the bridge. After visiting the park, retrace your steps to the trailhead.

Miles and Directions

- **0.0** Start at trailhead on Wolf Neck Road.
- **0.2** Reach Junction and Breakwater Trail; turn right.
- **0.9** Cross Holland Glade bridge—a perfect rest stop—and reenter the woods.
- **1.8** Turn right at trail marker.
- **2.0** Cross Holland Glade Road, and follow trail through the woods.
- **2.6** Reach Hebron Avenue; turn left and continue to end of road.
- **2.8** Turn right onto sidewalk.
- **3.0** At end of road turn right and then immediate left onto Rehoboth Avenue.
- **3.1** Reach Lewes and Rehoboth Canal drawbridge.
- **3.2** Rest awhile at The Grove Park before retracing your steps.
- **6.4** Arrive back at the trailhead.

Options: Here is the ultimate way to enjoy the Junction and Breakwater Trail: Drive to the trailhead and walk the trail into Rehoboth; then rent a bike in Rehoboth to pedal back to the car. Or take the Delaware Resort Transit bus to the trailhead and walk into Rehoboth.

54 Burton's Island Loop, Delaware Seashore State Park

An easy, interpretive hike on boardwalks, sand, and soft upland soil through salt marsh and coastal forest. With good facilities near the trailhead and interesting options, a walk on the nature trail at Burton's Island makes a great family outing.

Location: Burton's Island is just north of Indian River Inlet in Delaware Seashore State Park, 50 miles southeast of Dover and 7.5 miles south of Rehoboth Beach.
Type of hike: 1.5-mile loop.
Difficulty: Easy.
Season: October through May.
Fees and permits: No fees or permits required.
Maps: USGS Bethany Beach, Delaware.

Special considerations: Bring binoculars for birding and insect repellent during summer.
Camping: Camping is available; a fee is required.
For more information: Delaware Seashore State Park.
Trailhead facilities: On the access road, about 150 yards before the trailhead, there are restrooms, a snack bar, picnic tables, telephones, and an observation deck.

Finding the trailhead: From Rehoboth Beach, travel 7.5 miles south on Delaware Highway 1, and exit to the right into Delaware Seashore State Park Marina, just north of Indian River Inlet Bridge. Turn right at the park office and proceed on Inlet Road 0.5 mile past the marina and public boat storage area to trailhead parking.

The Hike

Burton's Island is the largest island in an archipelago of small islands that separates Rehoboth Bay from Indian River Bay, just behind the barrier beach of Delaware Seashore State Park. This easy 1.5-mile walk around the island affords great views of inland bays and close-up observations of the creatures of the salt marsh and upland forest. From boardwalks over tidal creeks, you will see wading shorebirds, muskrat tracks, and skittering fiddler crabs as well as ospreys, great blue herons, and egrets gliding over the wetland grasses. A shady picnic table on the Indian River Bay shoreline is a perfect place for lunch. Bring the kids!

From the trailhead, cross the causeway to Burton's Island and proceed on hard and soft sand through short cedars and marsh grass. To the right, out across the marsh, look for osprey on a nesting platform. Nearly extinct thirty years ago, ospreys—or fish hawks—have made a strong comeback and may now be seen nesting and fishing all along the Delaware coast.

At 0.2 mile the return loop intersects from the left. Continue right to a boardwalk at 0.3 mile, one of several that cross the tidal marshlands. At low tide look for muskrat tracks or watch a retreating fiddler crab disappear into a hole in the mud, waving his oversized claw. This is also a good place to gaze across the marshland flats,

Burton's Island Loop

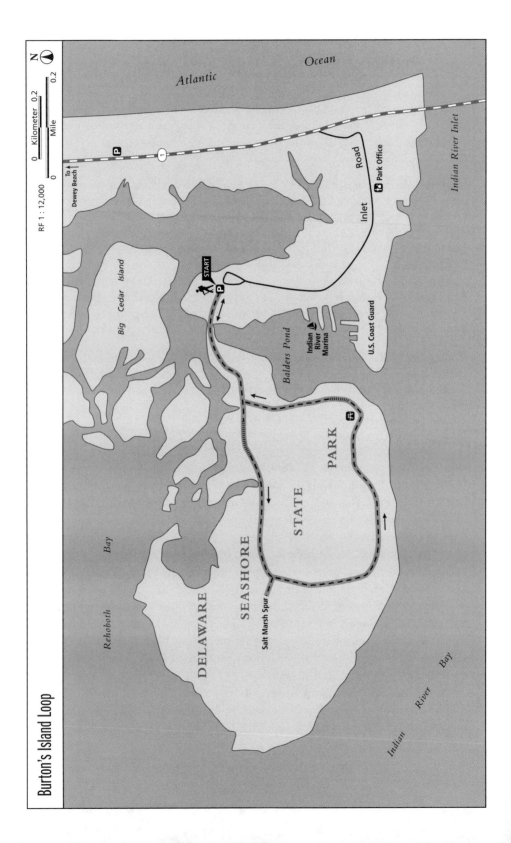

where sandpipers, herons, and egrets feed in the spawning grounds of crab, bluefish, and flounder.

After the boardwalk the trail enters a shady grove of cedar, pine, and holly, at 0.4 mile. Here the path changes from sandy to a soft upland soil that supports a more varied community of trees, vines, and shrubs. At 0.5 mile the trail bends left at a short spur. A 10-yard detour takes you into the marsh for wide-open views and, if you wish, a few steps in the salty marsh grass. This is another great spot for heron watching.

Back on the trail, wind through woods and wetlands to a sandy rise at 0.8 mile. Here a picnic table sits in the shade overlooking a narrow beach on Indian River Bay. Refreshing breezes and a lovely view of the inland bay make this an ideal spot to rest, eat, or daydream.

The trail continues along the beach for 30 yards before entering the woods and then crossing a boardwalk with the marina to the right. At 1.3 miles the trail completes the island loop. Turn right and proceed on the sandy trail back to the causeway and the trailhead.

Miles and Directions

0.0 Start at trailhead 0.5 mile past marina.

0.2 Return loop intersects from left; continue right.

0.3 Reach boardwalk; Rehoboth Bay salt marsh.

0.4 Enter cedar, pine, and holly grove.

0.5 Trail bends left at short spur. Take 10-yard detour into a salt marsh before returning to trail.

0.8 Reach Indian River Bay beach; trail continues along beach 30 yards, then enters woods and crosses boardwalk.

1.3 Reach loop junction; turn right and proceed back to trailhead.

1.5 Arrive back at trailhead.

Options: Swim in the Atlantic or walk along the shore at a guarded swimming beach on the south side of Indian River Inlet. Walk the docks of the active marina, just south of the trailhead.

55 Seahawk Nature Trail, Holts Landing State Park

On the shore of one of Delaware's inland bays, a walk along the edges of marsh, pond, forest, meadow, and bay shore.

Location: Holts Landing State Park is in Sussex County, Delaware, on Indian River Bay, about 6 miles northwest of Bethany Beach.
Type of hike: 1.7-mile loop.
Difficulty: Easy.
Season: Year-round.
Fees and permits: Fee of $3.00 collected during summer and on weekends and holidays in spring and fall.

Maps: USGS Bethany Beach, Delaware.
Special considerations: Check trailhead information board for information on trail closures due to shorebird nesting.
Camping: Youth camping only.
For more information: Holts Landing State Park.
Trailhead facilities: Restrooms, picnic pavilion, shady picnic areas.

Finding the trailhead: From Delaware Highway 1 in Bethany Beach, travel west 3.5 miles on Delaware Highway 26 to White's Neck Road (Road 347). Turn right onto White's Neck Road, go 2 miles, and turn right onto Road 346. Go 0.4 mile to the Holts Landing State Park entrance, and continue 0.7 mile to trailhead parking at the ball field.

The Hike

Seahawk Nature Trail does not cover a lot of ground, but the lands it does cross are quite diverse. From sandy beach to wildflower meadow, from salt marsh to freshwater ponds and poplar groves, the path winds through many worlds. Short, easy, and interesting, this is a great trail for introducing children to the outdoors.

From the parking lot, cross the ball field toward the bay and the log gateway marked SEAHAWK NATURE TRAIL. The path begins by crossing a grassy flat and a short bridge, and then follows the shoreline of Indian River Bay. Proceed on a narrow, wild beach with beach grass and marsh on the left and the shallow inland bay on the right, the first of the many "edges" you will encounter. Just 0.1 mile into the hike, you have already reached a nice view of the bay, its far shore to the north, and Burton's Island to the east.

Continue along the beach, and follow the trail left at the osprey nest platform and into a broad meadow busy with bees, butterflies, and wildflowers in spring. At 0.3 mile the trail splits to the right, crossing the meadow to a stand of loblolly pines and then following the forest edge.

The trail then cuts left, back across the meadow, and soon follows yet another margin, this between a forest of pines, oaks, and dogwoods on the right and a pond and marsh on the left. As with all edges, this one is teeming with life. Songbirds dart in and out of the woods, a squawking blue heron sails above the trees and perches on a pine branch over the pond, and egrets wade carefully in the dark, shallow water

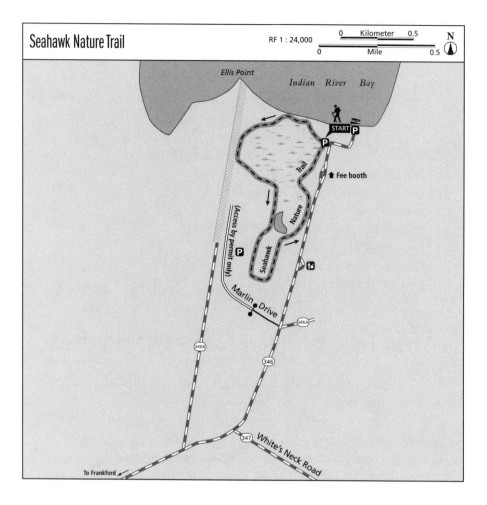

RF 1 : 24,000

0   Kilometer   0.5

0   Mile   0.5

N

Ellis Point

Indian River Bay

START P

P

P

Fee booth

Seahawk Nature Trail

(Access by permit only)

P

Marlin Drive

346A

346B

346

347 White's Neck Road

To Frankford

while jabbing for minnows and frogs. Along a row of phragmites, the invasive and pervasive marsh reed, the trail bends right into the woods at 0.5 mile, and continues through skinny pines, maples, and sweet gum.

A pond on the left, at 0.7 mile, is partially hidden by a hedgerow of pine and oak. At the end of the pond, the trail begins a 0.5-mile rectangular "loop"—or box—through the woods that will lead back to this spot. Follow the well-marked trail to the right, proceed about 50 yards, and then go left, traveling through a young stand of poplars growing in the shade of oaks and pines. The trail intermittently crosses primitive camping clearings, turns left at 1.0 mile, turns quickly left again, and then returns to the beginning of the box at the pond shore, at 1.2 miles.

Follow the trail to the right, and proceed between two ponds dotted with bird-houses mounted on posts. The houses provide nesting sites for wood ducks and other cavity nesters, birds that typically nest in now-rare climax forests. The metal collars on the posts protect the ducks' eggs from raccoons and snakes. In the light of day, it is unlikely that you will see those predators lurking around the ponds, but the sunning turtles will wait a long time before they slide off their logs into the dark green water.

The trail bends around the pond on the left and then breaks into the woods to the right, emerging in a clearing near the fee booth at 1.4 miles. The path bends left at the edge of the clearing, cuts back into the trees, and winds through the forest to the trailhead.

Miles and Directions

0.0 Start at trailhead at ball field.

0.1 Reach view of Indian River Bay, then continue along the beach.

0.3 Trail splits to right.

0.7 Reach woodland pond; at end of pond, trail begins loop.

1.2 Return to beginning of woodland pond loop.

1.4 Emerge into clearing near fee booth.

1.7 Arrive back at trailhead.

56 Paul Leifer Nature Trail, Furnace Town Historic Site

A short, easy walk through bald cypress swamps and upland forests in The Nature Conservancy's beautiful, 3,000-acre Nassawango Creek Preserve.

Location: Furnace Town Living Heritage Museum is in Worcester County, Maryland, 135 miles southeast of Washington, D.C., and 15 miles southeast of Salisbury, Maryland.
Type of hike: 1.0-mile loop.
Difficulty: Easy.
Season: Fall and winter.
Fees and permits: $4.00 entrance fee in season.

Maps: USGS Snow Hill, Maryland.
Special considerations: Bring insect repellent in summer; check for ticks after your hike.
Camping: No camping is available.
For more information: Furnace Town Foundation.
Trailhead facilities: Restrooms and a nature shop at the visitor center, April through October.

Finding the trailhead: From the Salisbury, Maryland, bypass, travel 13.5 miles southeast on Maryland Highway 12 and turn right onto Old Furnace Town Road. Proceed 1 mile to Furnace Town parking on the left. The trail begins in the historic village at the old Nassawango Iron Furnace.

The Hike

Before European settlement, much of the farm country of the Delmarva Peninsula was a vast forest. Along the creeks of southeastern Maryland, the woodlands were lush groves of giant bald cypress, Atlantic white cedar, and loblolly pine. There were lady's slippers and other orchids, butterflies and salamanders, hawks and warblers,

Furnace Town Historic Site and the adjacent Nature Conservancy Preserve connect natural and human history. PHOTO COURTESY OF FURNACE TOWN FOUNDATION INC.

otters and snakes. While much of the original forest has been cleared, a sliver much like the original survives on Nassawango Creek. Here, on the Paul Leifer Nature Trail in a Nature Conservancy preserve, you can walk among the old groves and see an especially rich community of wild creatures. Bring the kids. The trail is short and easy, and the forest is wonderfully diverse, active, and mysterious, making this a great introduction to the outdoors.

The short loop trail begins near the old brick furnace, used by settlers between 1828 and 1850 to make pig iron from bog iron ore dug from Nassawango Creek, oyster shells from the bay, and charcoal produced from the surrounding woodlands. From a tended lawn at the base of the furnace, the path enters a forest that was clear-cut from 1825 to 1850. In just a few steps, you truly are in the woods. The loblolly pines are giants, the birdsong is sweet, and the forest floor is dense with groves and tangles. Beneath the old, thick-trunked pines are maples and oaks, sweet gums and sassafras. Holly, highbush blueberry, and sweet pepperbush form a lush understory. And springing up at trailside are jack-in-the-pulpits, cranefly orchids, and the luscious flower of the pink lady's slipper orchid.

At the preserve boundary, at 0.2 mile, the trail bends and winds through holly groves, soon crossing a series of boardwalks through a bald cypress swamp. An aquatic tree, the bald cypress sends many of its roots up for air rather than down into the soaked, oxygen-poor soil. From the boardwalks, at 0.3 mile, look to the left where

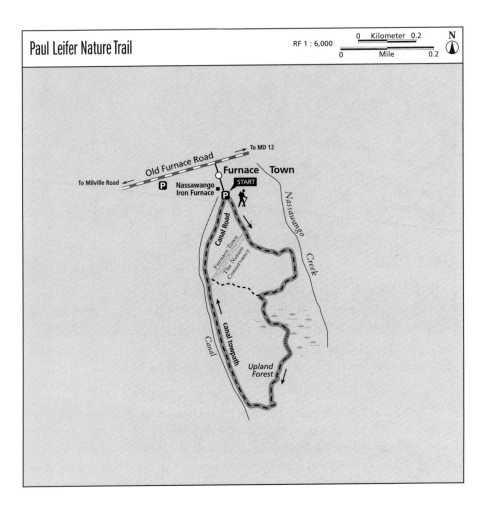

To MD 12

Old Furnace Road

Furnace Town

To Milville Road

START

P   Nassawango
Iron Furnace

P

Nassawango Creek

Canal Road

Furnace Town
The Nature
Conservancy

canal towpath

Canal

Upland
Forest

the knobby roots—or "knees"—rise up out of the shallows. Along with swamps in southern Delaware, the Nassawango swamps are home to the northernmost stands of bald cypress in North America.

After the boardwalks the trail leaves the wetlands and enters the drier upland forest at 0.4 mile. Here the path is covered in holly leaves and spiny sweet gum balls, and the woods are thick with ferns and Muscadine grapevines. The birds are lively, and there are deep shade and dappled sunlight. Proceed through the woods to Furnace Town Canal, and turn right onto the canal towpath at 0.6 mile. Follow the towpath back to the trailhead.

Dug in 1825, the mile-long canal carried barges from the creek to the furnace loaded with oyster and clam shells for smelting or with pig iron on its way up the Chesapeake to the port of Baltimore. Following the canal towpath with the forest on your right, look to the left for an interpretive sign pointing out an iron seep. Here iron-rich water sinks into the sandy streambed, forming the "bog iron" that drove the Furnace Town boom in the mid–1800s. Walking the towpath back to the furnace beneath the tall loblolly pines, be thankful that Nassawango Creek's iron was too impure to compete in the marketplace, ending a local industry that may very well have left little of the forest we enjoy today.

Miles and Directions

0.0   Start at trailhead at iron furnace.

0.2   Reach preserve boundary; continue on trail.

0.3   Cross series of swamp boardwalks.

0.4   Trail enters upland forest.

0.6   Turn right onto canal towpath.

1.0   Arrive back at trailhead.

57 Pocomoke State Forest Hiking Trail

An easy loop hike through the woodlands and along the swamps of the Pocomoke State Forest on Maryland's Eastern Shore.

Location: Pocomoke State Forest and Park is in Worcester County, Maryland, about 140 miles southeast of Washington, D.C., and 22 miles southeast of Salisbury, Maryland.
Type of hike: 4.5-mile loop.
Difficulty: Easy.
Season: October through April.
Fees and permits: No fees or permits required.

Maps: USGS Snow Hill, Maryland.
Special considerations: Where the trail is grassy, ticks are plentiful.
Camping: Camping is available at nearby Milburn Landing State Park.
For more information: Pocomoke State Forest.
Trailhead facilities: None.

Finding the trailhead: Travel 16 miles south on Maryland Highway 12 from the Salisbury bypass. Turn right onto Nassawango Road (also called River Road) and proceed 5 miles to Camp Road, a dirt road on the right just after the Nassawango Country Club. Turn right onto Camp Road, and go 0.6 mile to trailhead parking on the left.

The Hike

The Pocomoke River runs through southeastern Maryland from southern Delaware down to the northern border of Virginia. Before emptying into the Chesapeake Bay at Pocomoke Sound, the river drains the fertile farmlands west of Ocean City and the deep, shady woods of southern Worcester County. In Pocomoke State Forest, you can experience the river's wilder side as you walk among the pine, poplar, magnolia, and mountain laurel that flourish on its banks.

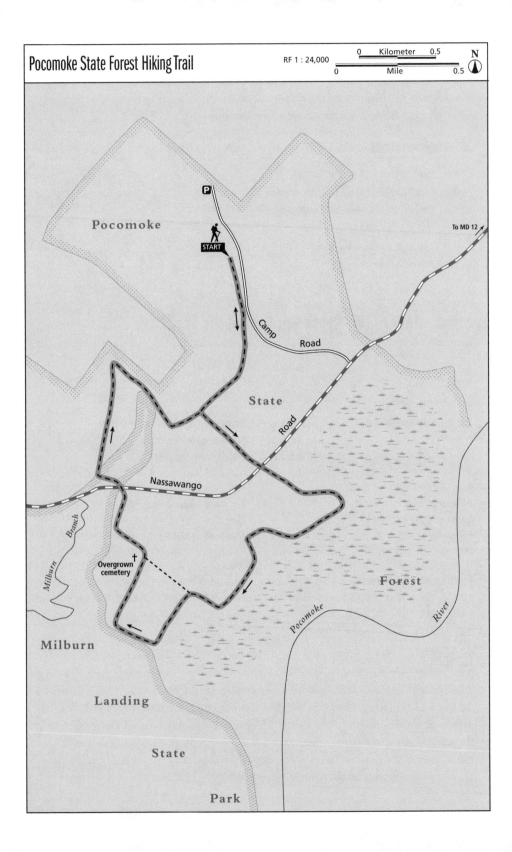

Pocomoke State Forest Hiking Trail

RF 1 : 24,000

Kilometer
0   0.5

Mile
0   0.5

N

Pocomoke

To MD 12

P

START

Camp

Road

State

Road

Nassawango

Milburn Branch

Overgrown
cemetery

Forest

Pocomoke

River

Milburn

Landing

State

Park

From the parking lot, turn right on Camp Road and proceed 0.3 mile to the trailhead on the right. Cross a shallow gully, and walk into the woods following white blazes. The forest along the dirt road and the footpath is a classic example of the diverse mix of trees in Maryland's coastal-plain woodlands.

Loblolly pines, common in the South, are growing with hardwoods, common in the piedmont to the north. There are sweet gum, sassafras, and oak as well as a lush evergreen understory of holly and sweetbay magnolia. In spring the blossoming mountain laurel is particularly showy.

Walking the footpath, you are soon traveling through holly groves in the shade of the oaks and pines. At 0.6 mile the trail bends left and can be a bit wet for a stretch. With the branches of young sweet gums and oaks offering shade, you may have to step over ruts in the trail that often hold enough water to harbor bugs, frogs, and tadpoles in the spring. But the path levels and grows grassy before long, and soon the going is easy again.

At 0.9 mile the trail crosses Nassawango Road. Duck under the gates on either side, and proceed on the white-blazed footpath with young, skinny pines on the left and a mixed forest on the right. Pass a bench where the pines begin to give way to hardwoods, and follow the trail as it bends left through mountain laurel and descends slightly into a grove of big tulip trees on the edge of the Pocomoke River wetlands at 1.2 miles.

Turn right, and travel along the edge of the forested wetlands. This is a very nice stretch. The tulip trees are tall and stately, and where they dominate, the ground is carpeted in ferns. In some places loblolly pines mix in, and at others the groves of holly and laurel are dense. At 1.7 miles the trail bends left, descending slightly to cross a streambed on an old, mossy culvert, and then ascends, bending right, into a more spacious wood where you can see far down the trail and into the trees.

At 2.1 miles the trail dips into a grassy meadow and forks. Turn left, following white blazes (if you go straight here, the trail does rejoin the loop, but it misses a nice stretch of forest and an old graveyard hidden in the woods), and proceed through another lovely grove of tulip trees and fern meadows. At 2.4 miles the trail turns right and then, shortly, right again at a log bench in a small clearing. Proceed into the woods, staying right and following white blazes.

On the left, at 2.8 miles, is an old, overgrown cemetery, where the mostly illegible gravestones collect moss or lay toppled against trees. For all its eeriness, the graveyard is a surprisingly lively place. There are white-tailed deer about, birds flitting in the sapling branches, and a busy hive of bees buzzing around a long crack in the trunk of an old loblolly pine.

Just after the cemetery, the trail travels through tall grasses, turns left into the woods, and then turns right, heading back to Nassawango Road. The trail is grassy here and infested with ticks. You may want to stop and pick them off as you go.

At 3.2 miles cross Nassawango Road, turn left, and pick up the trail on the right, where it continues through the woods to the forest boundary at 3.7 miles. At the boundary are a bench and a field visible through a thicket. The trail turns sharply right here, following white blazes and continuing through the forest. At 3.9 miles the trail bends to the right and then splits sharply left. Although this section of the trail is narrow, it is well marked. Follow it through the woods to the beginning of the loop trail; turn left and proceed to Camp Road at 4.2 miles. Turn left onto Camp Road and return to the parking area.

Miles and Directions

0.0 Start at trailhead parking on Camp Road; turn right onto road.

0.3 Reach trailhead on right.

0.9 Cross Nassawango Road; proceed on white-blazed footpath.

1.2 Enter Pocomoke River wetlands, fringed by a grove of tulip trees.

1.7 Trail bends left, descend slightly to cross streambed on culvert.

2.1 Turn left at fork, following white blazes.

2.8 Reach overgrown cemetery. Just after cemetery turn left into woods, then turns right heading back to Nassawango Road.

3.2 Cross Nassawango Road; turn left and pick up trail on right.

3.7 Reach forest boundary and bench.

3.9 Forest trail turnoff; trail bends to right and then splits sharply right.

4.2 Reach Camp Road; turn left.

4.5 Arrive back at parking area.

58 Milburn Cypress Nature Trail, Milburn Landing State Park

A short but enchanting walk through one of the northernmost stands of bald cypress in the United States. You may not think to drive all the way from Baltimore or Washington, D.C., for this quick stroll—but it just might be worth it. This hike is ideal for a short detour en route to the beach.

Location: Pocomoke River State Park is in Worcester County, Maryland, about 145 miles southeast of Washington, D.C.
Type of hike: 1.0-mile loop.
Difficulty: Easy.
Season: September through May.
Fees and permits: No fees or permits required.
Maps: USGS Pocomoke City, Maryland.

Special considerations: The environment here is extremely fragile; stay on the trail.
Camping: Developed campsites and small cabins are available; registration and a fee are required.
For more information: Pocomoke State Forest.
Trailhead facilities: Comfort station.

Finding the trailhead: From Salisbury, Maryland, travel south on Maryland Highway 12 for about 13 miles from the Salisbury Bypass. Turn right onto Nassawango Road and go 6 miles; turn left into Milburn Landing State Park. Turn right onto the boat launch access road, following signs to the launch. The trailhead is at the opposite end of the parking area from the river. Look for a big sign.

The Hike

This hike is very short and is out of the way for most hikers, except for local residents and visitors to the family campground. Although your leg muscles will forget the walk before you have left the park, the magic of the swampland is, without exaggeration, unforgettable.

From the nature trail sign, enter pine forest and bear right at the fork. Giant loblolly pines grow straight to a towering height of 80 feet, forming the upper story above some of the tallest holly trees you will ever see.

Cross the park road at 0.3 mile and, 175 yards farther, reach the cypress swamp. The bald cypress grow in shallow, brackish swamps. To keep from drowning, the root systems develop knobby, kneelike outcrops that protrude from the water. These "bald" knees are the tree's breathing mechanism.

The trail is easy to follow; it would be difficult to get lost. Just plan to take longer to walk a mile than you usually do, because you will continually stop in wonder. Follow the signs and blazes. Cross the park road again at 0.7 mile, passing beneath the white pines and more loblolly. At the fork turn right to return to the parking lot.

Milburn Cypress Nature Trail

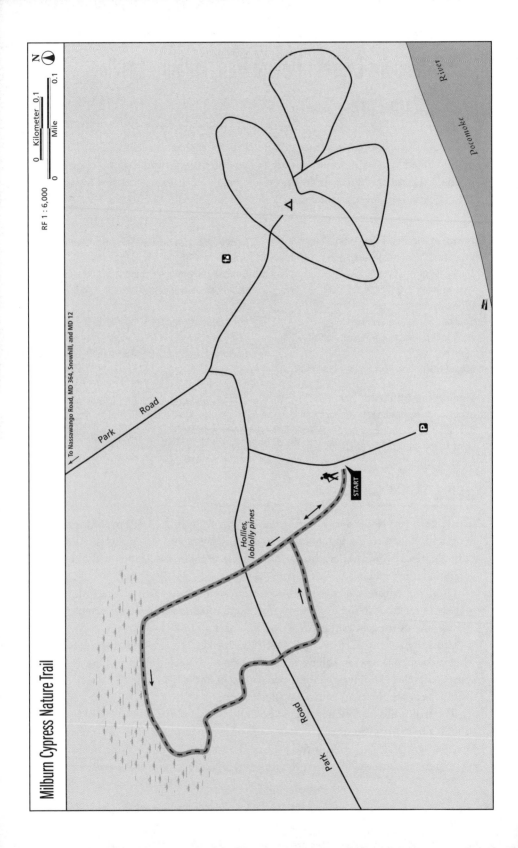

RF 1 : 6,000

N

To Nassawango Road, MD 364, Snowhill, and MD 12

Park Road

Hollies, loblolly pines

START

P

Park Road

Pocomoke River

Maryland's wide tidal creeks are a distinctive feature of the Chesapeake Bay region. PHOTO COURTESY OF MARYLAND DNR

Miles and Directions

0.0 Start at nature trail sign; bear right at fork.

0.2 Stroll through hollies and loblolly pines.

0.3 Cross park road.

0.4 Reach cypress swamp.

0.7 Cross park road again.

1.0 Arrive back at trailhead.

59 Trap Pond State Park Loop

An easy circuit hike on three park trails in a forest of stately conifers and hardwoods. Circle a pond and bald cypress swamp, the northernmost stand of bald cypress trees in the United States.

Location: Trap Pond State Park is in southwestern Sussex County, about 55 miles south of Dover and 5 miles east of Laurel, off Delaware Highway 24.
Type of hike: 4.8-mile loop.
Difficulty: Easy.
Season: Year-round.
Fees and permits: Entrance fees daily May 31 through October 31; $3.00 per car for state residents, $5.00 for nonresidents.
Maps: USGS Trap Pond, Delaware; state park map.

Special considerations: Entrance fees are required during summer and on weekends and holidays in May, September, and October. Wear a cap, and thoroughly check your scalp and skin for ticks after your hike. During summer, bring a cap and sunglasses for the road portion of the loop.
Camping: There are 142 campsites on the pond's northern shore, as well as eight cabins and two yurts.
For more information: Trap Pond State Park.
Trailhead facilities: Restrooms, bathhouse, telephone, picnic pavilion, nature center.

Finding the trailhead: From Delaware Seashore resorts, take Delaware Highway 1 North to Delaware Highway 24 and travel west 29.5 miles to Trap Pond Road. Turn left onto Trap Pond Road, and drive 1.2 miles to the main entrance of Trap Pond State Park. Turn left into the park, pass the entrance station, and continue 0.25 mile to the end of the bathhouse parking lot. The Trap Pond Loop begins along the shore of the pond beneath the log gateway marking the Island Trail trailhead.

The Hike

Tucked in the southwest corner of rural Sussex County, Trap Pond State Park is a jewel of a state park. Amid broad, flat fields of wheat and soybeans, the park protects a wonderful 3,500-acre parcel of wetlands, forest, and bald cypress swamp. In an afternoon on the park's trails, you can stroll through towering stands of loblolly pine and shady groves of oak, holly, dogwood, and sweet bay. Among the trees and swamps, bird life is abundant; walk quietly and you are likely to see kingfishers, ducks, great blue herons, ospreys, hawks, kestrels, and a great variety of songbirds. Where the trail hugs the shoreline of the pond, there are great views of tall, thin-trunked bald cypress with their knobby roots bulging out of the shallows.

The loop begins on Island Trail, a singletrack hiking path that runs parallel to the wide, sandy Boundary Trail to the right and the Trap Pond shoreline to the left. The trailhead is marked by a log gateway; the trail by directional markers.

This is a perfect place to enter the woods. For about 0.25 mile, the trail meanders through a lovely example of southern Delaware's lowland forest, with its canopy

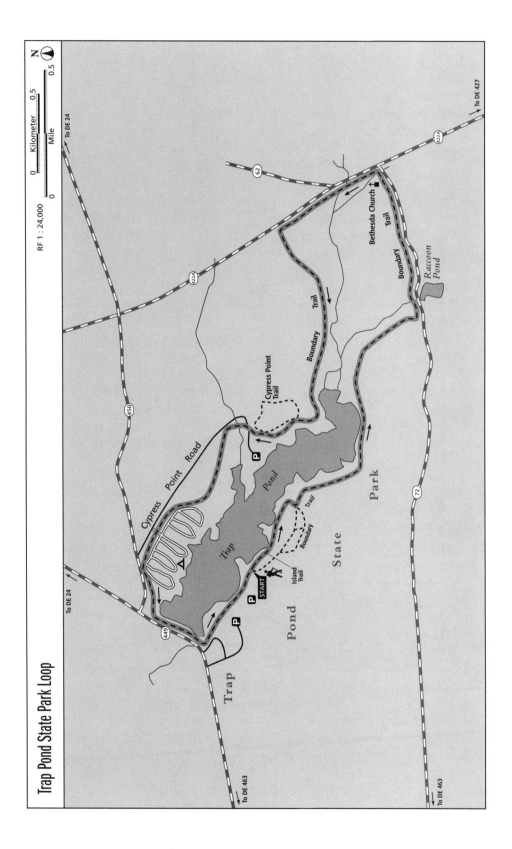

Trap Pond State Park Loop

RF 1 : 24,000

N

Kilometer   0   0.5

Mile   0   0.5

To DE 24

62

24

450

Cypress Point Road

To DE 24

449

P

P

Trap
Pond

Trap
Pond

Island
Trail

START

P

Boundary
Trail

Cypress Point
Trail

P

Boundary   Trail

State

Park

Bethesda Church
Trail

Boundary
Trail

Raccoon
Pond

72

To DE 463

To DE 463

To DE 427

of tall pines, oaks, and sweet gums and its ornamental, gardenlike understory of holly and sweet bay. The pine duff path runs along the shoreline and then bends deeper into the forest beneath abundant dogwoods, flowering white in spring and bearing red leaves and berries in autumn. A bridge crosses a sliver of bald cypress swamp, and then the trail rejoins the shoreline for open views of the pond. Along the water's edge, look for great blue herons, loons, and canvasback ducks, or peer up above the tree line for soaring ospreys or black vultures.

Island Trail turns sharply right just before a group camping area and crosses Boundary Trail at 0.4 mile. At the crossing turn left onto Boundary Trail. Bear right at the campground fork, and follow the wide, sandy path into a shady grove of tall, stately pines. A quarter of a mile farther, the trail bends left, drawing close to the pond and, rather suddenly, into a stand of mixed hardwoods. Look to the left through the trees to get a closer look at a majestic bald cypress stand and rows of turtles sunning on fallen logs.

The trail then bends away from the pond into a much thinner—and sunnier— pine grove; at 1.5 miles it meets Road 72 at Raccoon Pond. Turn left onto Road 72, passing Raccoon Pond on the right, and proceed around a bend past an old corncrib and down the arrow-straight roadway toward Bethesda Church, which you will reach at 2.0 miles. This 0.5 mile stretch of road could be much worse. There is little traffic on this rural route. To the right is a wide-open soybean field; to the left is a planted stand of pine, which makes up for its regimented look with the soothing music of the wind in its branches. In the middle of the day, it can get rather bright and hot here, so bring a hat, sunglasses, and a little extra water to help you stay cool.

Bethesda Church is worth 0.5 mile on the road. Built in 1878, the weathered clapboard church sits abandoned in a clearing, surrounded by nineteenth-century gravestones. The church's tall windows are shuttered, wildflowers shoot up through the brick walkway, and the headstones bear wonderful carvings and interesting epitaphs. This is a great place to pause for a rest and a quick look around.

Just past Bethesda Church, cross Thompson Branch and turn left onto Road 62. The road is straight for 0.25 mile, bends to the right, and then turns sharply left onto Road 422A at 2.3 miles. Proceed on the roadway, past several homesteads on the left and a wheat field on the right, to the Boundary Trail marker at 2.6 miles. Turn left into the woods.

Back in the forest, you will appreciate the strong pine scent, the soft duff underfoot, and the shade of the big tulip trees as you walk the straight path to Cypress Point Trail, at 3.3 miles. Cypress Point Trail is another marked nature trail; the short loop parallels Boundary Trail and then circles back into the woods. It is a little hard to find because it is marked for hikers traveling in the opposite direction. The first marker you see, on the left, is for a 50-yard path to the swamp. Take a look if you like. Then proceed on Boundary Trail another 200 yards. There you will see a marker on the right, at 3.4 miles. Go left here. You will quickly see the backside of a Cypress Point Trail marker (number 10) on the left.

Follow Cypress Point Trail along the edge of the pond for about 0.25 mile. It passes a boardwalk that extends into a bald cypress swamp, rejoins Boundary Trail for 50 yards, and then cuts back to the water's edge and a lovely spot for viewing the expanse of a bald cypress stand. This is the northernmost grove of this aquatic tree in the United States. Once an extensive bald cypress swamp, the area was logged and the swamp dammed to power a sawmill in the late 1700s. It was not until the 1930s that the federal government purchased 1,000 acres around the pond, and the forest began to recover. In this spot, to the left of a bench beneath a big pine, you can touch the soft, copper-colored bark of a giant bald cypress and feel the sturdiness that drew the attention of so many loggers.

At 3.9 miles cross a footbridge through a grove of sweet bay, and travel 250 yards to a youth group campground. Cut right across the campground parking lot to the entrance, follow the hard sandy road 200 yards, and then turn left at 4.4 miles into the woods on Boundary Trail. Follow the trail 0.25 mile to the public campground. Enter the campground, go 50 paces, and proceed through a post-and-rail walkway and across a bridge over a swampy branch. Turn left sharply; walk to the pond and follow the trail along the water's edge to the boat ramp at the far side of the campground. At the stop sign at 4.5 miles, turn left onto Road 449.

Follow Road 449 across the Trap Pond dam, which was rebuilt in the 1930s by the Civilian Conservation Corps. Look left for a great open view of the pond and the surrounding forest. Cross the spillway and turn left toward the park office and the beginning of the Trap Pond Loop.

Miles and Directions

- **0.0** Start at Island Trail trailhead.
- **0.4** Reach junction with Boundary Trail; turn left onto Boundary Trail.
- **1.5** Trail meets Road 72 at Raccoon Pond; turn left onto Road 72.
- **2.0** Reach Bethesda Church; just past church turn left onto Road 62.
- **2.3** Turn left onto Road 422A.
- **2.6** Reach Boundary Trail junction; turn left into woods.
- **3.3** Reach Cypress Point Trail junction; stay on Boundary Trail.
- **3.4** Turn left onto Cypress Point Trail.
- **3.7** Reach boardwalk.
- **3.9** Cross footbridge.
- **4.4** Turn left onto Boundary Trail after campground parking lot.
- **4.5** At stop sign, turn left onto Road 449; follow road across dam.
- **4.8** Arrive back at trailhead.

60 Nanticoke Wildlife Area Loop

An easy stroll through mixed hardwood and pine forest along the edges of fields and hedgerows. A nice blend of rural and woodland landscape.

Location: The Robert L. Graham Nanticoke Wildlife Area is in the southwest corner of Sussex County, Delaware, about 45 miles south of Dover and 5 miles west of Laurel.
Type of hike: 2.5-mile loop.
Difficulty: Easy.
Season: Year-round, except during deer hunting season.

Fees and permits: No fees or permits required.
Maps: USGS Sharptown, Delaware.
Special considerations: Do not hike during deer hunting season.
Camping: No camping is available.
For more information: Nanticoke Wildlife Area.
Trailhead facilities: None.

Finding the trailhead: From U.S. Highway 13, travel west on Delaware Highway 24 through Laurel and continue 1.2 miles to Road 494 (Old Sharptown Road). Turn right on Road 494 and, at 2.2 miles, bear left, staying on Road 494. Travel another 1.6 miles to the Nanticoke Wildlife Area entrance sign, and turn right on the access road. Proceed 0.2 mile to the parking area for deer stands 1 and 2, on the right.

The Hike

The Nanticoke Wildlife Area is primarily managed as a hunting area, and the trails are mostly travel routes to deer stands tucked into the wooded corners of small clearings. Hiking here during deer hunting season is not advised, but during the rest of the year walking the area's paths is thoroughly enjoyable. Passing through dense forest and along the edges of cultivated fields, the trails provide an opportunity to stroll in both bright, open spaces and shady groves.

From the parking area, continue up the access road on foot beneath the branches of big oaks. On the left, at 0.1 mile, is a nineteenth-century graveyard—the burial plot for the Adams family, presumably a clan of Sussex County farmers. The old white stones, some listing and propped up, sit among wildflowers beneath a cedar tree bearing birthdates as early as 1806 and inscriptions such as that on the stone of Hyram M. Collins, who died in 1852: IN FULL HOPE OF IMMORTALITY.

Just past the graveyard, follow the access road right and then turn right again onto the trail leading to deer stands 10 and 11. There is a barrier here that defines a small parking area for hunters. Proceed on the trail with the forest on the left and a wooded hedgerow backed by a small field on the right. For the next 0.6 mile you will walk along the edge of a typical coastal-plain forest of loblolly pines mixed with red maples, oaks, and sweet gums. Although this woodland community may be commonplace in Sussex County and the southern coastal region, it is hardly without charm. The tall loblollies are wonderfully fragrant and musical in the wind, the oaks

RF 1 : 24,000

0   Kilometer   0.5

0   Mile   0.5

N

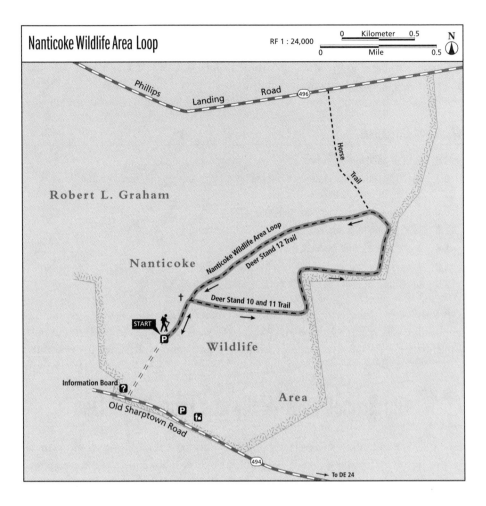

stand strong and majestic. The sweet gums, with their star-shaped leaves, medicinal sap, and prickly fruit, are distinctive and beautiful.

On the right, the trail passes wood-bordered fields lined with wildflowers in the spring. These open areas are prime habitat for birds and other wildlife who favor browsing in the fields and perching on its edges. It is no accident that most of the hunting stands sit just inside the woods on the margins of clearings; at dusk you are likely to see deer gather here. Areas such as these are also good places to watch and listen to birds.

At the end of the field, the trail crosses a concrete barrier at the wildlife area boundary, at 0.8 mile. Turn left here and follow the trail along the edge of a large cornfield on the right. Keeping to the field edge, the trail turns right, bends left at 1.3 miles, and soon breaks into the woods to an intersection with a marked horse path at 1.5 miles. Turn left onto the horse path, continue 100 yards, and then go left again on the trail to deer stand 12, where a gate blocks the path to stands 13 and 14.

The sun-dappled path winds through the woods and then passes a small clearing where you will see deer stand 12 in the back left corner. Beyond the clearing, the path is soft and grassy and passes through nice stands of oak and pine with spacious groves of holly growing beneath their sheltering branches. At 2.2 miles the trail crosses a barrier and joins the sandy access road leading back to the trailhead.

Miles and Directions

0.0 Start at trailhead at parking area.

0.1 Reach Adams family graveyard. Just past graveyard, turn right onto access road and then right again onto trail.

0.8 Come to wild area boundary; turn left.

1.5 Reach horse trail; turn left.

1.6 Deer stand 12 trail junction; turn left.

2.2 Cross barrier and join access road back to trailhead.

2.5 Arrive back at trailhead.

Options: If you like walking on rural roads, you could extend your circuit hike, continuing past stands 13 and 14 to Road 496, traveling west (left) on 496, and then south (left) on the unpaved access road for stands 15 and 16 back to the trailhead.

61 Old Schoolhouse–Holly Tree Loop, Wye Island

The Old Schoolhouse—Holly Tree Loop is an easy hike that showcases old-growth woods featuring towering trees, a beautiful tidal cove, and a 250-year-old holly tree.

Location: Wye Island Natural Resources Area is in Queen Anne County, Maryland, 20 miles east of the Chesapeake Bay Bridge, 5 miles off U.S. Highway 50.
Type of hike: 2.0-mile loop.
Difficulty: Easy.
Season: Year-round.
Fees and permits: No fees or permits required.

Maps: Queenstown, Maryland.
Special considerations: Wye Island Natural Resource Area is open to hunting; check the kiosks or at the office for schedules.
Camping: No camping is available.
For more information: Wye Island Natural Resource Area.
Trailhead facilities: Kiosk with trail map. Trail maps are for sale at the office.

Finding the trailhead: from the junction of US 50 and U.S. Highway 301 east of the Chesapeake Bay Bridge, go east on US 50 for 5 miles. Turn right onto Carmichael Road and travel about 5 miles; bear right onto Wye Island Road and cross the bridge onto the island. Follow signs to the park office on Wye Hall Road, or go directly to the trailhead, on the right a mile past the office road. Signs at each trailhead identify the trails reached from the lot.

Old Schoolhouse—Holly Tree Loop

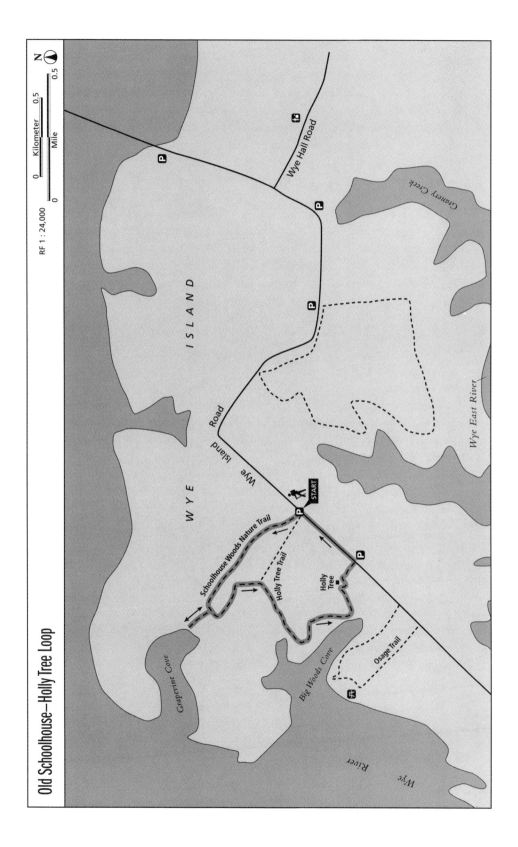

RF 1 : 24,000

N

Kilometer 0 0.5

Mile 0 0.5

ISLAND

WYE

Wye Island Road

Wye Hall Road

Cranberry Creek

Wye East River

Grapevine Cove

Schoolhouse Woods Nature Trail

Holly Tree Trail

Holly Tree

Big Woods Cove

Osage Trail

Wye River

START

The Hike

Wye Island Natural Resource Area is a wonderful spot for kids. Every trail offers a scenic reward for very little effort—most also include a visit to a cove or bay. This loop, which incorporates the Schoolhouse and Holly Tree Trails, travels through the largest remnant old-growth woods on Maryland's Eastern Shore. On the way to Grapevine Cove on the Wye River, the trail passes a small wetland pond where wood ducks can be seen in summer. The hike is topped with a stop at a huge holly tree older than the United States.

The trail enters the woods just behind the kiosk. Immediately you get the sense that you have entered the land of the giants. Oaks and poplars 15 feet around dominate. This remnant forest, left untouched when the land was cleared for pasture, is 0.5 mile long but only a couple hundred yards wide. Because it is so narrow, you don't get that feeling of utter darkness and isolation you might expect in such an old woods. Still, even on a bright day the sunlight does not penetrate to the ground. And unless you have been lucky enough to live in an area of old growth, you rarely see this many trees of this size.

Pass a wetland pond just outside the woods line at 0.2 mile. The pond is a low spot that drains the spongy forest floor. You might see a wood duck or perhaps a hawk hunting the fields just beyond the pond.

Reach the first of four wooden footbridges on a spur trail at 0.4 mile. The last bridge leads to a clearing at Grapevine Cove on the Wye River. If you have brought your gear, you can fish for bass. Or just find a soft spot in the leaf litter, have a seat, and watch the birds above the water.

Retrace your steps over the four bridges, then turn right. Follow the trail toward an opening in the woods. Just before entering the clearing, a blue-blazed trail sign leads left. Or step into the clearing and turn left to follow the woods line. In 300 yards pass through a hedgerow and turn right onto the Holly Tree Trail. Begin circling the field, with the woods line on your right.

At the end of the long field, Big Woods Cove is visible beyond the trees. The cove, a scenic location for a picnic lunch, is accessible by the Osage Trail.

The ancient Wye River Holly Tree is enclosed within a wooden fence at 1.5 miles. You can get up close and walk beneath it. Almost as noteworthy as the holly's age is its shape. We've become accustomed to manicured, conical holly trees. This one is round and stately, like a big white oak.

Leaving the holly, continue on the path to Holly Tree trailhead parking at 2.0 miles. Turn left and follow the unpaved, unhurried road back to the Schoolhouse Woods parking lot.

Miles and Directions

0.0 Start at trailhead, just behind the kiosk.

0.4 Cross first of four bridges.

0.5 The last bridge leads to a clearing at Grapevine Cove; retrace your steps over four bridges, then turn right.

0.9 Turn right onto Holly Tree Trail.

1.5 Reach Wye River Holly Tree.

2.0 Arrive back at trailhead.

Options: For a detour to Big Woods Cove, turn right on the road, walk 0.2 miles, and turn left onto Osage Trail. It's just over a quarter mile to the cove and a picnic.

62 Tuckahoe Creek Loop, Tuckahoe State Park

Tuckahoe Creek might be the quietest stream valley in Maryland, offering a rich diversity of trees, terrain, creeks and bogs, and passage through the Adkins Arboretum.

Location: Tuckahoe State Park is in Talbot County, Maryland, 8 miles west of Denton.
Type of hike: 5.3-mile loop.
Difficulty: Easy.
Season: Late summer through spring.
Fees and permits: No fees or permits required.
Maps: USGS Price; Ridgely, Maryland.
Special considerations: As in many other

Maryland Parks, there are managed hunting periods during deer season. Check with park office for information.
Camping: Tent sites and cabins are available through the park office.
For more information: Tuckahoe State Park.
Trailhead facilities: Park office has restrooms and a display of historical photographs.

Finding the trailhead: From the Maryland Route 50/301 split, 9.5 miles east of the Chesapeake Bay Bridge, take Route 50 east. Turn left onto Route 404 toward Denton and travel approximately 8 miles. Turn left onto Route 480 (Ridgely Road), then almost immediately turn left onto Eveland Road. The park entrance is 3 miles ahead on the left; the office is a white farmhouse.

The Hike

Follow the path behind the park office through the field and toward the woods in the distance. At the woods edge are two posts; one leading right to Arboretum Spur Trail, and the other pointing left toward Tuckahoe Creek. Turn right and enter a plantation of loblolly pines. It has been thinned to allow a variety of wildflowers and berry-bearing shrubs to create an understory. A spring runs alongside the trail here. If you take time to explore, you will see fox scat and the furry remains of their prey.

At 0.5 mile turn right at the junction of Tuckahoe Valley Trail; follow the blue blazes into a stand of beech and tall tulip poplars. In spring you will delight to the hundreds of "tulips" that drop from the poplars and scatter among the flowers on the forest floor. The woodland through here is remarkable for its silence. Busy MD

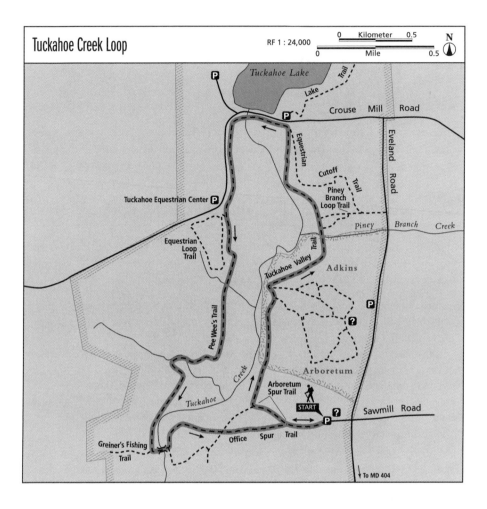

Tuckahoe Creek Loop

RF 1 : 24,000

0   Kilometer   0.5

0   Mile   0.5

N

Tuckahoe Lake

Lake Trail

Crouse   Mill   Road

Eveland Road

Equestrian

Cutoff

Piney Branch Loop Trail

Trail

Piney   Branch   Creek

Tuckahoe Equestrian Center

Equestrian Loop Trail

Tuckahoe Valley Trail

Adkins

Pee Wee's Trail

Arboretum

Creek

Arboretum Spur Trail

START

Sawmill   Road

Tuckahoe

Office   Spur   Trail

Greiner's Fishing Trail

To MD 404

404, 3 miles south, might be packed with cars heading toward the beaches, but the land surrounding the park is rural to the roots. This is quiet.

Entering Adkins Arboretum, a number of winding trails intersect Tuckahoe Valley Trail, creating several opportunities for diversions. The Creekside Trail departs from Tuckahoe Valley Trail at 1.1 miles; it follows the creek for a few hundred yards then rejoins Tuckahoe Valley Trail. Adkins Arboretum is worthy of an extended detour. The well-marked paths lead through a variety of habitats native to the Delmarva Peninsula. The facility, owned by the state of Maryland and managed by a nonprofit organization, is one of a few in the region dedicated to restoring and stewarding native forests and meadows. Maps are available at the visitor center.

It seems no hike is complete without crossing a stream called Piney Branch (or some other Piney name). Cross the stream on a footbridge, leaving arboretum lands. Just beyond, at 1.7 miles, is the first junction with Piney Branch Loop Trail. Turn left and follow the wide path through mature stands of hardwoods just above the creek.

Emerge from the woods at Crouse Mill Road at 2.3 miles, turning left toward scenic Tuckahoe Lake. The boat rental concession is just across the road beside the lake. You can take some time to paddle around the lake, or put in below the dam and float back.

After taking time to enjoy the lake, continue past the lake, turning left on the road and following it 0.25 mile to the equestrian center. Here pick up Pee Wee's Trail and follow it through an old field in succession to a new forest. For the next couple of miles, enjoy the easy terrain changes as you walk into and out of the forest and cross two small streams.

Reach Greiner's Fishing Trail at 4.3 miles. Turn left onto Tuckahoe Valley Trail, and climb a small hill from the creek to a junction with the Office Spur Trail at 4.8 miles. Go straight; wander through tall loblolly pines to reach the clearing where you started, at the junction with the Arboretum Spur Trail. Retrace your steps through the field 0.25 mile to trailhead parking.

Miles and Directions

0.0 Start at trailhead behind park office.

0.5 Junction with Tuckahoe Valley Trail; turn right.

1.1 Adkins Arboretum; Creekside Trail separates from Tuckahoe Valley Trail.

1.7 Reach first junction with Piney Branch Loop Trail; turn left.

2.3 Emerge from woods at Crouse Mill Road; turn left toward Tuckahoe Lake.

2.6 Reach equestrian center; pick up Pee Wee's Trail.

4.3 Reach Greiner's Fishing Trail, Tuckahoe Creek. Turn left on Tuckahoe Valley Trail.

4.8 Come to junction with Office Spur Trail; go straight.

5.3 Arrive back at trailhead.

Options: Hike north from the office or from Route 404, then rent a canoe at the concession at Tuckahoe Lake for your return. Or begin your hike at the arboretum and make their trail system a part of your loop.

Appendix A: Resources

Maryland

American Chestnut Land Trust
Box 204
Port Republic, MD 20676
(410) 586–1570

Antietam National Battlefield
P.O. Box 158
Sharpsburg, MD 21782-0158
(301) 432–5124

Bear Branch Nature Center
300 John Owings Road
Westminster, MD 21158
(410) 848–2517

Blackwater National Wildlife Refuge
2145 Key Wallace Drive
Cambridge, MD 21613
(410) 228–2677

Calvert Cliffs State Park
c/o Point Lookout State Park
P.O. Box 48
Scotland, MD 20687
(301) 872–5688

C&O National Historical Park
P.O. Box 4
Sharpsburg, MD 21782
(301) 739–4200

Catoctin Mountain Park
6602 Foxville Road
Thurmont, MD 21788-1598
(301) 663–9330

Cedarville State Forest
11704 Fenno Road
Upper Marlboro, MD 20772
(301) 888–1410

Cunningham Falls State Park
14039 Catoctin Hollow Road
Thurmont, MD 21788
(301) 271–7574

Deep Creek Lake Recreation Area
898 State Park Road
Swanton, MD 21561
(301) 387–4111

Eastern Neck National Wildlife Refuge
1730 Eastern Neck Road
Rock Hall, MD 21661
(410) 639–7056

Fort Frederick State Park
11100 Fort Frederick Road
Big Pool, MD 21711
(301) 842–2155

Furnace Town Foundation
Box 207
Snow Hill, MD 21863
(410) 632–2032

Gambrill State Park
c/o Greenbriar State Park
21843 National Pike
Boonsboro, MD 21713
(301) 791–4767

Green Ridge State Forest
28700 Headquarters Drive NE
Flintstone, MD 21530
(301) 478–3124

Greenwell State Park
25420 Rosedale Manor Lane
Hollywood, MD 20636
(301) 373–2320

Gunpowder Falls State Park
2813 Jerusalem Road
Kingsville, MD 21087
(410) 592–2897

Herrington Manor State Park
222 Herrington Lane
Oakland, MD 21550
(301) 334–9180

Howard County Recreation and Parks
7120 Oakland Mills Road
Columbia, MD 21046-1677
(410) 313–4700

Little Bennett Regional Park
23705 Frederick Road
Clarksburg, MD 20871
(301) 972–6581

New Germany State Park
349 Headquarters Lane
Grantsville, MD 21536
(301) 895–5453

Ocean City Convention and Visitors
Bureau
4001 Coastal Highway
Ocean City, MD 21842
(800) OCO–CEAN (800–626–2326)

Oregon Ridge Park
13555 Beaver Dam Road
Cockeysville, MD 21030
(410) 887–1815

Patapsco Valley State Park
8020 Baltimore National Pike
Ellicott City, MD 21043
(410) 461–5005

Patuxent Research Refuge
National Wildlife Visitor Center
10901 Scarlet Tanager Loop
Laurel, MD 20708
(301) 497–5760

Patuxent River Park
16000 Croom Airport Road
Upper Marlboro, MD 20772
(301) 627–6074

Pocomoke State Forest
3461 Worcester Highway
Snow Hill, MD 21863
(410) 632–2566

Potomac State Forest
1431 Potomac Camp Road
Oakland, MD 21550
(301) 334–2038

Rocky Gap State Park
12500 Pleasant Valley Road
Flintstone, MD 21530
(301) 777–2139

Savage River Complex
349 Headquarters Lane
Grantsville, MD 21536
(301) 895–5453

Seneca Creek State Park
11950 Clopper Road
Gaithersburg, MD 20878
(301) 924–2127

Soldier's Delight Natural Environment
Area
5100 Deer Park Road
Owings Mills, MD 21117
(410) 922–3044

Susquehanna State Park
3318 Rocks Chrome Hill Road
Jarrettsville, MD 21084
(410) 557–7994

Swallow Falls State Park
c/o Herrington Manor State Park
222 Herrington Lane
Oakland, MD 21550
(301) 387–6938

Tuckahoe State Park
13070 Crouse Mill Road
Queen Anne, MD 21657
(410) 820–1668

Wye Island Natural Resources
Management Area
632 Wye Island Road
Queenstown, MD 21658
(410) 827–7577

Delaware

Blackbird State Forest
502 Blackbird Forest Road
Smyrna, DE 19977
(302) 653–6505

Bombay Hook National Wildlife
Refuge
2591 Whitehall Neck Road
Smyrna, DE 19977
(302) 653–9345

Brandywine Creek State Park
P.O. Box 3782
Wilmington, DE 19807
(302) 577–3534

Cape Henlopen State Park
42 Cape Henlopen Drive
Lewes, DE 19958
(302) 645–8983

Delaware Division of Fish and Wildlife
89 Kings Highway
Dover, DE 19901
(302) 739–5297

Delaware Seashore State Park
Inlet 850
Rehoboth Beach, DE 19971
(302) 227–2800

Fenwick Island State Park
c/o Holts Landing State Park
P.O. Box 76
Millville, DE 19970
(302) 539–9060
(302) 539–1055 (summer only)

Holts Landing State Park
Box 76
Millville, DE 19970
(302) 539–9060

Killens Pond State Park
5025 Killens Pond Road
Felton, DE 19943
(302) 284–4526

Lums Pond State Park
1068 Howell School Road
Bear, DE 19701
(302) 368–6989

Nanticoke Wildlife Area
RR 3, Box 205A
Laurel, DE 19956
(302) 539–3160

New Castle County Department of
Parks and Recreation
Department of Special Services
187-A Old Churchman's Road
New Castle, DE 19720-3115
(302) 395–5790

Prime Hook National Wildlife Refuge
RD 3, Box 195
Milton, DE 19968
(302) 684–8419

Redden State Forest
RD 4, Box 354
Georgetown, DE 19947
(302) 856–2893

Trap Pond State Park
Route 2, Box 331
Laurel, DE 19956
(302) 875–5153

White Clay Creek State Park
425 Wedgewood Road
Newark, DE 19711
(302) 368–6900

Appendix B: Further Reading

Abercrombie, Jay. *Walks and Rambles on the Delmarva Peninsula.* Woodstock, Vt: Backcountry Publications, 1985.

Delaware Trails Guidebook. Dover: Department of Natural Resources and Environmental Control, 1994.

Fisher, Alan. *Country Walks near Baltimore.* Baltimore: Rambler Books, 1993.

Fisher, Alan. *Country Walks near Washington.* Boston: Appalachian Mountain Club, 1994.

Gosner, Kenneth L. *A Field Guide to the Atlantic Seashore: Invertebrates & Seaweeds of the Atlantic Coast from the Bay of Fundy to Cape Hatteras.* Boston: Houghton Mifflin, 1979.

Harding, John J., and Justin J. Harding. *Birding the Delaware Valley Region.* Philadelphia: Temple University Press, 1980.

Hikes in Western Maryland. Vienna, Va.: Potomac Appalachian Trail Club, 1997.

MacKay, Bryan. *Hiking, Biking, and Canoeing in Maryland.* Baltimore: Johns Hopkins University Press, 1995.

Maryland and Delaware Atlas and Gazetteer. Freeport, Me.: DeLorme Mapping, 1993.

Peattie, Donald Culross. *A Natural History of Trees of Eastern and Central North America.* Boston: Houghton Mifflin Company, 1991.

Phillips, Claude E. *Wildflowers of Delaware and the Eastern Shore.* Hockessin, Del.: Delaware Nature Society, 1978.

Sutton, Allan. *Potomac Trails.* Golden, Colo.: Fulcrum Publishing, 1997.

Sutton, Ann, and Myron Sutton. *Eastern Forests.* New York: Alfred A. Knopf, 1985.

Taber, William S. *Delaware Trees: A Guide to the Identification of the Native Tree Species.* Dover: Delaware Department of Agriculture and Forest Services, 1995.

Trails of the Mid-Atlantic Region. Washington, D.C.: National Park Service, 1990.

Willis, Nancy Carol. *Delaware Bay Shorebirds.* Dover: Delaware Department of Natural Resources and Environmental Control, 1998.

Appendix C: Hiking Organizations for Maryland and Delaware

Abbotts Mill Trail Club
RD 1, Box 12413, SR 36
Greenwood, DE 19950

American Discovery Trail
P.O. Box 20155
Washington, DC 20041-2155

Anacostia Headwaters Greenway
4112 Thirtieth Street
Mount Rainier, MD 20712-1834

Annapolis Amblers
539 Shore Acres Road
Arnold, MD 21012-1903

Appalachian Trail Conservancy
P.O. Box 807
Harpers Ferry, WV 25425

Audubon Society of Central Maryland
7166 Winter Rose Path
Columbia, MD 21045-5134

Baltimore Blaze Stoppers
6904 Beech Avenue
Baltimore, MD 21206-1209

Baltimore Walking Club
8426 Pleasant Plains Road
Baltimore, MD 21286

Capital Hiking Club
6519 Bannockburn Drive
Bethesda, MD 20817

Chesapeake & Ohio Canal Association
P.O. Box 366
Glen Echo, MD 20812

Columbia Parks and Recreation Association
10221 Wincopin Circle, Suite 100
Columbia, MD 21044-3410

Delaware Greenways Inc.
P.O. Box 2095
Wilmington, DE 19899

Delaware Outing Club
117 Dallas Avenue
Newark, DE 19711-5125

Delaware Wild Lands Inc.
303 Main Street
Odessa, DE 19730

Diamond State Trekkers
11 North Railroad Avenue, B
Wyoming, DE 19934-1043

Footprints Only
201 West Padonia Road, Suite 600
Lutherville, MD 21093-2115

Fort Ritchie Volksmarchers
Building 834
Outdoor Recreation Center
Cascade, MD 21719

Frederick Flatfooters
6803 Falstone Drive
Frederick, MD 21702-9478

Freestate Happy Wanderers
8548 Pineway Court
Laurel, MD 20723-1238

Friendly Trails Wandering Club
5457 Enberend Terrace
Columbia, MD 21045

Great Greenbelt Volksmarchers
4617 Lincoln Avenue
Beltsville, MD 20705

Greenbelt Parks
6565 Greenbelt Road
Greenbelt, MD 20770

Maryland Volkssport Association
1343 Huntover Drive
Odenton, MD 21113-2122

Mason-Dixon Wobblers
10886 Rock Coast Road
Columbia, MD 21044-2734

Metropolitan Branch Trail
4112 Thirtieth Street
Mount Rainier, MD 20712-1834

Mountain Club of Maryland
8442 Each Leaf Court
Columbia, MD 21045

National Handicap Sports
451 Hungerford Drive, Suite 100
Rockville, MD 20850-4151

The Nature Conservancy
260 Chapman Road, Suite 201D
Newark, DE 19702

Northern Central Railroad Trail
P.O. Box 50
Glen Arm, MD 21057

Outdoor Education Association
5110 Meadowside Lane
Rockville, MD 20855-1812

Piedmont Pacers
2102 Woodview Road
Finksburg, MD 21048-1118

Potomac Appalachian Trail Club
118 Park Street SE
Vienna, VA 22180

Seneca Valley Sugar Loafers
10513 Neckleby Way
Damascus, MD 20872

Sierra Club, Catoctin Chapter
12 East Third Street
Frederick, MD 21701-5311

Sierra Club, Potomac Chapter
1116 West Street, Suite C
Annapolis, MD 21401-3657

Star Spangled Steppers
809 East Farrow Court
Bel Air, MD 21014-6903

Walter Reed Wandervogel
146 Fleetwood Terrace
Silver Spring, MD 20910-5511

Wanderbirds Hiking Club
6806 Delaware Street
Chevy Chase, MD 20815-4166

Washington Women Outdoors
P.O. Box 345
Riverdale, MD 20738-0345

Wilmington Trail Club
P.O. Box 1184
Wilmington, DE 19899

Appendix D: Hiker's Checklist

Always make and check your own checklist!

If you've ever hiked into the backcountry and discovered that you've forgotten an essential, you know that it's a good idea to make a checklist and check the items off as you pack so that you won't forget the things you want and need. Here are some ideas:

Clothing
- ❏ Dependable rain parka
- ❏ Rain pants
- ❏ Windbreaker
- ❏ Thermal underwear
- ❏ Shorts
- ❏ Long pants or sweatpants
- ❏ Wood cap or balaclava
- ❏ Hat
- ❏ Wool shirt or sweater
- ❏ Jacket or parka
- ❏ Extra socks
- ❏ Underwear
- ❏ Lightweight shirts
- ❏ T-shirts
- ❏ Bandana(s)
- ❏ Mittens or gloves
- ❏ Belt

Footwear
- ❏ Sturdy, comfortable boots
- ❏ Lightweight camp shoes

Bedding
- ❏ Sleeping bag
- ❏ Foam pad or air mattress
- ❏ Ground sheet (plastic or nylon)
- ❏ Dependable tent

Hauling
- ❏ Backpack and/or day pack

Cooking
- ❏ 1-quart container (plastic)
- ❏ 1-gallon water container for camp use (collapsible)
- ❏ Backpacking stove and extra fuel
- ❏ Funnel
- ❏ Aluminum foil
- ❏ Cooking pots
- ❏ Bowls/plates
- ❏ Utensils (spoons, forks, small spatula, knife)
- ❏ Pot scrubber
- ❏ Matches in waterproof container

Food and Drink
- ❏ Cereal
- ❏ Bread
- ❏ Crackers
- ❏ Cheese
- ❏ Trail mix
- ❏ Margarine
- ❏ Powdered soups
- ❏ Salt/pepper
- ❏ Main course meals
- ❏ Snacks
- ❏ Hot chocolate
- ❏ Tea
- ❏ Powdered milk
- ❏ Drink mixes

Photography
- ❏ Camera and film
- ❏ Filters
- ❏ Lens brush/paper

Miscellaneous
- ❏ Sunglasses
- ❏ Map and a compass
- ❏ Toilet paper

- ❑ Pocketknife
- ❑ Sunscreen
- ❑ Good insect repellent
- ❑ Lip balm
- ❑ Flashlight with good batteries and a spare bulb
- ❑ Candle(s)
- ❑ First-aid kit
- ❑ Your FalconGuide
- ❑ Survival kit
- ❑ Small garden trowel or shovel
- ❑ Water filter or purification tablets
- ❑ Plastic bags (for trash)
- ❑ Soap
- ❑ Towel
- ❑ Toothbrush
- ❑ Fishing license
- ❑ Fishing rod, reel, lures, flies, etc.
- ❑ Binoculars
- ❑ Waterproof covering for pack
- ❑ Watch
- ❑ Sewing kit

Index

About the Author

David Lillard is the author of six books and is a former president of the American Hiking Society, a national organization serving hikers and hiking organizations. A Delaware native, he grew up walking northern Delaware's stream corridors, railroad beds, and the farm fields once common there. He is a trail volunteer with the Potomac Appalachian Trail Club and the Potomac Heritage Trail and a member of several grassroots hiking groups. His books include *Journey through Hallowed Ground: A Trail Guide; Exploring the Appalachian Trail: Hikes in the Virginias;* and *Appalachian Trail Names: Origins of Place Names along the A. T.*